INNER STATE 80

YOUR JOURNEY ON THE HIGH WAY

DR. JOEL C. HUNTER

with SUSAN CHESSER BRANCH *and* CONSTANCE RAINWATER

Acknowledgements

I'm so grateful to the very talented and dedicated people who made this book a reality. These 80 "Miles" of devotionals are derived from messages I have preached over a span of a decade, and it is their efforts that moved the spoken word into this written format. I'm blessed by their help, and I hope you will be blessed as you choose the High Way.

First, a big thank you to my wife and best friend, Becky, who envisioned this book, and who, for the past five years has stayed on top of this project.

And I want to recognize publicly and thank profusely the following people for their great contributions of time and expertise. Each of the following has played a very significant part in bringing this book to life.

Sincere appreciation to Connie Rainwater, Northland's director of content development and a good friend for decades, for compiling, into a single volume of text, the heart of ten years of preaching: The Journey to Spiritual Maturity.

Thanks to Susan Branch, a gifted professional writer and longtime Northland family member, for her time and expertise in arranging and editing the manuscript.

My gratitude to Dr. Jo Sykes Chesser, Ed.D. , an educational administration and supervision qualitative research consultant in Little Rock, Arkansas, whose work shaped the initial direction of the questions that help each of us make progress on our own individual journey.

Huge thanks to Rob Andrescik, Northland's director of public relations, for the brilliant superintending of this manuscript and its design.

Thanks to Tracy Bardwell, a Northland designer, for the dynamic cover and layout, as well as for her hand in polishing the chapter-ending questions—all of which help to inspire us to keep moving toward spiritual maturity.

INNER STATE 80

YOUR JOURNEY ON THE HIGH WAY

DR. JOEL C. HUNTER

with SUSAN CHESSER BRANCH *and* CONSTANCE RAINWATER

INNER STATE 80: Your Journey on the High Way
by Dr. Joel C. Hunter with Susan Chesser Branch and Constance Rainwater

© 2009 by Dr. Joel C. Hunter with Susan Chesser Branch and Constance Rainwater
All rights reserved.

Published by HigherLife Development Services, Inc., 2342 Westminster Terrace, Oviedo, Florida 32765 | (407) 563-4806 | www.ahigherlife.com

ISBN 13: 978-1-935245-16-2
ISBN 10: 1-935245-16-3

09 10 11 12 13 — 8 7 6 5 4 3 2 1

Printed in the United States of America

Dedication

As Becky and I journey toward spiritual maturity, many choices we make along the way are a direct result of our love, respect and hopes for our grandchildren: Noah, Jada, Ella, Ava, Lincoln, Luke and any additional ones who may yet join our family. We pray that each one will always choose the High Way and will one day teach their grandchildren to take that road as well.

Children's children are a crown to the aged,
and parents are the pride of their children.
— Proverbs 17:6

Road Map

On-Ramp

Preparing for Your Journey

DAY IN AND day out, we take the same roads—to work, to run errands, and to get back home. We take them because they're the fastest, or most direct, or most convenient routes to our destinations. The focus is on getting where we're going, and, truth be known, the routine can become mind-numbing.

Perhaps you're feeling this way about your spiritual journey ... you take the same "roads" every day—devotions in the morning, prayers at night, and church services every Sunday. The focus is on fulfilling your religious duty, and, truth be known, the routine has become soul-numbing.

You're on spiritual cruise control—moving at a steady pace, but no longer engaged in the process. You may wonder now and then why you're not making as much progress as you'd like or if you'll ever reach your destination. ("Are we there yet?") Even the apostle Paul, who wrote two-thirds of the New Testament, was frustrated at times during his spiritual journey and by his growth as a believer. He wrote, "It happens so regularly that it's predictable. The moment I decide to do good, sin is there to trip me up. I truly delight in God's commands, but it's pretty obvious that not all of me joins in that delight."[1]

Whether you're on spiritual cruise control and need to be roused from the routine, or you're in a ditch and need to get back on the road, or you just need encouragement as you travel the "High Way," this book was written for you.

I'll refer to the chapters of this book not as chapters, but as "Exits." There are ten Exits, divided into eighty short readings, or "Miles," which combine strong biblical teaching with inspiring, educational, and even light-hearted stories. How you proceed on this journey is totally up to you. You might want to do one Mile every day over the next few months, or one in the morning and one at night over forty days. Or, you might want to read in long stretches, from one Exit to the next. The choice is yours.

As you travel through these "Miles," you'll discover some of what we tend to miss when we speed down the congested road of Christian routines. Will you look back one day on a life of efficient familiarity that minimized your need, and eventually your ability, to take note of all that God placed around you, or will you be among those adventurous people who made the choice to take note of more than what a passing glimpse can reveal? Will you have chosen a relationship with God that gave you a profound degree of spiritual depth and an ever-growing love for Him, or will there be mile markers you missed because you were unengaged, letting spiritual cruise control set the pace of the most important aspect of your life's journey?

Progress in spiritual depth and maturity is inevitable as we begin to value the "along the way" aspects of the Christian life. So, as you're reading this book, you'll find tools along the way that will help you on your journey. With each Mile, you'll find both a "GPS," or God-Positioning Scripture, and a "Rest Stop." The GPS provides spiritual direction, and the Rest Stop provides a place for you to "pull over and ponder" what God is saying to you.

The journey to Christian maturity and real spiritual depth leads away from error and regret. When you follow the High Way, your "Inner State" will take you toward a fully confident faith, bringing you to a place where you can bless and encourage others.

Let the journey begin …

FOOTNOTES: 1. Romans 7:21-23 (The Message)

EXIT 1: *HIGHER WAY*

Mile 1

The Quest for the True God

The most well-traveled roads of religion lead to understanding of a god who is safe and manageable—a god who is easy to comprehend or easy to live with. Not so with the road to spiritual maturity. It leads us to the one true triune God, who is neither safe nor manageable. He is infinitely beyond our comprehension or control.

A S PART OF my college training, I taught history at Shaw High School in Cleveland, Ohio. Much of the student body was made up of disadvantaged inner-city kids. It wasn't long before my students realized I was a Christian and asked me who God is. Not knowing any better, I answered, "Well, God is kind of like a father." Unaware that most of these kids' fathers had walked out on them, or slapped their mothers around, and oblivious to the fact that most of their fathers were nothing but a big disappointment, my telling them "God is like a father" set them up to see God as yet another source of disappointment. To this day, I regret my youthful ignorance of their situations.

Unfortunately, a lot of people imagine God to be a source of big disappointment. Most atheists are like this. While they claim not to believe in God at all, most of them demonstrate anger or disappointment with the God whom they claim does not even exist.

A skewed picture of who God is limits our ability to make progress on our journey to spiritual maturity. J.B. Phillips wrote a valuable little classic titled *Your God Is Too Small*, in which he argued that spiritual immaturity stems from an inadequate understanding of who God is. Tempted to define and create our own version of God, ironically, we will always make Him less powerful, less just, less knowing than the true God is. Defining Him often leads us to this mistake since the One who made us will never be Someone we can fully comprehend this side of heaven. Idolatrous and incomplete images of God that we create limit our understanding of and interaction with the one true God.

> "The better we know God, the better we'll know ourselves, and the less likely we'll be to confuse the two."

Yet we cling to our skewed images of Him as we would a security blanket. And that's not surprising, given the time we invest in strategically picturing Him in limited dimensions. Motivation to replace these simplistic profiles with a vibrant multi-faceted portrait of the living God is hard to come by. Since it is "a terrifying thing to fall into the hands of the living God,"[1] we prefer to pay attention to our skewed views of God even though they allow us to see little resemblance to the true God. Let's take a moment to look at some of those warped images of Him that you may be carrying with you.

God of disappointment: Many of us, at one time or another, have said to God, "God, if You are real, give me this." And when God in His sovereign wisdom chose not to give us what we asked, we determined not to believe in Him or to trust Him.

God as a cop: Picturing God as a sort of cosmic police officer is not uncommon. Many people imagine Him sitting up in heaven just waiting for us to break the law, and when we do … WHAM! He pulls us over and writes us a ticket. The good thing about this view is that people holding it rarely do anything terribly immoral. Unfortunately, they just as rarely do anything wonderfully good. They just want to stay below God's "judging radar."

God as Superman: Those of us who see God as Superman, rescuing us every time we get into a tight spot, often take unnecessary risks in the name of "faith," pursuing foolhardy courses of action with the assumption that God will bail us out if we get in over our heads. It is a shock to learn that God does not always rescue us from the consequences of our actions or shield us from the painful parts of life.

God as a critical parent: When we view God as a critical parent, we go around anxiety-ridden all our lives. No matter what we do, we never feel we can live up to God's expectations. Oddly, there is a kind of security in this view. People who are never able to measure up seldom risk anything, because they assume God wouldn't like it anyway.

God as Father Christmas: We love this picture of God as the benevolent Father who never gets angry, never punishes us, never makes us suffer the consequences of our actions, and gives us warm fuzzies. We like our "gentle Jesus, meek and mild" and cherish the pose that emphasizes Christ's compassion, kindness, mercy, and forgiveness to the exclusion of His holiness, righteousness, wrath against evil, and judgment.

Most well-traveled roads of religion lead to such limited or skewed understandings of God—a god who is safe, manageable, easy to comprehend, or easy to live with. Not so with the road to spiritual maturity. It challenges us to approach the one true triune God, who is neither safe nor manageable, but infinitely beyond our comprehension and control. The journey that we're on is fundamentally a quest for the true God.

Our quest will lead us not only to a deeper and broader knowledge of God, but to a better understanding of ourselves as well—how we're wired, how we relate to each other, what our weaknesses are, and so on. The better we know God, the better we'll know ourselves, and the less likely we'll be to confuse the two.

Taking the High Way requires us to let go of our limited pictures of who God is. Once we do that we will find God to be much more than we could ever ask for or imagine.

FOOTNOTES: 1. Hebrews 10:31

GPS: *God-Positioning Scriptures (to Reorient Your Life)*

For now we see in a mirror dimly, but then face to face; now I know in part, but then I will know fully just as I also have been fully known. —1 **Corinthians 13:12**

 REST STOP: *Pull Over and Ponder*

A.W. Tozer, in *The Knowledge of the Holy*, wrote, "What comes into our minds when we think about God is the most important thing about us." Who is God to you? Consider today how your view of God—His traits and your expectations—compare to the true and living God found in Scriptures.

Mile 2

Approaching the Light

Having left our idols behind, the road now leads us into an open space illumined by a brilliant light. This light is harsh and unflattering. There is no place to hide from it. What will it expose to our sight?

I REMEMBER WHEN ONE of my cousins first accepted Christ. Like many new Christians, he wanted everyone he knew to become saved, so it wasn't long before he had a rather pointed conversation with my grandmother about being a sinner. Now, my grandmother had been a staunch member of a mainline denominational church in a small Midwestern town all her life, and sin was not something that got mentioned much. So when my cousin told Gran she was a sinner, she came to me with tears in her eyes and said, "Joey, I'm not that bad, am I?" To Gran, sinners were people who murdered or stole or drank or cussed on Sundays, not people whom she knew personally and certainly not she herself. She did not see that sin infects each one of us and that it runs very deep.

In direct contrast to this story is another one involving a friend's conversation with a prison inmate, serving time for robbery. My friend mentioned that he had recently read in the paper about a man who had robbed a house and killed the family who lived there. "You know," the inmate replied, "it's people like that who give robbery a bad name." When my friend remarked that he didn't know it had a *good* name, the prisoner explained that *his* kind of robbery wasn't so bad because he only stole from rich people and he never harmed them. Even sitting in a prison cell, he was able to tell you with a straight face why he's not so bad. Although he could recognize sin in theory, he could not (or would not) see it in himself.

John Calvin was right when he said that knowledge of God inevitably leads to knowledge of self. The more we delve into the depths of who God is, the more we come to understand the depths of who we are. Unfortunately, that means discovering our sinfulness. So if it's true that "God is Light, and in Him there is no darkness at all,"[1] the more we enter into the light of God's true nature, the more our "deeds will be exposed," and the more we'll be forced to realize just how sinful we really are.

> "Sin encompasses more than just 'evil deeds'; it is a deviation from the mark of perfection."

To understand the gravity of sin, it is helpful to look at some of the words used to describe sin in the Old and New Testaments. The primary Old Testament word for sin is *hata*, which literally means "to miss," based on the idea that when we sin, we "miss" the road to righteousness. Sin encompasses more than just "evil deeds"; it is a deviation from the mark of perfection.

The New Testament uses two more words to describe sin; the first of these is *hamartia*. It is the most used word in the New Testament, most often used to refer either to individual acts of wrongdoing or to the very nature of sin within us. The double meanings reveal the inextricable link between sinful acts and a sinful nature. Paul describes his struggle with sin in Romans 7:15-20 as an overpowering tendency to do what he does not want to do. In this sense, *hamartia* is not merely the act itself, but the driving force behind the act. We are not sinners because we sin. We sin because we are sinners.

To this some might say, "Well, if my sin springs from my very nature, how can I be condemned for being what I was meant to be?" Many people today prefer to see their sin as "liberating," or as an expression of who they "really are." They fail to grasp the extent to which their sinful nature is wrecking them from within.

My brother-in-law, Mark Beeson, once traveled to Belize to study the insects and wildlife. Walking through the jungle, his guide grabbed his shoulder and jerked him to the ground. From there they were able to see, in a nearby clearing, a tarantula being attacked by a huge insect known as the tarantula wasp. The wasp kept diving at the tarantula, and the tarantula kept rearing back in an attempt to catch it. Finally, the tarantula wasp swooped down, flipped the tarantula onto its back, and stung it right in its abdomen. But this allowed the tarantula to grab the wasp and sink its fangs into it, injecting it with its venom. For a few moments, they both lay still. Then, the tarantula turned itself over, shook off the dead wasp, and crawled slowly away. Mark looked at his guide and said, "So the tarantula won." "That's the way it would seem," the guide replied. "But what you do not know is that as that tarantula wasp was stinging him, she was also depositing her eggs in his stomach. Surrounded by the nourishment they need, those eggs will begin to grow inside of him until they eventually kill him, and out of him will hatch his enemy."

What a graphic picture of the devastating effects of sin. There are some who wallow in their sin, cherishing it as a freedom to "enjoy life." But they naïvely fail to realize that their sin has taken residence deep inside and is gradually eating away all that is vital to them. Yet even this graphic depiction of sin is not enough to get many of us to see the absolute viciousness of our vices. We have a tendency to cling to the sins to which we are addicted even when we realize they are killing us. We say, "I know I am ruining my life, but it's my life to ruin." That is where the second New Testament word for sin, *adikia*, comes in. Often translated as "injustice" or "wrongdoing," *adikia* has to do with the effects of our sin on other people. The fact of the matter is that it's not just my life to ruin; it's the lives of my wife, my kids, my family members, my friends, and everyone else who loves me and is connected to me.

The Bible usually treats sin in one of two ways: either from a legal perspective or from what we could call a "medical" perspective. The legal perspective treats our sinfulness as a kind of crime that deserves to be punished. The "medical" perspective treats our sinfulness as a kind of pernicious disease for which we are in need of a cure. There is yet another way to look at sin, however, and it is only from this perspective that we perceive its full impact. Only when we look at sin through the eyes of love do we clearly see the absolute devastation and heartache it can cause. If you see a drunk woman staggering along the street, you might think that she is breaking the law by disturbing the peace, or you might say that she is sick and in need of help. Both of these perspectives may be completely accurate, but if that drunk woman happens to be your mother, that's something else altogether.

If you see a little girl who has been molested, you might say that she needs counseling, a loving environment, and so on, but if she happens to be your daughter, the sin that has affected her takes on a whole new significance. No clinical or legal terms can take away the hurt and anguish that sin causes. When we say, "Sure, I know I'm a sinner," we need to understand that to the extent that we are making sinful choices, we are actually working to destroy the lives of the people who love us.

Taking the High Way means heading in the direction of the Light that will expose who we are, warts and all. When we see the depths of our own depravity, we will begin to explore the depths of God's mercy toward us as demonstrated through Christ.

FOOTNOTES: 1. 1 John 1:5

GPS: *God-Positioning Scriptures (to Reorient Your Life)*
For everyone who does evil hates the Light, and does not come to the Light for fear that his deeds will be exposed. —John 3:20

 REST STOP: *Pull Over and Ponder*
When viewed in the light, is there anything in your life that qualifies as a hindrance to your relationships and spiritual growth? How can you distance yourself from that sin today?

Mile 3

The Cross: Barrier or Gateway

Having been exposed to our true nature by the light of God's holiness, we now come upon an impassable barrier. Rising up like a monolith, it blocks our way.

THE CROSS STANDS as a potential crisis on our road to spiritual maturity. It is our response to the cross that determines whether or not we will choose the High Way or an entirely different and misleading road. Some people when faced with the cross insist that making a choice isn't necessary, or can be delayed. Indecision, though, is itself a road—a dead-end one, but nonetheless, a road many have chosen. Others, having come this far, become determined to find a way past this apparent obstacle. They attempt to climb over it, go around it, knock it down, or even try to ignore it. However, there is a group that sees the cross as a gateway to the rest of the road. They have realized that the solution to the dilemma of the cross is not to ignore it, to retreat from it, or to try to get past it by one's own efforts, but to go *through* it.

The execution of Christ is the central event of all history. All years preceding it (B.C.) are counted backward, and all subsequent years (A.D.) are counted forward. The cross was originally a symbol of death, like a gallows or electric chair would be for us today. Why don't we consider it rather morbid that this instrument of execution should adorn our churches and our necks? Christ's atonement for sin has been understood in a variety of ways throughout history and among various traditions and denominations, but there are three primary views of the atonement that have been widely held.

The substitutionary view: This view found its most articulate expression in the works of Augustine, Anselm, and John Calvin. According to this view, sin is a transgression of God's standards of holiness. In the last Mile, we saw how deep and how devastating our sinful nature is. As such, it is an affront to God, a crime for which the only just punishment is our death and damnation. The only way for God's justice to be satisfied apart from our own death is for Him to pay the penalty for us. Christ came in the form of a man, to become a fitting substitute. He willingly took our death upon Himself, thereby paying the penalty for our sin and freeing us from our death sentence.

Christ had to remain sinless; otherwise, He, too, would have been an affront to God. By remaining spotless, He was able to take our sins upon Himself. His sacrifice had to be voluntary. If the Father had simply forced Him to die, it would be like a judge letting a murderer go free because he arbitrarily chose someone else to die in the murderer's place. Because of Christ's atonement, we, as believers, have been justified by God's grace, and our transgressions are forgiven. The cross stands as a symbol of God's mercy toward us in Christ.

The Christus Victor view: Irenaeus, a second-century bishop, said that Christ's life is the recapitulation of the lives of all mankind. In other words, just as Adam was the prototype for all of us in our sinful condition, so Christ is the prototype for all in our spiritual condition. Here it is not Christ's substitutionary death that is the focus, but His spotless obedience to the Father and His victory over evil. Satan tried many times to entice Jesus to sin. As He was about to face the cross, Jesus was tempted to avoid it, but He was obedient. It was through this ultimate act of righteousness that Christ achieved victory over Satan. Through our identification with Christ, His victory becomes our victory. We are no longer slaves to sin or Satan. The cross is not only the symbol of God's mercy toward us in Christ; it is also the symbol of the turning point in the spiritual war—the point at which sin and death were destroyed once and for all.

The Christ as our example view: This particular theory found perhaps its most articulate expression in Horace Bushnell, a nineteenth-century theologian who was most interested in the believer's compassion and willingness to suffer on others' behalf. This perspective understands sin to be more than merely falling short of a certain standard. In Bushnell's mentality, sin is a closure of one's spirit to the inflowing righteousness of God. Until your heart is broken, until your heart is open to the compassion of Christ, you have not understood the full significance of the cross. We need to realize that a major element of sin is hardness and obstinacy. We need to be broken, but God never breaks a strong person by loading on more law or by strong-arming him. God connects with us at the point of our weakness; He does not try to break us of our strength.

"...we respect strength, but we connect at weakness."

I can remember my mother telling me I was the most strong-willed person she knew. She was raising my sister and me alone, and sometimes I was a lot to handle. There were many times when she would make me sit down, and I would think to myself, *I'll sit down, but I'm still standing on the inside!* I remember her coming to me one day and saying, "Joey, I'm sorry I yelled at you the other day. I've got to remain strong, but I don't feel strong. I feel like I'm weak. I feel like I'm just not doing a very good job, and I'm sorry." Everything melted in me immediately. I would have charged the gates of hell with a squirt gun for her at that moment. That is because we respect strength, but we connect at weakness.

There is something about vulnerability that draws us in and connects us, that opens us up. God knew that. So He came down in a weakened fashion, because He did not just want our obedience; He wanted our hearts.

Taking the High Way means understanding what we mean when we say that Christ died for our sins. The true and comprehensive view of atonement through the cross of Christ is multi-faceted and includes aspects of the views presented.

GPS: *God-Positioning Scriptures (to Reorient Your Life)*

Since the children share in flesh and blood, He Himself likewise also partook of the same, that through death He might render powerless him who had the power of death, that is, the devil, and might free those who through fear of death were subject to slavery all their lives. —Hebrews 2:14-15

REST STOP: *Pull Over and Ponder*

Consider the aforementioned views as you reflect on what Christ has done for you. How might having a more accurate understanding of the cross of Christ improve your relationship with God and others today?

Mile 4

A Spirited Journey

The cross of Christ is the birth canal of spiritual life. Once we have passed through it, our journey will never be the same again. For that matter, neither will we.

BECOMING A CHRISTIAN is a classic case of getting more than you bargained for: You put your faith in Christ and His love for you on the cross, and next thing you know, you're being told that you've been born of the Spirit, that you're a "new creature," that you need to be "filled" with the Spirit, and all manner of other mystical-sounding expressions! Who exactly is this Spirit? When Jesus said, "Unless one is born of water and the Spirit he cannot enter into the kingdom of God,"[1] the Spirit He was referring to was, of course, the Holy Spirit, the third person of the Trinity. The doctrine of the Trinity that God consists of three distinct persons—the Father, the Son, and the Holy Spirit—is difficult to explain without sounding polytheistic on the one hand or Unitarian on the other. But the Trinity is the God we worship, the God

15

we have set out on a quest to find. The Bible makes it clear that the persons of the Trinity are inseparable in their essence and attributes, so that God is not divided. Yet Scripture also makes it clear that the singular works of God are accomplished through the distinct efforts of each of the three persons: Father, Son, and Holy Spirit. In other words, when God sets out to do something, the three persons of the Trinity do not all participate in the act in the same way-Creator, Savior, and Sustainer do not all do the exact same thing. Rather, they each participate in the work in a distinct way. God is, within Himself, a relationship.

> "The extent to which we are 'filled' with the Spirit is the extent to which we are not filled with anything else."

The Bible repeatedly makes it clear that the Holy Spirit, like the Father and the Son, is fully God. The Holy Spirit acts as a kind of liaison between God and those who have been "born of the Spirit," directing our attention to the Father and the Son, and presenting our needs to God. Where Christ became the visible manifestation of God with us, the Holy Spirit has become the invisible manifestation of God within us. The Holy Spirit, who dwells in our "hearts" from the time we put our hope in Christ, is a wonderful taste of eternal life with God.

Not only is the Holy Spirit a "taste" of eternal life with God, He is the necessary condition for life itself. Eternal life did not begin for us until we were "born of the Spirit." The Bible continually equates our pre-Christian existence with death and our new spiritual existence with life. We were dead, yet walking around.

Perhaps I watched too many monster movies as a kid, but the images that come to mind when I think of the dead walking around are of those fictitious creatures classified as "the undead," like zombies and vampires. They are beings who have died some kind of unnatural death, who are now trapped somewhere between death and life. They possess powers that the living do not have, such as supernatural strength. Yet they are unable to exist in the world of the living, and most horribly of all, they have an insatiable need to feed on the lifeblood of others in a futile attempt to regain the life they once had. Stories about such creatures are strangely fascinating for most of us because in the midst of their evil rampages, there is something terribly forlorn about them. One gets the feeling that they want nothing more than to live again. In a very real sense, this is exactly the situation Scripture describes when it speaks of our being dead in the trespasses and sins in which we used to walk. It was as though, like the vampire, we were trying to fill ourselves up with that which would make us feel alive. But sooner or later, the forlorn sense of emptiness and lifelessness would return.

Thankfully, by the grace of God, He "made us alive with Christ even when we were dead."[2] We have escaped the "walking death" we once knew, and are now about to "walk by the Spirit." What does it mean to be "filled with the Spirit"? The extent to which we are "filled" with the Spirit is the extent to which we are not filled with anything else. We are filled with whatever holds the biggest place in our hearts and our minds. The beauty of this process is that God does not ask us to become like Him by emptying ourselves of sin; He fills us up with Himself so there is no longer any room in our lives for sin. D.L. Moody, the nineteenth-century evangelist and preacher, used to illustrate this by putting an empty glass on the table and challenging people to get the air out of it. They would suggest a variety of things, such as suctioning the air out with a vacuum pump, but Moody would say, "Yes, but that would crush the glass." When no one could think how to do it, he would take a pitcher of water and fill the glass to overflowing. There would no longer be any air in the glass, only water. In the same way, inasmuch as we are filled with the Spirit of Christ, that is how much sin no longer has any place in our lives. Therefore, if we want to be rid of the sin that is so ingrained in us, we need to focus not on rooting it out directly, but on being filled to overflowing with the Spirit of God—on having Him crowd it out.

What is being filled with the Holy Spirit like? To begin with, being filled with the Holy Spirit results in the discernment of one's purpose and giftedness. Secondly, it results in a greater obedience to God. Finally, when we are filled with the Spirit, we are given the assurance that our faith is genuine and that we really do belong to Christ. In short, being filled with the Holy Spirit results in no longer having to live life in a defensive posture. No longer do we try to "keep from sinning," because we are so saturated with God's righteousness that sin, although still present in our lives, is no longer able to gain a lasting foothold there.

Taking the High Way is about a life of purpose and direction not about the religious duties we perform. The Holy Spirit will guide us through this journey to the end.

FOOTNOTES: 1. John 3:5; 2. Ephesians 2:5 (NIV)

GPS: *God-Positioning Scriptures (to Reorient Your Life)*

Therefore if anyone is in Christ, he is a new creature; the old things passed away; behold, new things have come. —2 **Corinthians 5:17**

REST STOP: *Pull Over and Ponder*

Is there something other than the Holy Spirit occupying space in your heart and mind lately? What steps can you take today to crowd it out with the Holy Spirit?

Mile 5

Sharing the Road

Once we have passed through the gateway of the cross and have discovered that we have been born to an entirely new nature, we look around to see that we are not alone ...

WHEN I THINK of a covenant, I am reminded of some of the old Westerns I watched as a kid. Occasionally, two screen friends (usually an Indian and a white man) would become "blood brothers" to show their commitment to one another. Each man would cut his hand with a knife—a very cool thing to a young boy—and they would put their hands together to allow their blood to intermingle. Whenever one of them was in need, the other was supposed to come to his aid. To fail to honor this bond was an act of cowardice and treachery. This covenant was a "bond in blood" that must never be broken!

Every Christian has become Christ's "blood brother," and as such we are obligated not only to Him, but also to each other. If any of us is struggling, the rest of us must assist him, because we are bound to him by the blood of Christ. It's a covenant relationship, and the differences we may have pale in comparison to this Lord we share.

Too often, covenant relationships degenerate into contract relationships, and the results are always devastating. Marriage is a covenant relationship, and most marriages begin with excitement and dreams for the future, but somewhere along the way, we slip into a nitpicking preoccupation with our spouse's faults and a desire to be treated better. And what about the relationship between parents and children? We begin as parents thinking we're going to be the best moms and dads in the world, but eventually, we settle for doing what we can to get a little "peace and quiet." We begin our Christian lives with dreams of changing the world, but somehow we become disillusioned and focused on our unfulfilled desires. We replace our passion for knowing and serving Christ with a stale, but safe, religious formula: If we live the "good Christian life," we'll be blessed and accepted. Throughout the Old and New Testaments, God initiates covenant relationships with His people, and time and again His people settle for easy (but empty) formulas. And those of us living today are equally likely to take the easy route, setting the "cruise control" rather than involving ourselves in a dynamic relationship with God.

> *"We begin our Christian lives with dreams of changing the world, but somehow we become disillusioned and focused on our unfulfilled desires."*

The church was never meant to be an institution built by a contract with God; it was meant to be a community established by a covenant with Him. When people speak negatively about "organized religion," they are describing what remains after the church has forgotten its "first love." We must be careful to avoid slipping into the kind of contract relationships devoid of life and meaning, for we belong to an eternal covenant with the living God.

The Bible goes even further in describing the relationship we have with each other as brothers and sisters in Christ. It goes so far as to say we are all members of a single body, "the body of Christ"; the most detailed description is found in 1 Corinthians 12. We must understand that we share a common life, health, and vitality, as different members of a single organism. By describing the church as a body, Scripture is not only depicting the unity that should exist among its members, but the diversity out of which this unity comes.

Several years ago, Northland Church had some air-conditioning units stolen. A few weeks later, I came in one morning and was told, "Boy, we had another one stolen!" So I checked, and sure enough, it looked like an AC rapture had come— "One will be taken and one will be left."[1] Throughout the day, I had the chance to tell several different people about it, and I was surprised by the variety of reactions I got. The first person I told said something like this: "You know, it's drugs. ... The culprits probably thought they could get some good money for the copper tubing those units hold. And I can't imagine the kind of family life the person who stole that has had, the poor guy." This person almost started crying just thinking about it. The next person I told said, "What is this society coming to when someone will steal from God's church? We're all just going down the tubes!" The third person said, "How do you steal a ten-ton air conditioner? I mean, they must have had some big monster truck out there!" The fourth person said, "How much does one of those cost? Are we talking thousands and thousands of dollars, or what?"

None of these individuals necessarily responded the right way or the wrong way; they simply reacted according to the way they were wired. Each one addressed the same situation from a very distinct perspective. That is the kind of diversity that exists within the church because God has called a rich variety of people to Himself. He has not limited His calling to those who meet a certain set of requirements. The church is not made up of people who got the same score on some personality profile, or who have a certain kind of ancestry, or are members of a particular political party or the same social class.

God has wired and gifted each of us with a specific purpose in mind. Each of us has something unique to offer the church at large. And amazingly, the things that God calls us to be and do are the very things for which we are perfectly suited, and from which we will derive the greatest satisfaction.

Taking the High Way means depending on each other for the strength to finish the journey. We share a common destiny. We are connected, like members of a single organism. In the midst of a world consumed by loneliness and the pain of isolation, we who are in Christ have become part of a genuine community. Because we have passed through the cross, we shall never be alone again.

FOOTNOTES: 1. Matthew 24:40

GPS: *God-Positioning Scriptures (to Reorient Your Life)*

A body isn't just a single part blown up into something huge. It's all the different-but-similar parts arranged and functioning together. If Foot said, "I'm not elegant like Hand, embellished with rings; I guess I don't belong to this body," would that make it so? If Ear said, "I'm not beautiful like Eye, limpid and expressive; I don't deserve a place on the head," would you want to remove it from the body? If the body was all eye, how could it hear? If all ear, how could it smell? As it is, we see that God has carefully placed each part of the body right where he wanted it. —**1 Corinthians 12:15** (**The Message**)

REST STOP: *Pull Over and Ponder*
Take a mental inventory of the people God's put in your life. Is there anyone whose purpose you've been underestimating? Anyone whose talents you've been taking for granted? How can 1 Corinthians 12 alter how you perceive the people you come in contact with?

Mile 6

Warning! Danger Ahead

As we look ahead, we discover that the road to spiritual maturity cuts straight through a war zone. We must face an enemy—one with a major stake in diverting us from the High Way.

BY PASSING THROUGH the cross and being born of the Spirit, we have declared our allegiance to God. We face all the forces of hell, who are well aware that our journey signifies their ultimate demise, and who will do whatever is necessary to divert us, turn us around, cripple us, and, if possible, destroy us. God's enemies are now our enemies, and we must learn how to deal with them if we are to follow this road to the end. In short, we must learn how to engage in "spiritual warfare."

The key to victory in any war is knowing your enemy. The key to victory in spiritual warfare is understanding Satan, and the key to understanding Satan is accepting the reality of hell. Hell is not a very popular subject these days. We have come to emphasize God's love and forgiveness so much that we have a hard time reconciling the existence of hell with our concept of God. Hell is Satan's ultimate destiny, and it is that knowledge that drives him in his war against God. Because of his failed attempt to fight God directly, Satan vents his fury on mankind, in order to injure God by destroying those whom He has lovingly created. He is driven by the knowledge that he will soon be confined to hell for eternity. Although hell has not been prepared for us, all who follow Satan into continual rebellion against God will also follow him into continuous torment in hell and eternal separation from the presence of the Lord.

We know that those who have acknowledged Christ's atonement for their sins are eternally secure from the threat of damnation. With regard to getting us to suffer with him for eternity, Satan has lost, where we are concerned. That does not mean he has given up on us. We are a potential hindrance to him. By becoming Christians, we have not only escaped his power, we may now be used by his hated Enemy to set others free. Every soul that escapes Satan's grip is a maddening reminder to him of his impotence in his fight against God.

> "Yes, God gives Satan some leeway, but it is only because He is using Satan's own schemes against him."

Even though we, as Christians, are free from the power of hell, it takes discipline, focus, and intentionality to travel on the High Way. "For the gate is small and the way is narrow that leads to life, and there are few who find it."[1]

We will be tempted to disregard our spiritual battles because we are content to remain on the road to destruction, indulging in what the Bible calls the "acts of the sinful nature."[2] If we are already following this road, Satan need not waste his efforts on us. Satan is limited, and his Enemy is formidable, so my hunch is he must ration his efforts as much as possible in his war against God. He waits for his best opportunity, and did so even when he was directly dealing with Jesus. We read in Luke 4:13: "When the devil had finished every temptation, he left Him until an opportune time."

A most significant spiritual reality is that Satan is not free to act on his own; he is on a leash, and God is holding onto the other end.

Contrary to popular opinion, Christianity is not dualistic. Dualism is the belief that the world is caught in the middle of a war between two equally powerful gods, one good, and the other evil, each of whom is continually trying to achieve victory over the other. Christianity, on the other hand, affirms that God is all-powerful and perfectly good. Satan is at war with God, but he can do nothing more than God allows him to do. God is not trying to achieve dominance over Satan, because He has always had it. In the blink of an eye, He could utterly destroy His adversary. In fact, God has already accomplished Satan's defeat, so there can be no doubt of His supremacy.

Of course, this raises some pretty serious questions about God's justice. After all, we know that Satan does nothing but inflict pain, suffering, and death upon anyone he can get his hands on. If he does so with God's full consent, then doesn't God's righteousness become questionable? What are we to make of this? How good is a God who uses evil? Romans 8:28 gives us the answer to our dilemma: "God causes all things to work together for good to those who love God, to those who are called according to His purpose." God's leash on Satan means that He is working for our ultimate good, and that although He may allow Satan to cause us suffering, He will not allow Satan to interfere with the ultimate good He has planned for us. Yes, God gives Satan some leeway, but it is only because He is using Satan's own schemes against him. It's kind of like Judo, where you use your enemy's force against him. If he takes a swing at you, you use his momentum to throw him off balance, so that what he intended to hurt you with becomes the means by which he hurts himself. God does the same thing with Satan. In the case of Peter, Satan asked for the chance to "sift" him "like wheat"[3] in order to destroy his loyalty to Christ, but God used Peter's threefold denial to break him of his overconfidence in himself and to make him into the one who could "feed (Christ's) sheep."[4]

Another biblical example of God's putting limits on Satan is found in Job 1:2. There we see that Satan was given permission to test Job, but God instructed Satan on his limitation as he dealt with Job. Satan was given orders not to put his hand of destruction on Job personally.

The fact that God has a "leash" on Satan is more than an indication of God's justice, as it might seem at first glance. It is our assurance that Satan's attacks can never derail God's purpose for our lives. Taking the High Way means we need not fear the onslaughts of the devil and his forces. Just as a man trained in Judo need not fear someone taking a swing at him; God will use his attacks to bring about his own defeat!

FOOTNOTES: 1. Matthew 7:14; 2. Galatians 5:19 (NIV); 3. Luke 22:31; 4. John 21:17 (NIV)

GPS: *God-Positioning Scriptures (to Reorient Your Life)*

My sheep hear My voice, and I know them, and they follow Me; and I give eternal life to them, and they will never perish; and no one will snatch them out of My hand. My Father, who has given them to Me, is greater than all; and no one is able to snatch them out of the Father's hand. —**John 10:27-29**

REST STOP: *Pull Over and Ponder*
How does knowing that God has a "leash" on Satan change how you view the current difficult circumstances in your life?

Mile 7

Your Safety Equipment

Driving through a war-zone, we begin to understand the necessity of being prepared with the right strategy and resources to make it safely to the other side.

WHEN IT COMES to spiritual warfare, much of the church behaves as if it is on a search-and-destroy mission. We have this tendency to get all worked up emotionally and to go out and try to fight Satan, but he has been defeated. It is now our job to advance in the victory Christ has already won. Our energies can be used in raising a new standard over conquered territory and building God's kingdom in depth as well as scope. Jesus said, "I chose you and appointed you to go and bear fruit—fruit that will last."[1] A Christian accomplishes the purposes of God by bearing fruit.

It would seem that if we are going to build God's kingdom, we need to settle down to the quiet task of actually conforming our daily lives to the Christian principles we profess. "Make it your ambition to lead a quiet life, to mind your own business and to work with your hands, just as we told you, so that your daily life may win the respect of outsiders ... "[2] We must not let Satan distract us from the calling we have received.

Undoubtedly, one of the best-known passages of Scripture dealing with spiritual warfare is Ephesians 6:10-18, which talks about the "armor of God." We need to be properly trained in the most effective use of this armor. Our failures are not necessarily due to a lack of zeal, but to a lack of knowledge. Paul commands us to put on the *full* armor of God, emphasizing it by saying it twice. To stand against the wiles of the devil is not possible unless we have all of the gear in place.

> "God has created us for, and called us to, relationships."

"Stand firm then, with the belt of truth buckled around your waist ... ," (v. 14, NIV). As Christians, we need to be committed to the truth, but too easily we become committed to, instead, proving we are right. There is a profound distinction between the two. The person committed to truth is willing to have his preconceived notions stretched or altered by the truth he discovers throughout his Christian journey. The one who wants to be right seeks merely to defend his preconceived notions of truth against all challengers. The first person is looking for that which is beyond himself, while the second person is trying to justify himself. Once Jesus said, "I am the way, and the *truth*" in John 14:6, believers understood that truth is an integral aspect of our God. As we grow in our knowledge of Him, our knowledge of truth grows as well.

" ... with the breastplate of righteousness in place ... " (v. 14, NIV). The biblical definition of *righteousness* can be summed up as follows: Righteousness is fulfilling the demands of a relationship. It is neither more nor less. God is always righteous in that He never fails to fulfill the demands of His relationships. Too often we, as Christians, think we are serving God and being righteous by defending His name against the slander and disbelief of those who do not yet know Him as Lord of their lives, but in reality we may be driving away the very people God has placed in our paths. Are we treating people who haven't met Christ in a way that creates in them a desire or even a willingness to know Him? God has created us for, and called us to, relationships. It makes sense that Satan's goal would be to drive a wedge between people, and especially to separate and isolate those who believe in Christ from those who do not. Our righteousness demands

compassion and interaction even with those who are not like us. In Matthew 5, Jesus tells us we should even love our enemies.

"... with your feet fitted with the readiness that comes from the gospel of peace." (v. 15, NIV). It may seem a little paradoxical to us to talk about readiness for warfare coming from peace, because our natural tendency when facing a struggle is to gear up by getting angry or aggressive. However, in a spiritual struggle, exactly the opposite is true. The calmer you are, the more at peace, the better you are able to stand in the face of the enemy's onslaught.

"In addition to all this, take up the shield of faith, with which you can extinguish all the flaming arrows of the evil one" (v. 16, NIV). The "flaming arrows" of Satan are intended to bring fear, chaos, and confusion to our ranks. The "shield," which enables us to extinguish those "flaming arrows" sent to intimidate us, is our faith in God's promise never to let us go.

"Take the helmet of salvation ... " (v. 17, NIV). Satan loves to attack our minds. Our salvation, our confidence in Christ, is the crowning piece of our spiritual armor. If our confidence in the security of our relationship with God can be shaken, we have no basis for peace, righteousness becomes a legalistic pursuit, and we will begin to doubt the truth. If you are going to, as Jesus instructed, love God with all your heart, soul, mind, and strength, then this helmet is crucial.

" ... and the sword of the Spirit, which is the word of God ... " (v. 17, NIV). The sword is the only offensive weapon that Paul lists among the Christian's equipment. Each time Satan tempted Jesus, Jesus responded with the words: "It is written," then He would quote a passage of Scripture. Our own knowledge and appropriate use of Scripture gives us the power to combat Satan. The words of the Bible have power because they carry God's authority.

Paul concludes his list with a call to prayer, saying, "And pray in the Spirit on all occasions" (v. 18, NIV). Taking the High Way means praying to love God well and serving others with compassion. Through acting on that prayer, Satan's opposing goals will not be reached.

FOOTNOTES: 1. John 15:16 (NIV); 2. 1 Thessalonians 4:11-12 (NIV)

GPS: *God-Positioning Scriptures (to Reorient Your Life)*

For I am convinced that neither death nor life, neither angels nor demons, neither the present nor the future, nor any powers, neither height nor depth, nor anything else in all creation, will be able to separate us from the love of God that is in Christ Jesus our Lord. —**Romans 8:38-39** (NIV)

REST STOP: *Pull Over and Ponder*
Are you ready for battle—fully suited up in the armor of God—or is there a piece of equipment you have yet to put on? Are you using the armor of God as it was intended to be used?

Mile 8

Guardrails

As we proceed on the High Way, we will notice places that are mesmerizing. Some will flood our mind with memories—actions and attitudes we practiced in our old selfish nature. We must avoid these enticements and remain on the course laid out for us.

ONE OF SATAN'S strategies for getting us to crash—for distracting us from God's purposes—is the use of strongholds. We commonly refer to strongholds today as addictions, and they come in tailor-made variations to perfectly suit each one of our unique weaknesses. Whether it's gambling, drugs, porn, or whatever else that snatches our valuable time and efforts from Kingdom progress, addictions ultimately create sadness and often, despair.

Strongholds are traps; disguised as various enticements and strategically placed at points where our spiritual journey is especially grueling or, ironically, where it is especially mundane, they invite us to take a wrong turn and keep going ... away from our intended destination.

31

Initially, the only power Satan's strongholds have is their ability to appeal to our old nature. They cannot jump out and grab us; they can only wait for us to turn to them. The more we turn to them and the deeper we enter into them, the greater their hold on us. There is scientific evidence our brains actually undergo some physical changes as we become addicted. These changes in the brain that result from feeding compulsions are not irreversible, so changes in our patterns of behavior can effect positive physical change. In short, the power addictions have over us is *the power we give to them.*

"We often fall for Satan's traps because we put little effort into prevention."

When I was a boy, I was a "victim" of several self-made accidents. I would always say, "Sorry, I didn't mean to do that." My family would accept my contrition, and I would get a little punishment and go on with my life. I thought that was just the way life was.

One day, though, a man who loved me and had confidence in me would not let me off the hook. I was playing around, not paying attention, and broke a glass. "Sorry," I said automatically, "I didn't mean to." "But," he interrupted, "you didn't mean not to, either, and that is your problem." It had never occurred to me that I could actually have less trouble in life by "meaning not to."

We often fall for Satan's traps because we put little effort into prevention. Like driving along a cliff without guardrails, we don't miss them until it's too late. I put up guardrails because I mean not to mess up my life. Here are some of my guardrails:

- I let my wife in on all my conversations with other women and important conversations with other men. She also has free access to all my e-mails and regular mail. She can often spot a potential problem before I do. I always keep her, or reminders of her, with me.

- I get with colleagues with a great sense of humor. We laugh about our struggles, which defuses them and offsets the temptation to sedate the frustrations of life with sin. We can be open (and accountable) about our struggles, because it just produces laughter at ourselves and a reminder of God's grace.

- I arrange my time with a schedule that produces, and keeps track of, enough little accomplishments in a day to: 1) not have much time to get into trouble; 2) feel good enough about the accomplishments that I don't want to reverse them with failure.

I also have these motivations for not messing up my life:

- I spend time enjoying the people I love. I have less need to find other fulfillment, plus I am continually reminded that if I mess up, they are the ones who will be hurt more than I.

- I dream big. Little accomplishments provide some reasons to not mess up, but big dreams for my church and for the ways I can serve are more motivating for me. I am motivated far more by dreams than by fear.

- I saved the best for last. For some strange reason, God has been enormously gracious to me. I should have self-destructed many times, but He saved me. Even today, when I mess up in little ways, He forgives me and blesses me anyhow. The awareness of His goodness and grace to me is my greatest motivation for not messing up big time.

I am not without sin. I am certainly not without making mistakes with great regularity. I still don't live life very carefully, but I do live carefully enough not to mess up big time. And I don't spend a great deal of time beating myself up for the little stuff. I simply ask for forgiveness and accept it and go on.

As I write these words, I can hear some of you asking, "But what if I already have messed up big time (or am in the middle of it right now)?" The great news is this: Our God is a God of new beginnings. You can (and should) start all over—forgiven, thankful, and wiser.

The late Donald Grey Barnhouse, one of our nation's greatest preachers, used to tell the story of a young man he knew. The young man had been in an unhealthy relationship before going away and meeting a wonderful Christian girl, who became his wife. Years later, he and his wife visited his hometown. One night his wife was out, and his old girlfriend dropped by. She made no attempt to hide her affection; he had only to reach out, and her body would be his. He was tempted.

Instead, he acted oblivious to her advances. He began talking about how wonderful his wife was, showing his old girlfriend the pictures of his wife he always carried with him. She said simply, "She must be quite a woman if she can keep you from reaching," and she left. He had never loved his wife so much as he did in that moment.

He used her pictures as little guardrails that night. They had not kept him from temptation, but they helped him not to crash. He meant not to crash.

Taking the High Way means recognizing that strongholds have inherent within them empty promises of comfort and security. Pass them by.

GPS: *God-Positioning Scriptures (to Reorient Your Life)*
No test or temptation that comes your way is beyond the course of what others have had to face. All you need to remember is that God will never let you down; he'll never let you be pushed past your limit; he'll always be there to help you come through it. —1 Corinthians 10:13 (The Message)

REST STOP: *Pull Over and Ponder*
What "guardrails" might you want to establish to help you pass up areas of temptation or addiction in your life?

Mile 9

Your Compass

Knowing the dangers that wait for us along the roadside, how can we possibly keep from losing our way on this journey? Our faith is the answer to this concern. It orients us on our journey; it's our compass amid the challenges.

IN MATTHEW 19:16-22, Jesus is approached by an evangelistic prospect. A young man with everything going for him—wealth, prominence, and morals—asks Him point-blank how to have eternal life. How does Jesus respond? Differently than you might assume! To begin with, He places an impossible demand on this rich young ruler: "If you wish to enter into life, keep the commandments" (v. 17). This should have driven the young man to despair, since we "all have sinned and fall short of the glory of God."[1] But remarkably, he makes the claim that he has kept all of the commandments! Yet even in spite of this confidence in his own righteousness, he still believed that there was something else he lacked, and he was hoping that Jesus would tell him what it was. Jesus replied, "If you wish to be complete, go and sell your possessions and give to the poor, and you will have treasure in heaven; and come, follow Me" (v. 21).

Isn't that an odd way for Jesus to present the Gospel? He doesn't even mention things like grace, faith, or redemption; He simply demands that this rich man give up all his possessions and follow Him. Why would He do such a thing? Why would He obscure the Good News of the Gospel by demanding the renunciation of wealth? Does this mean we must take a vow of poverty before we can enter heaven? No, but it does illustrate the essence of true faith.

"Faith is an adventure with Christ, in which our love for Him exceeds all other loves."

The rich young ruler was looking for some addition to his life, which would assure him of eternal life. Our Lord responded by challenging him to forsake everything he had in exchange for eternal life. True faith cannot merely be tacked on to our lives. On the contrary, true faith *orients* our lives. Faith is an adventure with Christ, in which our love for Him exceeds all other loves.

This is not a very popular view of faith in a culture that tells us we can have our cake and eat it too. Many Christians today believe they can put themselves at the center of the universe and that God will reward them for including Him in their worldview. There was a time in church history when most believers were willing to forsake their own lives rather than deny their faith. And still, all these centuries later, many believers around the world would willingly do so. But do you know what I hear people in the church talking about today? Cholesterol counts and Botox! They're trying desperately to prolong their physical lives or regain a youthful appearance. What happened? We've taken a wonderful adventure, which for the sake of an eternity with God might cost us our physical lives, and shrunk it down to fit us. We've reduced the Christian life to what was manageable and comfortable, to something we could add to our lives to make ourselves feel good. But in the process, we stripped it of its vitality, and left ourselves wondering, like the rich young ruler, what we still lack.

True faith is something that grabs us by the lapels and drags us wherever it wants us to go. It calls us to "consider everything a loss compared to the surpassing greatness of knowing Christ Jesus."[2]

Like the needle of a compass being pulled north, true faith has an object, and the strength of one's faith depends on the trustworthiness of that object. Faith is not merely believing something with all of our hearts. Someone may believe that he can fly, but no matter how convinced he is, he'll still drop like a stone if he jumps off a cliff. Our faith is strengthened by seeing that the object of our faith is truly faithful. How do you develop trust in someone? By seeing time and again that they are truly trustworthy. Our faith in God is built the same way. Scripture says, "Faith comes from hearing, and hearing by the word of Christ."[3] This means that as we hear what God says, and as we see that His actions are true to His word, our faith in Him grows.

Faith does not come naturally for fallen humanity. Ephesians 2:8 tells us that every element of our salvation, including our faith, is the "gift of God." Because of our stubborn unwillingness to trust God, God had to open our eyes so that we could see the truth, and He had to change our hearts so that we could put our faith in Him. Faith is not only a gift from God; it is also our guide to Him. Isaiah 30:20-21 contains a prophecy about man's relationship with God under the new covenant, which describes how God Himself will guide His people: "Your Teacher will no longer hide Himself, but your eyes will behold your Teacher. Your ears will hear a word behind you, 'This is the way, walk in it,' whenever you turn to the right or to the left." This is the essence of the walk of faith.

Taking the High Way means trusting the One who is faithful. Faith in God is nothing more difficult than that.

_____

FOOTNOTES: 1. Romans 3:23; 2. Philippians 3:8 (NIV); 3. Romans 10:17

GPS: *God-Positioning Scriptures (to Reorient Your Life)*
You've taken my hand. You wisely and tenderly lead me, and then you bless me.
You're all I want in heaven! You're all I want on earth! —**Psalm 73:23-25** (The Message)

REST STOP: *Pull Over and Ponder*
Are you trusting in anything or anyone other than God today? True faith revolutionizes our lives. In which parts of your life have you left faith out of the equation lately? What do you need to entrust to God today?

Mile 10

Checking the Directions

As the first part of your journey comes to an end, you begin to see that this is not a linear journey through space and time, but a spiritual journey that grows in several directions. There is no aspect of our lives that will remain unaffected.

YOUR JOURNEY HAS three dimensions: upward, outward, and inward. And as you take steps in each of these directions, you make progress in the ultimate journey toward Christian maturity.

The **upward journey** leads us to a more complete relationship with God. We began in Mile 1 by realizing that our tiny images of God were skewed, simplistic profiles that helped us feel like we really knew Him. Many of us approach God and try to localize Him, to confine Him to a particular place or a manifestation. We try to hold Him within a system that will make Him easy to understand. This is what the Samaritan woman did when she asked Jesus where people should worship. Jesus told her that God could not be confined to Mount Gerizim in

Samaria or Mount Sinai in Jerusalem, that He was far greater than any parish or place of worship. Jesus said, "A time is coming and has now come when the true worshipers will worship the Father in spirit and truth, for they are the kind of worshipers the Father seeks."[1]

Gothic architecture is not required for worship to take place. I doubt the early Christians built flying buttresses and elaborate spires in the sewers and catacombs where they were often forced to worship. Northland, A Church Distributed, where I have served as senior pastor since 1985, met for more than two decades in a dilapidated skating rink, and for a number of years, the atmosphere was more like the catacombs than Notre Dame de Paris. The restrooms were right next to the sanctuary, and the congregation could hear every flush! Occasionally, a big rat would crawl across the ceiling beams in the middle of a class. Conditions were less than ideal, but true worship was taking place. As wonderful as those places may be, God is not confined to churches with stained-glass windows and pipe organs.

> "As we grow in spiritual maturity, we being to learn that although we are an essential part of God's plan, we are not necessarily the central part."

While the upward dimension of our journey features our relationship with God, the **outward dimension** extends to our relationships with people. Our relationship with God and our relationships with others go hand in hand. God is at work in the lives of all people. We need to stop thinking of people in terms of "us" versus "them," Christian versus non-Christian, secular versus sacred, black versus white, Jew versus Gentile, male versus female, Democrat versus Republican, or any other kind of opposing categories. Beyond external appearances, provincial stereotypes, and differing perspectives, we find that all people have a fundamental problem with sin and therefore a fundamental need for Christ. The outward dimension of our spiritual journey will stretch us to the point where compassion turns into contribution. It draws our focus beyond our own needs and concerns to the needs and concerns of others. It will continually lead us into more significant, and more selfless, relationships with others.

Our journey inward highlights a thrilling and frightening realization that God knows us personally—that there is no place we can go to hide from Him.

We are completely open to His scrutiny, and He knows us by name. Realizing that our individual purpose is only one aspect of a grander purpose is a significant milestone on our inward journey. As we mature in Christ, we will begin to look beyond the initial thrill of being singled out, to a greater thrill—the discovery that He has also singled out others and has given each of them a special role in the advancement of His kingdom. As we grow in spiritual maturity, we begin to learn that although we are an essential part of God's plan, we are not necessarily the central part. It's ironic that our journey inward actually leads us to focus outwardly. We start to realize that we get to help prepare the way for what Christ will do in other people's lives.

Taking the High Way means coming to grips with the fact that the Christian life is the "road less traveled." If we choose it though, we shall see God face to face, and we will reflect His glory. Knowing this, how could any of us wish to remain where we are?

FOOTNOTES: 1. John 4:23 (NIV)

GPS: *God-Positioning Scriptures (to Reorient Your Life)*

The highway to hell is broad, and its gate is wide for the many who choose that way. But the gateway to life is very narrow and the road is difficult, and only a few ever find it. —Matthew 7:13-14 (NLT)

REST STOP: *Pull Over and Ponder*
Do you see evidence of upward, outward, and inward dimensions to your current spiritual journey? What can you do today to more fully engage every aspect of your journey?

EXIT 2: *PURPOSE DRIVE*

Mile 11

The Path to Purpose

As you continue on your journey to spiritual maturity, you begin to feel uncertain about the road ahead. You're tempted to pull over, to play it safe. But making progress requires venturing out into the unknown.

W E HAVE PROBABLY heard somewhere that God has a "wonderful plan" for our lives. But for all our ability to repeat platitudes, do we honestly live with any more of a sense of purpose and meaning than non-Christians do?

Could it be that we're afraid to face the nagging questions about the meaning of life? Are we worried that we might be disappointed with the answers to them? What if God's definition of wonderful plan doesn't match ours? What if our purpose is to sell all we have and take a vow of poverty? What if our purpose is to be something that's not very glamorous or maybe even weird? I think many of us are afraid to discover our purpose because it might not be exactly what we think we want, so we just keep busy and hope that maybe somehow, in some way, our life is counting for something. Or we are scared to ask the questions of purpose because we're afraid we might answer them wrongly. So we just keep living the way we've always lived, playing it safe by sticking with endless activity and its byproduct of nagging uncertainty.

The journey toward spiritual maturity involves surrender, risk, and an ever-increasing dependence upon God. The path to certainty about our purpose for living requires going beyond the familiar. As we look to God rather than our routine and circumstances, we will discover that what we must risk is not worth holding on to. In a C.S. Lewis paraphrase, we will realize we were like an ignorant child who wanted to go on making mud pies in a slum because he could not imagine what is meant by the offer of a holiday at the sea. In other words, we will realize we were far too easily pleased. If we are ever to find that which is meaningful and worthwhile, we must be willing to risk disappointment and face uncertainty.

> "The path to certainty about our purpose for living requires going beyond the familiar."

God alone is in control of what happens to us. He is the One who created us. Apart from Him, we never would have existed. Only by asking Him will we have a framework for understanding how every area of our lives fits together.

And He did not create us in a vacuum, as unconnected individuals who are complete in and of ourselves. We were born into the family of mankind. Although all creatures were created *ex nihilo*, "out of nothing," not one of them was placed *in nihilum*, "into nothing." Each one was born into the world that God had prepared, each created "according to their kinds"[1] with built-in characteristics, instincts, behaviors, and relationships to the environment and the other creatures. Man was no exception to this pattern.

We cannot find our purposes as individual men and women until we have grasped God's purpose for mankind as a whole. God created mankind because He wanted to build a people for Himself. "Now the dwelling of God is with men, and He will live with them. They will be His people, and God himself will be with them and be their God."[2]

Was God's purpose for creating man a vain or selfish one? Certainly not. Scripture says that God is love, God is *agape*. *Agape* is a full love, so full, in fact, that it seeks out someone to give to. Agape is for the good of the beloved.

God created a people who could experience that love. He created a people for Himself not for what they could give Him, but for what He could give to them. God created people able to reflect His own character, able to stand as the pinnacle of His creation, able to rule, protect, provide, cultivate, and love as He does. Ultimately, our reasons for existence are to love God and serve as the people of God.

In the final analysis, the question is not whether or not we will give our lives away, but what we will give our lives away for. Taking the High Way means making each day of our lives count for something, and even more importantly for Someone beyond ourselves.

FOOTNOTES: 1. Genesis 1:21 (NIV); 2. Revelation 21:3 (NIV)

GPS: *God-Positioning Scriptures (to Reorient Your Life)*
Whoever finds his life will lose it, and whoever loses his life for my sake will find it.
—Matthew 10:39 (NIV)

REST STOP: *Pull Over and Ponder*
Have you discovered your purpose in life? For *whom* or *what* would you say your actions and words indicate you're living?

Mile 12

Powered by Purpose, Part 1

To find your purpose, you must now turn to the Garden of Eden—to the ideal God had for mankind at the time of our creation, to the life people were originally intended to live.

WHEN WE LOOK for a life of purpose, nothing can compare to the lives of Adam and Eve in the garden. Our first parents were created for a life that was absolutely overflowing with purpose. As their children, who continue to bear the image of the eternal God, it only makes sense that we still long for that life we were originally intended to live. Yet we no longer live in the Garden of Eden, but in a fallen world, in which the original spheres of purpose seem like hopeless fantasies. How can we possibly hope to live as we were intended to?

Adam and Eve were given **Life** to enjoy, **Labor** to fulfill, **Limits** to preserve, **Learning** to explore, and **Love** to share. They were to reflect God's image in each of those spheres of life ...

Life: Our Purpose in Being

The first thing we need to realize about our purpose is that we have meaning simply by virtue of having life. This is a very difficult concept to accept, especially for those of us steeped in American culture, which is highly utilitarian. The American culture's attitude is this: Something is good only insofar as it is useful, and anything that has outlived its usefulness, we discard. If we embrace this attitude, we can begin to judge the worth of people's lives (including our own) by how useful they are.

"...work originally was intended to be a gift to mankind, an opportunity for us to leave our mark on the world."

The first thing that God did for Adam after sculpting his body from the dust was to "breathe into his nostrils the breath of life," and immediately the man became a "living being." God's appraisal of His creation, and His verdict of "very good,"[1] were not based on creation's functionality or usefulness. After all, of what use was creation to God? He lacked nothing! He was, and still is, complete and sufficient in and of Himself. Creation was good simply because it had been brought into existence. Just as a painting reflects the mastery of the painter, so creation reflects the genius and artistry of the Creator. Its primary value is in its existence, because its existence points to God. In Scripture, all of life is considered sacred and worth preserving simply because its existence reflects the glory of God.

Labor: Our Purpose in Work

In addition to giving Adam life, God gave him a job as well. He took him and "put him into the garden of Eden to cultivate it and keep it."[2] The name "Eden" is actually the Hebrew word for "delight." So, literally, God placed Adam in the garden of delight, in Paradise, and commissioned him to cultivate it and keep it. Part of the delight of Adam's Paradise was in the work he had been given to do. This may come as some surprise to us, since we tend to associate work with the curse God placed on Adam after the Fall, but work originally was intended to be a gift to mankind, an opportunity for us to leave our mark on the world.

Imagine if some master artist came to you and asked you to apply the finishing strokes to his masterpiece and to sign your name to the painting directly under his. This is precisely what God did with Adam. Adam was given the opportunity to add to what God had already done, to leave his own mark on the world, his own signature to creation. In the beginning, the purpose of work was not survival, or greed, or ambition, or obsession. God intended work to be a great adventure, a mirroring of His own great act of creation.

Taking the High Way means knowing that it is not the substance of our contribution but the act of contributing itself that is divine.

FOOTNOTES: 1. Genesis 1:31 (NIV); 2. Genesis 2:15

GPS: *God-Positioning Scriptures (to Reorient Your Life)*

When I look at the night sky and see the work of your fingers—the moon and the stars you set in place—what are mere mortals that you should think about them, human beings that you should care for them? Yet you made them only a little lower than God and crowned them with glory and honor. —**Psalm 8:3-5** (NLT)

Whatever you do, do your work heartily, as for the Lord rather than for men. —**Colossians 3:23**

REST STOP: *Pull Over and Ponder*
You can leave a much more significant mark on the world when you believe God has created you to do so. Are you motivated by God's ability (and desire) to use your life to glorify Him? How might you be able to "leave your mark" on the timeline of eternity today?

Mile 13

Powered by Purpose, Part 2

The journey toward Christian maturity is a great adventure! Having gained an understanding of the meanings of life and labor, you now explore God's purpose behind limits, learning, and love.

Limits: Purpose in our Contingency

God created man to be the pinnacle of His creation, His crowning achievement—and God treated him as such. He made man the master of all he surveyed, the keeper of the garden. He called Adam to contribute to His world, even to improve it. He imparted to Adam His own image, something no other creature had been permitted to bear.

Adam was given great authority over creation. Yet Adam was still a created being. He could bear the image and likeness of God, but he would never be God. He was, and forever would be, a contingent being. God alone is the only truly necessary Being. He is the only One who must exist.

God communicated this distinction to Adam through the forbidden tree. After telling Adam that he had been provided everything he needed for the sustenance of life, God said, "but from the tree of the knowledge of good and evil you shall not eat, for in the day that you eat from it you will surely die."[1] Out of all of creation, God had set apart this one tree as off-limits to Adam, a stark reminder to Adam of his dependence upon God. Think about it, if man is a contingent being, dependent upon God for his existence, then he will live only as long as he remains dependent upon God. Any creature that tries to sever its relationship with the Creator is cutting itself off from the Source of its life— quite literally, killing itself.

With the tree of the knowledge of good and evil, God established a simple boundary for Adam. The limitation was meant to underscore his continual need for the Creator, and to protect him from that which would result in his destruction.

Learning: Our Purpose in Knowledge

It is often supposed that Adam's state in Paradise was one of blissful ignorance, and that God wanted to keep it that way—hence His restriction on the tree of the knowledge of good and evil. But God's restriction of the tree was not meant to keep man in the dark, but to protect him from that which would destroy him. In fact, one of man's purposes in the garden was to acquire knowledge. Adam was given a world to explore, analyze, contemplate, and marvel. Clearly, God was not resistant to Adam's gaining knowledge. On the contrary, He fully intended that Adam should learn all that he could about his world.

In the beginning, all knowledge pointed to God. Whenever Adam learned something about the world around him, he was gaining insight into the nature of the Creator who had brought these things into existence. Thus, man's ultimate purpose in learning about the world around him was to gain a deeper understanding of the character of God. Adam knew no distinction between "sacred" knowledge and "secular" knowledge. To him, it all inevitably led back to God. Johannes Kepler, the father of modern astronomy, once remarked in the midst of his studies, "God, I am thinking Thy thoughts after Thee!" He understood well that the more we come to know about the universe, the more clearly we see God reflected in it. For Kepler, ignorance was not bliss, and neither was learning opposed to faith. Kepler had discovered what Adam had known long before—that mankind has been given the glorious opportunity to delve into the marvels and mysteries of what God has done.

Love: Our Purpose in Relationship

In addition to learning about the world around him and the character of his God, Adam learned of his need for relationship. God had recognized this need long before, but for some reason, had decided not to satisfy it right away. In Genesis 2:18, God stated for the first time that something in His creation was "not good." It was not good for the man to be alone. So He declared immediately that He would provide the solution to Adam's need for relationship. He would make a "helper suitable for him." God brought all the animals to the man to see what he would call them, but when all was said and done, no suitable helper was found for Adam.

> *"...the more we come to know about the universe, the more clearly we see God reflected in it."*

For most of us, the creation story is so familiar that we miss the dramatic tension that is introduced at this point. God actually seems to have failed! He simply has not yet delivered on His promise to provide Adam with a "suitable helper." By observing and naming the animals, Adam was becoming aware of a need that he never before knew he had. By making Adam wait to have this need satisfied, God was preparing him for the day when he would receive that "helper suitable for him," when he would enter into an entirely new sphere of purpose and meaning, when he would reflect God's image by giving love to another.

In Hebrew, the phrase "a suitable helper" literally means "a help like—opposite him." This "helper" would be "suitable" for Adam in that she would be enough like him to have a basis for relationship with him, yet different enough to be able to contribute something unique, or, stated another way, similar enough to be intimate, yet different enough to be necessary. When God finally created Eve from Adam's rib and brought her to him, Adam recognized immediately that she was the answer to his need for relationship. He exclaimed, "This is now bone of my bones, and flesh of my flesh; she shall be called Woman, because she was taken out of Man."[2] They were one—free to love one another, be completed by one another, and know one another completely. Though separate, they were one in essence, alike, yet distinct, both singular and plural at once. How better to reflect the image of God, who is three, yet one—united within Himself by perfect love.

Taking the High Way means understanding that we were created to bear God's image; to reflect the His likeness and splendor. When we really understand that, we are humbled and honored and sense the importance of the roles He offers to us.

FOOTNOTES 1. Genesis 2:17; 2. Genesis 2:23

GPS: *God-Positioning Scriptures (to Reorient Your Life)*

God commanded the Man, "You can eat from any tree in the garden, except from the Tree-of-Knowledge-of-Good-and-Evil. Don't eat from it. The moment you eat from that tree, you're dead." —Genesis 2:17 (The Message)

Then the Lord God made a woman from the rib, and he brought her to the man. "At last!" the man exclaimed. "This one is bone from my bone, and flesh from my flesh! She will be called 'woman,' because she was taken from 'man.'" This explains why a man leaves his father and mother and is joined to his wife, and the two are united into one. —Genesis 2:22-24 (NLT)

Above all and before all, do this: Get Wisdom! Write this at the top of your list: Get Understanding! Throw your arms around her—believe me, you won't regret it; never let her go—she'll make your life glorious. —Proverbs 4:7-8 (The Message)

 REST STOP: *Pull Over and Ponder*
Where might God's prevailing purposes in establishing limits, promoting learning, and initiating love intersect with your current circumstances in life?

Mile 14

Purpose Lost

Mankind's purpose-filled life in Paradise ended with the Fall. Adam and Eve had severed their personal relationship with God, wreaking havoc upon every dimension of their lives.

INTO THE GARDEN of Eden crept a shadowy figure. Satan, the prince of darkness, the sworn enemy of God, desired to leave his own mark upon the world that God had made. His heart was filled with hatred for the man and woman whom God had so richly blessed. How fervently Satan must have longed to unseat these new creatures from their place of honor, to lead them in hopeless rebellion against the Creator, to coax them into eternal damnation with himself.

How to do it? If Satan could get Adam and Eve to suspect that God had some ulterior motive for restricting the tree of the knowledge of good and evil, then they might voluntarily sever their relationship with God through disobedience. Satan promised Adam and Eve a different kind of knowledge—a secret knowledge that would make them equal with God. Adam and Eve bought into Satan's lie that God was trying to hold out on them, to keep them ignorant in order to control them. They began to suspect that God was not really good—that His plans for them were not the best. Through their doubt and ultimate disobedience, they severed their personal relationship with the Creator.

By embracing evil, they were now intimately acquainted with it. Their eyes were opened. They knew good and evil in the sense that they now understood that they were evil and no longer good. They now had the "wisdom" to see that what God had said was true: that in the day they ate of the forbidden tree, they would surely die. Not only had they lost their Paradise, they had lost their purpose as well. The Fall resulted not only in death, but in the distortion and disruption of **Life**, **Labor**, **Limits**, **Learning**, and **Love**, which give meaning to human existence.

Life: From Individuality to Individualism

The first thing Adam and Eve did after they damaged their relationship with God was cover themselves and hide from God.[1] Mankind had gone from being the pinnacle of creation to being a wretched, cowering creatures, desperately seeking shelter from the exposure of their sin. This catastrophic loss of security before God completely undermined man's sense of purpose in being. The Fall brought an end to the perspective that all life has value and purpose. Fallen man is too busy trying to protect his own worth to value anyone else's life as highly as his own.

"Individuality is an expression of the image of God; individualism is a reflection of the image of Satan."

The Fall resulted in a descent from individuality to individualism. Individualism is an insidious worldview in which the individual places himself at the center of the universe and considers the welfare of all others to be secondary to his own. Individuality is an expression of the image of God; individualism is a reflection of the image of Satan.

Labor: From Contribution to Consumption

Man's perspective on work has been skewed ever since the Fall. In Paradise, man's work was inherently connected with God's provision for him. Adam's purpose in work was not to "earn a living," but to cultivate and keep the garden.

He did not have to work for food, because his food had already been provided for him. The Fall changed all that. Man's work had now become his toil and travail, a desperate attempt to prolong his existence one more day. The irony of fallen man's situation was that his labor should have driven him back to God in the recognition that only He could supply his needs, but instead it became the catalyst for further rebellion. Human beings began to associate their provision with the work that they did. They became consumed with making their own ways in the world—earning their own places in the universe. The purpose of our labor changed from contribution to consumption.

Ever since the Fall, we have engaged in the desperate attempt to get what we want by our own efforts. Do we want fame, fortune, comfort, or recognition? Then we pursue our careers with reckless abandon. Do we want love? Then we work hard at getting it, trying to find ways to coax or manipulate people into loving us. Do we want salvation? Then we invent a system of religious duties by which we can earn divine approval. As fallen men and women, our lives are consumed with restless activity, in a desperate attempt to acquire the things God freely gave us in the garden. The proverbial "rat race" began with Adam and Eve, and it continues to this day.

Limits: From Refuge to Refugees

Man's purpose in his limitation was to recognize his continual need for God and to remain content with what God had provided. The limitation established a safe haven from the death and desolation of life apart from God, a refuge in which man was free to fulfill the purposes for which he had been created. Yet, prompted by the empty promises of the serpent, Adam and Eve chose to break out of this refuge in order to see what was beyond the boundary God had set. What they found was a life of separation from God, full of endless craving, continual struggle, and constant fear. In the words of Paul, "They exchanged the truth of God for a lie."[2]

Adam and Eve left behind the refuge of God's will and, as a result, became refugees, lost souls with no place they could truly call home. As fallen creatures, we continually forsake the abundance of God's provision in a hopeless quest for some forbidden fruit. We have become so distorted and perverse in our nature that we rebel against almost every restriction we are given. We abandon the refuge of God's will in order to become refugees in "the valley of the shadow of death."[3]

Learning: From Connection to Separation

In the beginning, all of life was connected, and the learning process involved tracing those connections. Human knowledge was intended to be like one of those connect-the-dot pictures we used to do as children. The picture was there all the time, but it was not evident until we drew the lines, making the connections.

With the Fall, no longer did man see learning as the making of connections between the various clues God had left throughout the world. On the contrary, man deliberately began to avoid making the connections that would point him back to God. The more clearly we come to see God, the more vividly our own sinfulness is exposed. Therefore, fallen man began to reconnect the dots in such a way as to erase God from the picture. The result was that his picture of the world became distorted and incomplete. Learning had become the process by which man attempted to dethrone God, rather than the process by which he discovered Him.

Love: From Complements to Competitors

Perhaps one of the most devastating consequences of the Fall is the effect it had on human relationships. Having lost the security that comes from having a relationship with God, man and woman became obsessed with asserting their own worth, typically by casting blame on someone else. The decline into individualism drove a wedge between people. Suspicious of each other, resentful, selfish, and cruel, the proverbial "battle of the sexes" began. No longer was woman man's "suitable helper." She had become his rival in a contest for dominance. God declared in the garden that it is not good for the man to be alone. The irony of the Fall is that men and women are now alone in the midst of their relationships.

Although we still long for the perfect love of a relationship, for the ability to give without fear of being taken advantage of, and to receive with no strings attached, fallen men and women have been left to sift through the shattered pieces of this love we were created to know. We continue to try to give love, to reach out for one another, but our love is tainted with fear, insecurity, suspicion, and the desire to possess.

There is no way we can go back to the garden, but God in His grace has established a way for us to go forward together. Taking the High Way means moving toward fulfillment in the five areas of purpose and enjoying a relationship with Him that is once again intimate and complete.

_____

FOOTNOTES: 1. Genesis 3:8; 2. Romans 1:25 (NIV); 3. Psalm 23:4 (NIV)

GPS: *God-Positioning Scriptures (to Reorient Your Life)*

Let us fix our eyes on Jesus, the author and perfecter of our faith, who for the joy set before him endured the cross, scorning its shame, and sat down at the right hand of the throne of God.
—Hebrews 12:2 (NIV)

 REST STOP: *Pull Over and Ponder*
The Fall significantly altered how we perceive our purpose in life. Where do you see the effects of the Fall still affecting you today? How has God's grace helped you reclaim purpose and meaning despite Satan's handiwork in the garden?

Mile 15

Purpose Found

Mankind's sense of purpose was lost when he stretched out his hand to take the fruit of the forbidden tree. Yet by God's grace, it was regained when Jesus Christ stretched out His hands upon the deadly tree of crucifixion.

FALLEN MAN HAD forgotten God, but fortunately, God had not forgotten man. While mankind was accelerating into rebellion against Him, God was establishing the Bridge to accomplish mankind's redemption, to reunite us with Him and to bring us back to the purposes for which we had been created.

"Redemption" is one of those buzzwords Christians often use but seldom understand. To "redeem" means to purchase, "to recover ownership of something by paying a specified sum."[1] The word was primarily used with respect to slaves who were purchased in order to be set free, or debtors whose debts were paid by someone else.

Christ came not only to save us from the penalty for sin, but also to redeem us from the futile way of life that resulted from the Fall. Christ entered a fallen world in order to reestablish life—and not just any kind of life, but full, abundant, and complete life. "I have come that they may have life, and have it to the full."[2]

He came so that Paradise might be regained, and to redeem us through **Life**, **Labor**, **Limits**, **Learning**, and **Love**.

Life: Christ, Our Identity

Christ came to redeem us out of the fear and insecurity of our fallen existence, in order to restore us to peace and security before God. He did so by way of an incredible transaction—the most uneven swap ever conceived. He took on our fallen identity so that we might take on His divine identity. He did this by taking our sins with Him, to the cross, so that they could no longer separate us from God. Since our fallen identity has been crucified with Christ and we have been endowed with Christ's own identity, we are able once again to have security and meaning on the basis of who we are, rather than what we do. Just as in the garden Adam and Eve lacked nothing, so in Christ we lack for nothing. We can now have life, and have it "to the full."

"By grace Christ gave us back everything that we had foolishly given up in the garden."

Labor: Christ's Contribution Evokes Ours

Into this world of poverty and destitution, Christ came to give redemption not as a reward for any effort we had put forth (since all our efforts deserved His condemnation, rather than His blessing), but as a free gift, completely undeserved and unmerited. "For by grace you have been saved through faith; and that not of yourselves, it is the gift of God."[3] What a radical truth! By grace Christ gave us back everything that we had foolishly given up in the garden. He completely canceled our debt to God, leaving nothing more for us to pay.

Because we have been completely provided for, we no longer need to worry about obtaining what we lack. Instead, we can give to others out of our abundance, even to the point of making great sacrifices for them. In Christ, we are once again free to leave our signatures on God's creation, to have a hand in the shape of eternity, and to make a difference in this world.

Limits: Our Weakness Becomes Christ's Strength

In order to redeem humanity, Christ set aside equality with God, "emptied Himself,"[4] of His omniscience, omnipotence, omnipresence, and immortality in order to assume human form, accepting such human limitations as frailty, hunger, weariness, pain, and vulnerability. What's more, in His humanity, He accepted even greater limitation, in that He came not as a King, but as a "bond-servant," birthed in a stable, laid in a feeding trough, raised as a carpenter, scorned by the political and religious elite, and rejected in His own hometown. How far had He descended from the throne room of heaven!

Through His humiliation, Christ won salvation for the world. Through His weakness, He won the victory over sin and death. His highest glory came through His acceptance of the most confining limitations. In the same way, we who are in Christ are called to accept the limitations that God has placed on us, because in them lies our greatest strength.

Learning: Christ, the Missing Link

Everything that mankind destroyed in the Fall, Christ came to restore. He came to restore humanity's knowledge of God through His incarnation, becoming God with a face, the visible "image" of the invisible Lord. He came to "show us the Father" and to make known to us the "mystery of His will."[5] In Him, the knowledge of God is once again an unspeakable joy, rather than a maddening torment; it is the knowledge of a love regained, rather than a love lost.

By restoring our knowledge of God, Christ restored our ability to acquire true knowledge of everything. He freed us to pursue knowledge without fear of where it would lead. He became the "missing link" in our picture of the universe, connecting the dots we were previously unable or unwilling to connect.

The learning process is like a jigsaw puzzle. The best way to complete it is to compare each piece to the picture of the finished puzzle in order to see where that piece fits into the larger pattern. Before Christ came, fallen man was able, with painstaking effort, to match up a few pieces of the puzzle of knowledge, but he refused to look at the overall picture that the puzzle made, because it was a picture of the God he had rejected. In Christ, we are once again equipped to pursue knowledge. No matter where we turn for it, whether to astronomy, mathematics, physics, literature, history, science, philosophy, art, music, or theology, we are able to see how what we learn fits into the pattern of who God is.

Love: Christ Forms "One New Man"[6]

In our fallen state, we no longer knew how to give the agape love we were created to give. By laying down His life for those whose lives were not worthy, Christ demonstrated God's perfect agape, the kind of love that gives without regard to self, that reaches out without fear of rejection, and that sacrifices for the sake of the other. Yet Christ went beyond merely demonstrating agape; He went so far as to make us one with Himself and with each other so that loving each other could become as natural as loving ourselves.

Scripture makes it clear that because there is no one beyond the reach of Christ's love, there is no one whom we cannot love. Differences of race, social standing, culture, sex, language, and so on are no longer the lines that divide us, but the diversities out of which Christ unites us. He makes us all "one new man" in Himself so that when we love each other, we love ourselves.

Taking the High Way means embracing the freedom that comes with redemption. We have been ransomed out of a position of slavery and bondage in order to be given freedom and a meaningful life.

FOOTNOTES: 1. The American Heritage Dictionary of the English Language, Fourth Edition, 2005, by Houghton Mifflin Company; 2. John 10:10 (NIV); 3. Ephesians 2:8; 4. Philippians 2:6-7; 5. Ephesians 1:9 (NIV); 6. Ephesians 2:15

GPS: *God-Positioning Scriptures (to Reorient Your Life)*

Yes, Adam's one sin brings condemnation for everyone, but Christ's one act of righteousness brings a right relationship with God and new life for everyone. Because one person disobeyed God, many became sinners. But because one other person obeyed God, many will be made righteous.
—Romans 5:18-19 (NLT)

REST STOP: *Pull Over and Ponder*

Grace is often defined as unmerited favor—something we cannot earn and something wholly undeserved. Do you feel transformed by the grace present in God's redemptive work through Christ? In which ways?

Mile 16

Purpose Perfected, Part 1

Through the Fall, mankind's sense of purpose was lost. Through Christ's redemption, it has been found. In heaven, it will be perfected. Don't stop until you reach that destination.

Life: Living in Exile

Though in Christ we are a "new creation,"[1] we continue to live in a fallen world. Our nature no longer corresponds to our environment, so we experience our new life in Christ as "aliens and strangers in the world."[2] We are like the exiles in Babylon who longed for the day when they would return to the Promised Land. How can we fulfill our purpose in Christ while we are living in exile? Many Christians conclude that we should just hunker down and wait for Christ to return and complete our redemption. Those who have this "hunker down" mentality tend to put their lives on hold, to avoid involvement in the affairs of this world, and to see a great distinction between the sacred and the secular. The problem with such an approach is that it ignores the fact that God has a reason for not immediately whisking us away to heaven. Christ left us here for a purpose. We must recognize our time of exile as a part of God's plan.

Thankfully, God's Word speaks a great deal about how we are to live as strangers in a strange land. In Jeremiah 29:4-11, God speaks to the Jews in the Babylonian captivity about how they should live during their period of exile. God commands them to carry on just as they would if they were still in the Promised Land. God had a purpose for their being in Babylon. In the same way, God has a purpose for leaving us here on the Earth, even though in Christ, we have become citizens of heaven. The challenge for us, just like the Jews in Babylon, is to live out our time of exile as though we were already home.

> *"You don't need to become a preacher or a missionary to serve Christ. Rather, you can serve Him perfectly well right where you are—doing what you can, with what you've got."*

Imagine how remarkable the Jews of the Dispersion must have seemed to their Babylonian captors. Most foreign peoples conquered by Babylon either assimilated completely, adopting the culture, dress, and customs of the Babylonians, or resisted, trying to overthrow their oppressors in an attempt to regain their independence. The Jews, however, did neither of these things. They were too proud to assimilate, refusing to adopt the culture of an uncircumcised people who did not worship the true God, yet they became some of the best citizens of the Babylonian empire. The Jews built homes right beside those of their Babylonian neighbors, they engaged in commerce, they obeyed the law, and they prayed for the welfare of their cities.

As Christians living in the midst of a fallen world, we are called neither to revolt in an attempt to impose our own will upon society, nor to conform to the pattern of our culture. Rather, we are to act as "salt" and "light."[3] Though we live in an environment that either tempts us to assimilate or tries to provoke us into revolt, we must remember that "all things" are ours in Christ. Like the Jewish captives who influenced their Babylonian captors, we can have a profound effect on the people around us, without having to do anything more than live out in their midst the new, full, abundant life we have been given in Christ. It is by our "quiet," purposeful lives in the midst of exile that we will "win the respect of outsiders."[4]

Labor: Improving Our Corner of the World

The Jews of the Dispersion went beyond merely living their own private lives among the Babylonians; they actually worked for the welfare of their captors! They worked to improve the corner of the world God had placed them in, even though it was foreign to them. If we were created to work for the improvement and enrichment of Paradise, how much more should we who are in Christ work for the improvement and enrichment of a fallen and corrupt world? God has called us, during our period of exile in this world, to work to improve whatever corner of the world we find ourselves in.

When we become Christians, we are not called to quit our jobs, leave our families, cut off all our hair, and move to Outer Mongolia to become missionaries. We are called to serve Christ and to contribute to the world right where we are. You don't need to become a preacher or a missionary to serve Christ. Rather, you can serve Him perfectly well right where you are—doing what you can, with what you've got. He put you there for His purposes. Does this mean that we're stuck forever doing whatever it was we were doing when we came to Christ? Not at all. What it means is that we start contributing to the world as Christians right where we are. It means that we don't have to become something we're not in order to be good Christians.

In Jesus' Parable of the Talents, it was on the basis of the servants' faithfulness with the little things that the master gave them more responsibility and the opportunity to make a more substantial contribution.[5] Our "calling" is to be faithful to make whatever contribution we can in our present situation, until God reveals to us that He has something more for us.

Many Christians today, because of their desire to do something great for God, rush into things for which they are not yet prepared. They typically end up disillusioned and burned out, having accomplished very little of real substance. God calls us instead to make it our ambition to lead a quiet life,[6] to be faithful in the little things, the things that are right in front of us to do. It is those people whom God puts in charge of "many things." It is the people who do what they can to improve and lift up their corner of the world that God uses to turn the world upside down.

Taking the High Way means being faithful to serve Christ and contribute to the world right where we are. Such faithful ministry service is quite often a major factor in serving more broadly and effectively down the road.

FOOTNOTES: 1. 2 Corinthians 5:17 (NIV); 2. 1 Peter 2:11 (NIV); 3. Matthew 5:13-14 (NIV); 4. 1 Thessalonians 4:12 (NIV); 5. Matthew 25: 14-30; 6. 1 Thessalonians 4:11 (NIV)

GPS: *God-Positioning Scriptures (to Reorient Your Life)*

Make it your goal to live a quiet life, minding your own business and working with your hands, just as we instructed you before. Then people who are not Christians will respect the way you live, and you will not need to depend on others. —1 Thessalonians 4:11-12 (NLT)

REST STOP: *Pull Over and Ponder*
God has a purpose for your life, and He's invested in your potential. Consider your present career, relationships, or even geographical location. Are there areas in which you could be a catalyst of improvement today?

Mile 17

Purpose Perfected, Part 2

Until that day comes when your journey is at an end, you will continue to travel the road toward spiritual maturity. Leaving behind your former life, you keep moving ahead in renewed purpose.

Limits: When God Says No

When God spoke to the Jewish exiles in Babylon, He made it clear that He was the One who had sent them into exile. Their limitation had been placed on them by God Himself, and as such, it was to be accepted, rather than resisted. Nevertheless, He assured them, their exile was all part of His plan for them, a plan for "welfare and not for calamity" to give them "a future and a hope."[1]

Likewise, God has left us in exile, living in a world that is no longer our own. We long to win decisive victories over the forces of greed, selfishness, cruelty, decadence, and destruction that so pervade the world around us. We wish we could hasten the day when the kingdom of God will come in power. But God says no. He makes us wait for that day. He refuses to remove our limitations. So

73

we live out our time of exile, clinging to the assurance that this is all part of His plan, and that our weaknesses really are our strengths.

How should we respond when God says no, when He leaves us to the struggle and adversity of exile? Our tendency is to adopt a refugee or squatter mentality. Christians with a refugee mentality see themselves as a persecuted minority, living in a world destined for destruction. They see the time they stay on earth as a frustrating necessity, rather than as an important part of God's plan. They have little interest in making a positive contribution to the world. Those with a squatter mentality see the limitation of exile as something to be overcome. They typically react to times when God says no by digging in their heels and refusing to budge until God changes His mind. In doing so, they ignore the fact that God has a purpose for our limitations.

God allows us to experience certain weaknesses, frailties, and difficulties during our time here on Earth so that we will not forget our dependence on Him. Because our weaknesses drive us into the arms of God, they can become our strengths. Knowing this, we are able to accept our time of exile as a gift, an opportunity to make a difference in this world, both through our strengths and through our weaknesses, until that day when God finally brings us home.

Learning: Our Exile, an "Engagement"

Our period of exile is, like a marriage engagement, a period of anticipation and preparation. We, like those who are engaged to be married, eagerly wait for the day when we shall "know fully,"[2] when our union with Christ will be even more intimate than that of a husband and wife. Until that day comes, we seek to know all we can about Him, straining to see Him more clearly in a world limited to, among other things, time and space.

We satisfy this desire to know Christ by fulfilling one of the purposes for which we were created: to learn. He has revealed Himself in everything around us. The world in which we live, while both limited and fallen, points to our Lord. The people around us, whether Christian or not, reflect the image of God. Even more explicitly, the Scriptures reveal Him to us. And His Spirit indwells us for the purpose of guiding us into all truth.[3] Our hunger for a deeper, more intimate knowledge of Him can be, at least partially, satisfied. We can read Scripture, watch a child play, admire the sunrise, engage in academic study, develop our skills, learn a trade, and pursue God-given passions. This is our time of engagement, when we actively wait for the day that the Bridegroom will take us to Himself.

Love: Giving Good Love

Several years back, a popular song proclaimed, "You Give Good Love." I'm not sure just what that song meant by the phrase (or if I even want to know), but it would make a great slogan for how we are to fulfill our purpose in love during our period in exile. Through the Fall, we traded agape, the kind of love that finds its fulfillment in giving, for eros, an empty, self-centered kind of love driven by appetite and the impulse to acquire and control. As followers of Christ living in exile, we are called to follow His example, to show agape for others as He showed it to us. We are to "give good love."

While we are in exile, we have an opportunity to love people who do not have the capacity to reciprocate our love. Here, we are surrounded by those whom it is difficult to love, the kind of

"Because our weaknesses drive us into the arms of God, they can become our strengths."

people we come across every day, the kind of people to whom Christ came to give His love. He has called us to love them, no matter how much they may revile, despise, hate, or reject us.

Most of us can embrace His command to love those who are unlovable because it's not really all that difficult to love "everybody"; it's loving individuals that we have a hard time with! You know I'm right about that, don't you? We dupe ourselves into thinking that we are loving as Christ loves by loving people in the abstract. Christ never called us to love "everyone," but to love our "neighbor" as ourselves.[4] We are not just to be "lovers of mankind," but lovers of the particular individuals we come into contact with *every day*.

Besides our tendency to love vague abstractions, rather than actual people, we also tend to substitute eros for genuine agape. Sometimes Christians approach those to whom we are witnessing not as fallen people desperately in need of genuine love, but as potential converts, notches in our belt that will serve as a tribute to our own holiness and spiritual maturity. The desire to get something for ourselves, or to attempt to use a person to whom we are witnessing in order to satisfy our own ends, is actually a form of lust. In Christ, we have no need to give in order to get. Christ said, "Freely you have received, freely give."[5] During our time of exile, we have the chance to demonstrate love to those who, *like us*, do not deserve to receive it.

Taking the High Way means loving Christ enough to willingly serve others, reflect God's character and live out His love. We have not arrived, but we have begun.

——

FOOTNOTES: 1. Jeremiah 29:11; 2. 1 Corinthians 13:12 (NIV); 3. John 16:13 (NIV); 4. Luke 10:27; 5. Matthew 10:8 (NIV)

GPS: *God-Positioning Scriptures (to Reorient Your Life)*

*You have heard that it was said, "Love your neighbor and hate your enemy." But I tell you: Love your enemies and pray for those who persecute you, that you may be sons of your Father in heaven. He causes his sun to rise on the evil and the good, and sends rain on the righteous and the unrighteous. If you love those who love you, what reward will you get? Are not even the tax collectors doing that? And if you greet only your brothers, what are you doing more than others? Do not even pagans do that? Be perfect, therefore, as your heavenly Father is perfect." —***Matthew 5:43-48** (NIV)

REST STOP: *Pull Over and Ponder*
It's an inspiring truth that we get to "leave a mark" on the timeline of eternity during our time on Earth. How are you actively pursuing God's purposes for your life? Could you be doing something more or anything differently to genuinely love God and others well while "in exile"?

EXIT 3: *BEATEN PATH*

Mile 18

Road Hazards

On the journey to spiritual maturity, you will be sideswiped by adversity.
Satan means this for our destruction, but God uses it for our benefit.

Life: Struggling for Identity

The comedy show "Saturday Night Live," aka SNL, once featured a series of sketches in which Dana Carvey played a character known as the "church lady." Quick to condemn the "evils" of the world, the church lady was constantly posing the question, "Could it be ... Satan?" The humorous tone of the skit didn't warrant a moment of theological concern from the audience, but the question that the church lady continually posed is a question that a Christian needs to ask sometimes. Satan is real: a destroyer who wants to hinder us from fulfilling the purposes for which God created us and Christ redeemed us.

In addition to the church lady's question, we must also ask, "Could it be ... God?" After all, if God is truly sovereign—in complete control of whatever comes to pass—then He is certainly able to prevent Satan from causing us so much trouble. Why, then, does He choose not to? One reason is because of His relationship with us: God wants us to draw closer to Him.

He assures us in Scripture that He "causes all things to work together for good to those who love God, to those who are called according to His purpose,"[1] we can find peace and contentment—even real joy—in the midst of the most intensely difficult circumstances. God is working to complete and perfect us in the areas of **Life**, **Labor**, **Limits**, and **Love**, and we know from Scripture that God is in control—victorious in each area over evil.

Yet, Satan works tirelessly to sidetrack us—striking at certain opportune moments ...

Being Attacked in Childhood

It's not easy to be a child, but God loves us and limits the damage Satan can cause. No matter what kind of injuries we suffered as children—even if we experienced abuse or neglect—we need to remember that there is much that God has spared us.

But what about the pain He has not spared us? Some of our wounds are deep. The pain we experience in childhood can leave us scars of insecurity and fearfulness. We can be suspicious and unwilling to trust. Anger, self-centeredness, and hopelessness often take over hearts that have experienced great pain. Yet to the extent that they show us our need for God, even deep wounds can become great blessings.

"When we center our lives on Him, we are able to find our place in the world..."

Biologists describe the process of physical healing as one of regeneration. When the body is damaged in some way, it heals by generating new tissue to replace the damaged tissue. If physical wounds are healed by a process of regeneration, why should spiritual and emotional wounds be any different? What leads us to try to overcome the hurts and disappointments of childhood by constantly picking at them and agonizing over them?

Christ, the "Great Physician," did not come merely to bandage our spiritual wounds but to make us new. It is in the new life that Christ gives that we find healing for the pain of the past. And scar tissue, whether physical or spiritual, is always tougher, stronger than that which has been pain-free.

Being Torn as a Teenager

The primary struggle of adolescence is one of identity. No longer a child but not yet an adult, the teenager feels torn, caught between two worlds, and is searching for a place where he can "belong." Teens are likely to begin their search by a process of negative comparison, clarifying who they "are not," rather than who "they are," or by announcing what they "don't like," rather than focusing on what they "do like." Sentiments are often expressed by the teenager in the negative: "But Mom, I'm not you!" or "I hate to _____."

Scripture, though, tells us that our real identity comes neither from within ourselves, nor from other people, but from our relationship with God. We are to become God-centered, building our lives around Him and His will for us, rather than around ourselves or other people. By learning to discern and follow our Lord's voice, we gain the confidence, security, and sense of belonging that we long for. When we center our lives on Him, we are able to confidently define ourselves in terms of who we are and find our place in the world, at last.

Being Yanked as a Young Adult

Many of us look back with fondness to our college days or to our first job as a time when the world seemed full of promise and opportunity. But what we always seem to forget in the midst of our nostalgia is that those days also offered some difficult times. Great uncertainty and fear of the future are part of that season of life in which we are expected to begin making our own way in the world.

Young adults are faced with so many choices that they are often crippled with indecision and the unwillingness to make any lasting commitments. Many young adults simply avoid making decisions until they are certain how things are going to turn out. But God never intended for a person to know beforehand the details of future events in his life.

Although God has chosen to keep the details of the future a secret, He has revealed that He will lead us through it. Isaiah assures us that "whether you turn to the right or to the left, your ears will hear a voice behind you, saying, 'This is the way; walk in it.'"[2] If we would know that call, we must come to know His voice, and we will be able to face the future as those who are called, rather than "yanked."

Being Muddled in Middle Age

I'll never forget the shock I felt the first time I bent over a shaving mirror and noticed that even though my head stayed in the same place, my face just kept going! There is an even more profound way to know that you are entering middle age, however: even your youthful idealism begins to droop.

The optimism of youth is typically shallow. It is based on the assumption that if we just put forth enough effort, we can accomplish anything we set our minds to. The experience of age tells us there is more to it than that. Middle age can be a time when we embrace the idea that it is best to ask God to set our minds on what He desires for us to accomplish and to provide the strength we need to aim for the ideal. If we are to live a life that is meaningful and productive, we must segue from our youthful confidence in ourselves, and place our mature confidence in God.

Fearing Obsolescence in Old Age

Old age is the time of life when we begin to surrender our independence. For most of us, this growing dependence on others is terribly frustrating, disheartening, and humiliating. We fear that we are becoming obsolete and unproductive—a drain on and a burden to other people.

Our fears offer us nothing but discouragement. Our worth will never be found in our fears; it will be found in our love. Forced dependence on others can be lived out as yet another gift from God. For most of us, it is not until we begin to be slowed by age that we start to develop a truly balanced perspective. When we can no longer keep up with life, we begin to take stock of it, and we acquire the patience, perspective, and peace that we lacked in our youth. Having traded youthful strength for elderly wisdom, we are now in a position to give the young people in our lives the benefit of our perspective and insight. We can guide them away from some of the mistakes that we have made and help them not to miss their "golden opportunities."

Taking the High Way means recognizing that God has a great purpose for every crisis of identity that we face throughout life. God deepens and fortifies our sense of purpose in being, giving us a solid foundation for fulfilling His will every day of our lives in each area of purpose ...

FOOTNOTES: 1. Romans 8:28; 2. Isaiah 30:21 (NIV)

GPS: *God-Positioning Scriptures (to Reorient Your Life)*

"For I know the plans I have for you," declares the LORD, "plans to prosper you and not to harm you, plans to give you hope and a future." —Jeremiah 29:11 (NIV)

REST STOP: *Pull Over and Ponder*

Think back on Satan's past attempts to thwart your progress on your spiritual journey. Taking the wisdom gleaned from past experience and today's reading, how can you guard against Satan's next potential stage of life attack?

Mile 19

Road Weary?

God created us to reflect His image by contributing to the world around us, but the enemy wants us to pull over. Keep your attitude in check ... and your eyes on the road.

Labor: Bringing Good Out of Work Problems

Whenever we begin to work for the glory of God, Satan will attempt to sidetrack us. It is not our activity itself that he is opposed to—he is not particularly threatened by clean diapers, swept streets, well-run businesses, or even eloquent sermons. It is when these things are done to the glory of God that Satan's agenda is sidelined. It may sound kind of silly, but a diaper that is changed out of love and care for the child is a hindrance to Satan's goals. Yet the same act of changing a diaper, when resented as being an unpleasant and demeaning task, is a reason for him to celebrate.

Satan tries to hinder our purpose in work. Yet God can use the struggle that elicits from us to give our work meaning. Personal victories in attitude alone can become our moments of greatest achievement.

Weird People at Work

One of the first ways Satan tries to strip our work of its meaning and significance is by using the people we work with to distract, frustrate, and discourage us. Why does God allow us to be distracted by coworkers who need us to bail them out, bosses who are wishy-washy or explosive, busybodies who are always trying to give us advice, and teammates who desert us in the middle of the work? In part, it is to teach us that patience is an *active*, rather than a passive, virtue. It involves persistence in serving others, no matter how hopeless or irritating they might seem.

"Personal victories in attitude alone can become our moments of greatest achievement."

The way we view ourselves also has a great deal to do with how we treat others. If we see ourselves as the only "normal" or "decent" people at work, then we will naturally see all of the annoying and difficult people as "weird." But if we realize that we also have our times of weirdness, then we will be a little more understanding and gracious toward all of the other "weird people." Can't you almost picture Satan cringing when the "weird people" he hoped would distract us become the people we grow to love and serve?

Unappreciated for Your Work

No matter how much we accomplish or how hard we work, we never seem to get the credit we deserve. The perception that we are not properly appreciated is a sign of what I call the "older brother mentality," from the parable of the prodigal son.[1] Like this older brother, many of us feel that our steady faithfulness to fulfill our responsibilities has gone unnoticed. Meanwhile, the "squeaky wheel"—those who habitually flub up but attract a lot of attention when they succeed—seem to get all the "oil" of praise and recognition.

Our first impulse is to try to "set things straight" by bringing our own faithfulness and hard work to the attention of others. But drawing attention to our accomplishments rarely has the effect we wish it would have. It doesn't make us look deserving, only petty and jealous.

God wants us to look to Him, rather than to men, to reward our faithfulness. Jesus makes it clear that those who receive their praise from men have received their reward in full, and will receive nothing further from the Lord. On the other hand, those who perform their "acts of righteousness" in secret, so that not even their left hand knows what their right hand is doing, will be rewarded by their Father in heaven, who sees and repays what is done in secret.[2]

Losing Balance in Busyness

Some of us consider busyness a virtue—as if how much we do matters as much or even more than what we do. Scripture paints a different picture. The apostle Paul writes, "Make it your ambition to lead a quiet life, to mind your own business and to work with your hands."[3] According to this passage, our ambition should be to lead a peaceful life, not to run around in a frenetic state of activity. The problem with being "busy" is not primarily that we are working too hard, but that we are distracted by all the wrong things. When Jesus paid a visit to the home of Mary and Martha, Martha busied herself with all the preparations, but Mary sat at the Lord's feet. When Martha complained that her sister should be helping her, Jesus chided her for having the wrong focus: "Martha, Martha, you are worried and bothered about so many things; but only one thing is necessary."[4] In her busyness, Martha had become so distracted by "many things" that she was drawn away from the one thing in her life that really mattered—her relationship with Christ.

God says to us, "Be still, and know that I am God."[5] Let's make sure we are consumed with the God who calls us to live a life that is quietly meaningful and productive, rather than consumed with "getting things done."

Losing Our Passion to Routine

When most of us began our careers, passion, excitement, and enthusiasm fueled our youthful dreams of making a difference in the world. Somewhere along the way, though, dreams began to fade. Losing passion to routine is a calamity not only in work, but in our relationships as well.

As newlyweds, we dream of a life full of passion and romance, but to cope with the relentlessness of life, we divide up adult roles and establish a routine that seems reasonable. And reasonable it is. But then we begin to get "used" to each other, and eventually, one day, we turn around and notice that the person we married isn't the same person anymore, and neither are we. The routines of life have drained the intimacy and passion out of our relationship, and we never even noticed it was happening. Once we do notice, though, we can make our way out of the ruts we've established by determining that we will again treasure the person we simply got "used" to. When we invest in that person, when we treasure that person, intimacy and passion return to the relationship. Jesus wasn't referring only to money when He said, "Where your treasure is there will your heart go, also."[6]

Our relationship with God is not exempt from the dangers of routine. In the beginning, we want "to know Christ and the power of his resurrection and the fellowship of sharing in his sufferings."[7] Then we start learning how to speak the lingo—the "Christian-ese"—and learning how the "system" works. We start concentrating on walking, talking, feeling, and thinking as a Christian is *supposed to*, and we forget to concentrate on the One for whom we are doing it all in the first place.

We must invest our lives in the people and efforts that count for eternity. We must learn to live each day with the perspective that even the little things we do can have an impact forever.

Disasters at Work

Occasionally, we will experience some form of disaster—a loss of a job, a debilitating injury, or a personal problem that interferes with our daily life in some way. We must remember that while Satan means to use these disasters to destroy us, no disaster can befall us except by God's consent. So rather than getting panicked and giving up hope, we need to look for God's purpose and provision in the midst of the calamity.

Too often we try to ease the pain by rushing off and busying ourselves with distractions. If we'll stick around until the dust settles, we'll be able to see that God has been there with us through it all. In fact, out of that disaster, He will bring new life—He is, after all, in the business of resurrection.

Working for Yourself

As we engage in whatever work God has called us to do, we need the mind-set of a steward even if our work is entrepreneurial. We must continually remind ourselves that we are not our own bosses. Whatever "capital" we invest (time, talent, or treasure) does not really belong to us. If we are faithful, we will be rewarded with the words "Well done, good and faithful servant! You have been faithful with a few things; I will put you in charge of many things. Come and share your master's happiness!"[8]

Taking the High Way means working "as unto the Lord and not unto man," trusting that God has a plan and pressing ahead even when the road gets rough.

FOOTNOTES: 1. Luke 15:11-32 (NIV); 2. Matthew 6:4 (NIV); 3. 1 Thessalonians 4:11 (NIV); 4. Luke 10:41-42; 5. Psalm 46:10 (NIV); 6. Matthew 6:21; 7. Philippians 3:10 (NIV); 8. Matthew 25:21 (NIV)

GPS: *God-Positioning Scriptures (to Reorient Your Life)*
Let us not lose heart in doing good, for in due time we will reap if we do not grow weary.
—**Galatians 6:9**

REST STOP: *Pull Over and Ponder*
Considering that we spend so much of our lives working, it only makes sense that Satan would try to hijack our efforts using the very careers God's called us to. How can altering your attitude about the perceived adversity in/at work help you to become a better steward in the place God's placed you today?

Mile 20

Speed Limits

God allows us to experience certain limitations in order to remind us of our need for Him. Satan, however, has another kind of limitation in mind for us: the entrapment of sin.

Limits: Bringing Good Out of Temptation

We all have a tendency, once we have experienced some degree of victory over sin, to begin thinking ourselves immune to it. Peter warned us to remain "self-controlled and alert," because our enemy the devil "prowls around like a roaring lion looking for someone to devour."[1] Whenever I think of that verse, I picture those National Geographic specials that show how lions hunt their prey. As the cameraman pans a herd of wild antelope or zebra, he soon focuses in on some cute little calf skipping playfully along. Then, on the outskirts of the scene, you see her—a lioness crouching in the grass. She begins prowling around the periphery of the herd, patiently searching for some animal that has grown overly carefree or too confident and strayed a bit from the safety of the group. In an instant,

91

everything explodes into action! The lioness charges. A feverish chase ensues as she savagely and relentlessly pursues her victim. The end comes quickly...

Just as the calf is in danger when it is isolated from its family, we are most vulnerable when we have strayed too far from the safety of our spiritual family. Satan waits for such times. Whether they result from our intentional wandering or from our lack of attention, he charges in, knowing we are never more likely to succumb to the ravages of sin than when we are isolated. We must not grow overly confident about our ability to avoid sin. The book of Genesis also warns us that sin is crouching at the door, desiring to devour us. But if we find ourselves in its grip, escape is possible. The enemy is not irresistible. God provides us with the way of escape. First Corinthians 10:13 tells us, "No temptation has overtaken you but such as is common to man; and God is faithful, who will not allow you to be tempted beyond what you are able, but with the temptation will provide the way of escape also, so that you will be able to endure it."

> *"...we do not escape temptation by following a lot of rules and regulations."*

Satisfying Our Appetites

How, then, do we avoid giving in to temptation? The answer will probably surprise you. To begin with, we do not escape temptation by living every day of our lives focused only on rules and regulations. It never ceases to amaze me how many Christians try to avoid sin by singularly focusing on following the letter of the law: constantly reminding themselves what they shouldn't do. But the more we think about the sins we are trying to avoid, the more tempted we are likely to become. We are hardwired to go in the direction of our thoughts. There is a true story about two little boys who climbed much too high in a tree. Due to the thick summer foliage, neither could see the other and neither could make his way back to the ground safely. Well, it wasn't long before their moms were standing at the base of tree. One mother was yelling to her son, "Don't fall!" The other was shouting to hers, "Hang on!" I don't think it was coincidence that the boy who was hearing "Don't fall!" fell, while the one who was hearing "Hang on!" stayed safely on the branch until someone showed up with a ladder. Likewise, in a spiritual sense it is helpful to focus on hanging on rather than on not falling.

Scripture tells us that to nullify our appetite for sin we focus on the satisfaction of another appetite, our spiritual appetite, by learning to crave that which is holy and pure. When Satan tempted Jesus to turn stones into bread to satisfy His physical hunger, Jesus replied, "It is written: 'Man does not live on bread alone, but on every word that comes from the mouth of God.'"[2] Because He was intent on satisfying His spiritual hunger, He was able to withstand His physical hunger. By setting our hearts and minds on "things above," rather than on "earthly things,"[3] we replace our sinful desires with wholesome ones.

Like Sheep Going Astray

When Jesus referred to His disciples as "sheep,"[4] He couldn't have picked a more appropriate metaphor. Neither could He have picked one less flattering! Sheep are, after all, incredibly stupid animals. They are interested in little else than satisfying their own appetites, and this single-minded devotion to their stomachs often gets them into trouble. It has been said that sheep get lost "tuft by tuft." That is, once they are finished grazing on one tuft of grass, they simply wander over to the next one, and the next one, and the next one. They literally nibble their way to becoming lost.

As we begin indulging our sinful desires, we are like the sheep that goes astray "tuft by tuft." Each step further into sin seems like such a small thing. But there simply are no "little" sins or "minor" indiscretions. The flesh, our sinful nature, and our evil desires lead us "tuft by tuft" away from our Lord's presence, just like sheep being led to the slaughter.

Rebel Sheep

At times, the fact that if we love God, we aren't free to do whatever we feel like doing infuriates us. In our frustration, we choose to become rebel sheep. Rebelling against the Shepherd, we attempt to escape the "tyranny" of His "rod" and "staff."[5] Tired of being mere followers, we decide to become the masters of our own fates.

Faithfulness to Christ requires us to embrace certain limitations. A Christian life isn't fully reflected in just doing good things. We must also choose, on a daily basis, not to do those things that offend our holy God. So there are limitations, but they are ones that simply help us more fully honor God. True freedom—the freedom for which we were created—is not to be found unless we embrace God-given limitations. "All things are lawful, but not all things are profitable. All things are lawful, but not all things edify."[6]

Sheep Without a Shepherd

Being described as "sheep" doesn't do much for the ego. It implies that we are utterly dependent on someone else to shepherd us, because, just like sheep, we are too weak and senseless to survive on our own. But if we are to live and thrive, we must humbly submit to the oversight of our Shepherd.

This is completely contrary to what our society tells us. We who live in the United States of America live in a nation of "rugged individualists" who prefer to think of ourselves as mavericks, rather than as one of the flock. We aspire to be leaders, entrepreneurs, and trailblazers. Operating under the mistaken premise that "God helps those who help themselves," we take charge of our own lives. We have a hard time accepting the idea that we are weak, helpless, or are in need of any kind of "watching over."

Whether we wander away from our Shepherd "tuft by tuft" or run away from Him, sooner or later, we will come face to face with our lack of self-sufficiency. Whenever we try to strike out on our own, to assume control of our own lives, we will inevitably become "distressed and downcast." Taking the High Way means rejecting isolated living and accepting that as "sheep," we experience peace and security only in the presence of the Shepherd.

FOOTNOTES: 1. 1 Peter 5:8 (NIV); 2. Matthew 4:4 (NIV); 3. Colossians 3:2 (NIV); 4. Matthew 9:36 (NIV); 5. Psalm 23:4 (NIV); 6. 1 Corinthians 10:23

GPS: *God-Positioning Scriptures (to Reorient Your Life)*

When tempted, no one should say, God is tempting me. For God cannot be tempted by evil, nor does he tempt anyone; but each one is tempted when, by his own evil desire, he is dragged away and enticed. Then, after desire has conceived, it gives birth to sin; and sin, when it is full-grown, gives birth to death. —James 1:13-15 (NIV)

We all, like sheep, have gone astray, each of us has turned to his own way; and the Lord has laid on him the iniquity of us all. —Isaiah 53:6 (NIV)

REST STOP: *Pull Over and Ponder*
Are you nibbling on any particular "tuft" of grass lately—tempted into slowly wandering away from the peace and security found in the Shepherd's presence? How does the promise in 1 Corinthians 10:13 help you face the temptation you are facing today?

Mile 21

Driver's Ed., Part 1

The road ahead is rapidly changing—you wonder if you have the skill to keep from spinning out of control. You do! And as the unexpected happens along the way, the Manual will give you the insights you need to stay on the High Way. God is working all things together to accomplish His purposes.

Learning: Seeing God in a Fallen World

Knowledge of God is not hidden, but plain for all to see. Naturally, Satan desires to obscure this knowledge. His goal is to convince people that God is not present in the world—that He is far off and unconcerned with human affairs, if, in fact, He exists at all.

Even among believers, who have already acknowledged God and come to an understanding of the truth, Satan does his best to interfere with our ability to see God's presence in the world. Typically, he does this by convincing us that the sacred and the secular are completely disconnected, and that God is interested only in the sacred. If we come to believe that God is not involved with the secular world, we will miss so much that God is doing and misunderstand who He is, as well. Those of us who think God is interested only in the sacred are likely to isolate ourselves from the world and then pat ourselves on the back for protecting our faith. Eventually though, we discover that we are no longer in a position even to contribute to its betterment. Hear me on this, we can't hide in our prayer closets. We go there, and we go there often, but it is to be filled up with His strength to live among those He loves. And the Bible clearly says, "God so loved the world …"[1]

The End of the World (as We Know It)?

At some point, every generation comes to the realization that the world as they have known it is rapidly coming to an end. However, recent generations know this reality like no other. The rules of the road have been changing. Christians must learn to see God in a world that declares there is no right or wrong, where truth is assumed to be a matter of personal taste, and where the church is seen as nothing more than another "special-interest group." God has ushered His church out of the relative stability of the modern era into the untamed wilderness of the postmodern age. It's the end of the world as we knew it, but not as God knows it. He is still here, in the midst of all the chaos and confusion, unflinchingly accomplishing His ends and achieving His purpose.

"The postmodern individual is alone in the midst of the crowd."

It isn't easy to live as a citizen of the global community. Our increased "interconnectivity" via technology has brought us into contact with more people than we can possibly get to know—much less know intimately. Many of us are more connected, yet more isolated than ever before. The postmodern individual is alone in the midst of the crowd. For many of us, our *virtual* lives and relationships, which are controllable, mean more than our *actual* lives and relationships, which are so much more complicated and difficult to manage. The technology isn't nearly as scary as the need that it proposes to answer: the compulsion within us all to believe that we are at the center of the universe and that we must create worlds in which everything takes place according to our own set of rules. It all boils down to the ancient desire to become "like God"[2]—to be in complete control of the world in which we live.

With or without the technology, the reality of our culture has generally become "virtual," because it is not rooted in anything other than ourselves. We can create our own virtual worlds simply by engaging in real life only when we can be at least "remote"-ly in control of it, if we can have relationships based solely on what will make us happy, and are able to move on to someone else when our definition of happy isn't met. Consider how we seek out relationships that we think will answer needs within us, but when those relationships cease to meet our needs or make us happy, we abandon them to move on to someone or something else. These self-centered relationships are not really about anyone except us. Neither are they about covenant, or even about commitment. They are essentially "virtual marriages" and "virtual friendships," because we can turn them off as soon as we get frustrated or unsatisfied with them. Even worse, Christians can do the same thing when it comes to their relationship with Christ. For some, Christianity is not about "glorifying God and enjoying Him forever,"[3] but about getting what they want, being blessed with wealth, health, and happiness.

Taking the High Way means learning to live in the real world. It requires looking beyond ourselves in order to find true fulfillment and significance: contributing to the world around us, engaging in meaningful relationships with other people, and building our lives around Him, rather than around ourselves. We must not evade the costs, struggles, and challenges of genuine relationship. If we succeed in meeting those issues head-on, we will experience a depth and vitality that "virtually" is difficult to find.

FOOTNOTES: 1. John 3:16; 2. Genesis 3:5 (NIV); 3. Westminster Catechism, Question 1

GPS: *God-Positioning Scriptures (to Reorient Your Life)*

Don't become so well-adjusted to your culture that you fit into it without even thinking. Instead, fix your attention on God. You'll be changed from the inside out. Readily recognize what he wants from you, and quickly respond to it. Unlike the culture around you, always dragging you down to its level of immaturity, God brings the best out of you, develops well-formed maturity in you. —**Romans 12:2 (The Message)**

REST STOP: *Pull Over and Ponder*
Which various forms of technology impact your daily life? Today's "virtual" world of easy networking and instant gratification is actually leaving gaping holes in relationships. How can you combat the pull of the superficial and immediate and instead move toward a deeper relationship with God and others?

Mile 22

Driver's Ed., Part 2

The road ahead keeps changing. You feel pressured by other drivers who seem to follow a different set of rules than you. Don't give in, but don't drive angry, either ... just stay on course.

WHEN I PLAYED high school football, I had a coach whose scouting reports always contained "good news" about our opposition for the upcoming game. He would say to one of his receivers, "Good news! All three of their defensive backs have been told to cover you before they even worry about covering anybody else!" Or he would say, "Good news! They'll have two of their offensive linemen keying on you the entire game!" Why was this good news? Because it meant that these players were doing their jobs well enough to be a source of concern to their opponent.

Well, I've got "good news" for you: In the postmodern world, the church is being viewed with increasing suspicion and hostility. In a culture that considers truth to be relative, the church is stubbornly clinging to a set of beliefs that is applicable for all people everywhere. In a nation where there are many new "messiahs" claiming to have solutions to all our problems, the church is narrow-mindedly sticking to its original one. By being unwilling to go along with all the changes taking place, the church is becoming an object of scorn for the rest of the world.

That really is good news! Why? Because to the extent that we endure hostility and persecution for the reasons listed, we can take comfort in the fact that we are doing our job well enough to become a source of concern to the opposition.

There is, however, another reason why the world may hate us: not because we bear the name of Christ, but simply because we are downright hateful. If people hate us because we try to impose our beliefs on them by political means, rather than by example, invitation, and gentle persuasion, then they have every reason to feel that way. If our culture persecutes us because we are arrogant and obnoxious, what right have we to complain?

We must be careful to make sure that the harsh treatment we receive is for righteousness' sake. If we are so concerned about losing our place of prominence in society that we try to dominate people and circumstances to keep it, we are veering off course. Many Christians, who are rightfully aware that Christ is the only solution to the problems of the postmodern age, have sought to gain control of government, education, and the media in an effort to "win back the world for Jesus." To some extent, this is a good thing. But if we're not careful when competing for positions of cultural influence, we risk being perceived as nothing more than another self-seeking ideological group trying to get its own way. That perception is bad enough, but may it never be the reality of why we are involved in our communities. The world needs what we have to offer. We are to be the hands and feet of Christ. We don't run for office, teach in the schools, or publish our thoughts to make it a better place for only those who are most like us. We do it because "God so loved the world ..."

> *"Our greatest impact on history will come from building the kingdom of God."*

Jesus described His kingdom as a tiny mustard seed that eventually grows into a large tree, and as a little bit of yeast that eventually works its way through the whole batch of dough.[1] His point was clear: Though at times the kingdom of God may appear small and insignificant, in the long term, its influence will be clearly seen. Those who succeed in forming the dominant paradigm of the postmodern age will not be those who win control of the most important social institutions, but those who win the hearts and minds of the people. Our greatest impact on history will come from building the kingdom of God. We may feel that what we have to offer for kingdom purposes is small and insignificant, but there is an old saying that a little can go a long way. Maybe your contribution is tiny enough to sink into the deepest parts of minds and hearts, or into the cracks of unnecessary walls built between neighbors or cultures. Offer what you've been given to contribute, and it will grow as surely as the mustard seed and spread as rapidly as the yeast.

As we remind ourselves that God has not lost His place in the world and that our mission is not to rule the world as much as it is to shine as a light within it, we will become more effective at fulfilling God's commands. Eventually, some of the church's persecutors may "be ashamed of their slander"[2] and come to see their own need for Christ. This is precisely how the church has not only been able to survive, but has actually managed to *thrive* during periods of the most intense persecution. The "good news" of growing opposition to the church is that the more we suffer for doing good, the more clearly the truth of Christ will become evident.

Taking the High Way means staying faithful even as the adversary works to destroy our witness for Christ. If we stay faithful, we will find that even his efforts inadvertently help to build the very kingdom he hopes to destroy.

FOOTNOTES: 1. Matthew 13:32-34 (NIV); 2. 1 Peter 3:16 (NIV)

GPS: *God-Positioning Scriptures (to Reorient Your Life)*

If the world hates you, keep in mind that it hated me first. If you belonged to the world, it would love you as its own. As it is, you do not belong to the world, but I have chosen you out of the world. That is why the world hates you. Remember the words I spoke to you: "No servant is greater than his master." If they persecuted me, they will persecute you also. If they obeyed my teaching, they will obey yours also. They will treat you this way because of my name, for they do not know the One who sent me. —John 15:18-21 (NIV)

REST STOP: *Pull Over and Ponder*
God desires to use people to plant the seeds of his kingdom and cultivate growth. That's a powerful image. Who helped plant the seeds in your life? Are you planting seeds for the kingdom in a way that truly honors God and displays love for others?

Mile 23

Your Travel Companions

Few things can bring you more joy than your family—your companions on the journey. Unfortunately, few things can bring you more pain, as well. Your enemy wants you to leave them behind, but don't give in to his lies.

Love: Bringing Good Out of Family Problems

In a "dog eat dog" world, we expect other people to try to hurt us, but our families are supposed to "stay off our backs" and be "on our side," right? That's why whenever they do something to hurt us, no matter how small or insignificant it might be, it feels like a betrayal.

Betrayal is one of Satan's favorite forms of attack, because it awakens within us such powerful emotions and desires that we can easily lose sight of God's love and provision. In response, some people want to strike back at the source of their hurt. Others get depressed and disillusioned. Still others blame themselves for the betrayal, becoming crippled with insecurity.

Our closeness to our family members is a blessing, but the frailties, sins, follies, and inequities that exist within every family can leave us feeling victimized and betrayed.

Yet, as devastating as any betrayal can be, God is able to use even the most sinister acts of treachery to achieve for us an "eternal glory that far outweighs them all."[1] Examples of this are scattered throughout Scripture. Consider how God used the blatant betrayal of Joseph by his brothers to save many lives.[2] Betrayal is always a masterful stroke on Satan's part, yet in every case, God can use it to achieve a far greater good.

Pain and adversity are inevitable, and God never promised to shelter us from them completely. What God did promise was that He would always be with us. Isn't this exactly what we have always wanted from our own families—to know that there will always be someone there to love and support us? We look to our families to give us a sense of security and stability, but because they have their own frailties and are fighting their own battles, they sometimes seem to let us down, or even sell us out. They are unable to be who we need them to be, but God is more than able to fill that role. We must come to depend on Him. He is the only One who will never betray us.

Under Attack as a Spouse

Have you ever wondered why "opposites" seem to attract? It's because we find it extremely difficult to love people who are just like us. While we love our own strengths, we absolutely detest the weaknesses we see in ourselves. We are naturally drawn to the people who do not share our weaknesses. A couple's differences often form the seedbed out of which their love grows. They see themselves as filling one another's gaps, so that they are stronger together than they were apart. However, it's amazing how quickly this perspective can change. The moment we shift our focus from our loved ones to ourselves, our entire outlook on the relationship darkens. We can choose to focus on getting our own way all the time, in which case we will inevitably see our spouses as a hindrance and source of frustration, or we can focus on loving our spouses in such a way as to bless them, even if that requires self-sacrifice.

Peter commands husbands and wives to show agape toward one another by sacrificing their own strengths in order to meet the needs of their spouses.[3] Only by yielding our own strengths can we benefit from the strengths of our partners. Just as the biceps and triceps of the arm exert their particular strengths in opposite directions, alternately yielding to one another depending on the need at hand, so husbands and wives must be willing to yield their individual strengths in order to live together as "one flesh." It is only through mutual submission that each will be able to exercise his or her own strengths to the fullest.[4]

Feeling Helpless as a Parent

Parenthood is one of the few careers in which the goal is to work yourself out of a job. It is one of the few relationships in which people are meant to grow more distant. From the time they are infants, children steadily push for greater independence. Parents must respond to this challenge by giving their children enough room to assert themselves, while holding them back from freedoms they are not yet adequately prepared to handle in a godly, mature way. Even the wisest and most discerning parents feel inadequately prepared to raise their children successfully.

One thing we can do to avoid feeling helpless in the experience is to learn how to play "outfield." The early years of our children's lives are like playing in the infield; the ball comes our way pretty often, so we pay close attention for that moment when we will be needed. But as our kids get a little older, they no longer require our constant interaction, and we find ourselves better positioned if we move to the outfield. There we can remain watchful for that moment when they will hit the ball our way, and we will be ready to spring into action when they come to us for help. Eventually, adult children are best

> *"Parenthood is one of the few careers in which the goal is to work yourself out of a job."*

served by parents who have found a seat in the bleachers where parenting requirements are met most often by simply cheering them on.

In the Bible, the father of the prodigal son knew how to play outfield.[5] He did not try to track down his son and save him from every problem; he merely waited for the day when his son would return to him. When that day came, he was ready to respond immediately.

Most of all, we must pray, pray, pray for our children. Recognizing that God is truly their Father, we must continually entrust them to His care. Hard as it is to imagine, He loves them even more than we do, and He will guide them through life more faithfully than we ever could.

The Family's Victory Over Destruction

So many Christians today bemoan the fact that the culture of the United States and some other countries as well has had such an anti-family flair. They believe that they must fight to "rescue" the family by stamping out every kind of evil that threatens it. What they fail to understand is that as an open system, the Christian family will be able to survive in the most bleak of cultural conditions. We can have confidence in the family's ability to survive the forces of evil because we know that it is the nature of evil to destroy itself. We need to focus our efforts on living our lives in ways that reflect the God we love and cling to the "Rock of our salvation"[6] until our enemies destroy one another.

The family's victory over the world comes whenever we seek God's protection from the forces of destruction. Every time a Christian husband chooses to love his wife and a Christian wife chooses to respect her husband and they stay in their marriage for a lifetime, and whenever a Christian parent decides to invest the time, energy, and finances required to "train up a child in the way he should go," there is kingdom progress. The choices we make every day in our homes matter. They result in family victory or in destruction. Taking the High Way means living as though we truly believe "greater is He that is in" us—and in our families—"than he that is in the world."[7]

FOOTNOTES: 1. 2 Corinthians 4:17 (NIV); 2. Genesis 45:5-7 (NIV); 3. 1 Peter 3:1-7; 4. Ephesians 5:21; 5. Luke 15:11-32 (NIV); 6. Psalm 95:1 (NIV); 7. 1 John 4:4 (KJV)

GPS: *God-Positioning Scriptures (to Reorient Your Life)*

See how great a love the Father has bestowed on us, that we would be called children of God; and such we are. For this reason the world does not know us, because it did not know Him. —1 John 3:1

REST STOP: *Pull Over and Ponder*

The attack being waged by Satan on the family demands a strategy. What practices of faithfulness and discipline are you willing to practice regularly to guard your family against damage and destruction?

EXIT 4: *LOVE'S WAY*

Mile 24

Driven to Love

You've come so far on this journey. But the farther you travel, the more you realize just how far you've got to go to reach spiritual maturity. Don't be discouraged by your seeming lack of progress. God's "love story" has never been about what we do for Him, but our response to what He does for us.

THE CONSUMMATE ARTIST, God, created because He had to create—not out of any need or deficiency, but out of the abundance of His nature. Imagine what God must have felt when, before the dawn of time, He looked out upon a universe that was "formless and void."[1] The perfect fullness of God's nature had to be released into the void, so that it might share in that fullness and be filled. Thus, God spoke into the darkness, and the dawn broke forth for the very first time.

Genesis relates that after six days of creative activity, God paused for a moment of reflection. His canvas was no longer bare, but it was not yet complete. God brought forth His plan of making a man, someone who would bear His own image and likeness. More than a creature, this would be a son, born to reflect His image and rule over the earth.

Imagine a novelist developing a persona who could then update the story with new twists and developments. This would be a kind of living art! This is precisely the kind of masterpiece that God was preparing to create: a living work that would fulfill what He Himself had initiated.

Imagine Adam opening his eyes for the very first time to look up into the glorious face of his heavenly Father. And what must it have been like for God as He gazed into the eyes of His son?

Love's great tale had begun, and no starry-eyed poet could possibly dream up a more auspicious beginning. As they walked through the garden together, God soon demonstrated His intention to groom Adam for the purpose of showing love as He had shown it.

Not Good Alone

God called his son into relationship with the creatures that populated Eden. Adam was indeed to be king over all the earth, but not as an absolute despot. On the contrary, Adam was to be benevolent, wise, gracious, and good, reflecting the heart of God toward His creation.

> "Created in the image of God, man was made for relationship, to give and receive love (agape), to pour his life into another."

God had observed that it was "not good for the man to be alone."[2] Adam, though, was alone in the sense that he was not yet complete. He did not yet fully reflect the image of God, who is both singular and plural at once, experiencing perfect relationship among the three Persons of the Trinity. Created in the image of God, man was made for relationship, to give and receive love (agape), to pour his life into another. God's masterpiece was not quite finished, so He determined to add the finishing touch: "I will make a helper suitable for him,"[2] He said.

Causing him to fall into a deep sleep, God took one of Adam's ribs and fashioned it into a woman. In creating Eve, God made a person who was enough like

Adam to be intimate and different enough from him to be necessary. God had created Adam for relationship—not only with Himself, but with others as well.

Why would God do this? One reason was that He had created mankind to reflect His image—something that could only be done in the context of relationship. Relationship is, after all, intrinsic to the nature of the Godhead, as Father, Son, and Holy Spirit exist together in perfect love and unity. By creating mankind in His own image, God had hard-wired the need for relationship into the human soul.

By directing Adam's attention toward the garden, the animals, and his remarkable wife, God was actually drawing him closer to Himself than he might otherwise have been. God chose to reveal more of Himself to Adam by means of these relationships.

Saint Frances of Daseo once observed: "We learn to study by studying; we learn to run by running; we learn to work by working; and we learn to love by loving. But we learn to love God by serving an apprenticeship with people." By learning to love each other, Adam and Eve were serving an apprenticeship in which they were preparing to love God more fully.

When God gave Eve to Adam, he received a precious gift designed to complement and complete him, to bring him untold joy and delight. Yet Adam's relationship with Eve was not only a gift, for he had given up a part of himself to receive her. Love, while being an incredible gift, nevertheless cost Adam a great deal. In forming Eve from Adam's rib, God was graphically demonstrating that love has a physical cost. Relationships demand more of us than our mere "emotional involvement"—they require the investment of a tremendous amount of physical and spiritual energy.

Relationships cost us so much for two reasons. First, our similarity to our loved ones costs us time and attention. When Adam recognized that Eve was "bone of my bones" and "flesh of my flesh,"[3] he was admitting that she was a presence he could not ignore. He was placing her on an equal plane with himself, which meant that he was compelled to treat her as he would himself want to be treated.

In addition, Eve's dissimilarity to Adam placed another kind of demand on him. The fact that we must relate to someone different from ourselves—someone whose thoughts, perspectives, opinions, feelings, and dispositions may differ significantly from our own—costs us comfort. It requires us to bridge the distance between us by overcoming or looking past differences or learning how to cooperate in spite of them.

Eve's similarity to Adam warranted that he regard her as an equal. Her dissimilarity to him warranted that he reach out to her as his mate. It stretched him to look beyond his own ideas and perspectives, to temper his strength with gentleness, to complicate his decision-making by consulting her opinion, and to express his thoughts and feelings in a way that she could understand and appreciate. The fact that Eve was "other" forced Adam to give true agape—the kind of love that gives no thought to itself.

This kind of love sounds almost like a fairy tale. For most of us, such a pure selfless love is difficult to imagine. But if we are ever going to learn what true love is, we must dare to imagine it. Taking the High Way means never forgetting the ideal, the original perfection that we were created to know. If we are ever to learn to love, if we are ever to give and receive true agape, we must never lose sight of the Creator's love for us.

FOOTNOTES: 1. Genesis 1:2; 2. Genesis 2:18 (NIV); 3. Genesis 2:23

GPS: *God-Positioning Scriptures (to Reorient Your Life)*

My beloved friends, let us continue to love each other since love comes from God. Everyone who loves is born of God and experiences a relationship with God. The person who refuses to love doesn't know the first thing about God, because God is love—so you can't know him if you don't love.
—1 John 4:7-8 (The Message)

REST STOP: *Pull Over and Ponder*
Consider the important relationships in your life. How do those relationships bring you closer to God on a regular basis? What do they teach you about Him?

Mile 25

Detoured, Part 1

In spite of God's great love for them, Adam and Eve followed Satan's directions. While mankind continues to wander away from Him, God's love remains at work to turn this defeat into victory.

ENTER LOVE'S GREAT antagonist. Having lost his place in heaven through his foolhardy and ill-fated rebellion, Satan is bent on hideous revenge. He knows well that he cannot assault God directly, but now he perceives what he considers to be God's Achilles' heel, a weakness that can be used to injure and torment Him. This "weakness" is His unfathomable love for the creatures who bear His image. By striking at them, Satan hopes to break the very heart of God, and by that wound to avenge his expulsion from heaven.

One day, Adam and Eve wander toward the center of the garden, where Eve begins to gaze thoughtfully at the tree filled with that which God had forbidden them to eat. Here at last is the opportunity Satan has been waiting for! He directs his comments to the woman. "Did God really say, 'You must not eat from any tree in the garden'?"[1] The question is a subtle one. Twisting God's words to imply that He had restricted every tree in the garden, Satan poses a question that begs for more than a simple "yes" or "no." So she answers, "We may eat fruit from the trees in the garden, but God did say, 'You must not eat fruit from the tree that is in the middle of the garden, and you must not touch it, or you will die.'"[2]

Eve's answer reveals not only an exaggeration (God never said don't touch it) but also a fundamental misunderstanding of God's prohibition against the forbidden tree. The deadly poison that God has warned them against was not simply internalizing the fruit of the tree of the knowledge of good and evil, but the dreadful and damning sin of disobedience.

"You will not surely die," the tempter says, flatly contradicting God. "For God knows that when you eat of it your eyes will be opened, and you will be like God, knowing good and evil."[3] Here Satan slips in the lie that the tree is the key to becoming like God. He pushes Eve to consider the possibility that the tree is not merely good, but the highest good, the one thing in the world most worth experiencing. The implication of this is that God is the deceiver, that He had led Adam and Eve to believe the tree was evil only because He had wanted to keep them from becoming equal with Himself!

Having planted the seed of doubt in Eve's mind, Satan's work is now done. All he needs to do is wait for her to convince herself that he is telling the truth. Eating the forbidden fruit seems like such a little thing, but it constitutes a betrayal of satanic proportions, for Eve, like Satan, has chosen to spurn God's love and to separate herself from His presence in order that she might assume His place.

Eve has now eaten the forbidden fruit, but she has not yet died or suffered any ill consequences. She turns to her husband, who has been with her the whole time. Satan now catches his breath. The deception of the woman was a master strike, a great blow to the God whom she betrayed, but the linchpin of his plan resided with the man. If Adam followed his wife in the betrayal of his Father, if he submitted to the will of the evil one, then all humanity would be plunged into sin, and all the world would be handed over to Satan. The fate of the world was quite literally hanging in the balance.

Apparently, without careful deliberation, Adam chooses his relationship with Eve over his relationship with God. He takes the fruit and eats it, in open defiance of God's command and in irresolute conformity to the wishes of his wife. Created to lead, Adam chooses to follow, and in so doing, he betrays himself and Eve, in addition to his God.

True to the serpent's promise, their eyes were indeed opened, but not as they had hoped. Rather than realizing the joys of heaven or unlocking all the hidden mysteries of the universe, the only insight they had gained was the knowledge of their own sin. They saw that they were unworthy to stand before the Lord their God. Shame and fear of being rejected had entered paradise.

In a feeble attempt to hide their sinfulness, Adam and Eve cover themselves with fig leaves. Fallen humanity has had "fig leaves" ever since, whether they be in the form of religion, science, philosophy, wealth, power, or whatever else we believe will restore the significance and security that we lost in that single act of disobedience.

Thus began what appeared to be Love's great defeat. Man and woman together had chosen to betray the love of their Father in order to pursue the satanic dream of equality with God. The tragic irony of this was that they had already been like God, in that they had been created to bear His image and to live out His love. Now the world was forced to wait in silent shame for God's response to this scandalous betrayal. What answer could Agape possibly have for this seemingly total triumph of evil over good?

In the Cool of the Day

It had been customary for Adam and Eve to enjoy the presence of God in the cool, breezy part of the day. No sooner do Adam and Eve take the fruit and taste the bitter shamefulness of sin than they feel the first gentle breezes. They look at each other in dismay, knowing that they have grievously betrayed the God they love, and, fearing rejection, they try to hide themselves among the dense foliage of the garden.

They can hear the sound of Him walking through the garden, and to their guilty ears, it is a sound both terrifying and ominous. Coming near to the place where Adam and Eve are hiding, God calls out to His son, "Where are you?" I assure you, this was not a question about geography. This was a question about their relationship. Even so, Adam begins by explaining why he has hidden himself: "I heard you in the garden, and I was afraid because I was naked; so I hid."[4] In doing so, he admits his shame and his fear, but he does not go so far as to confess his sin. His focus is on himself and his own feelings of guilt, shame, and insecurity. See how sin strips love of its outward focus, leaving behind only selfishness and egotism!

God, therefore, presses him further. Adam has admitted his shame, but he has not given any indication of what brought it about. There is perhaps no feeling in the world more alarming than the feeling you get when you realize that your sin has been exposed. In desperation, he blurts out an accusation: "The woman you put here with me—she gave me some fruit from the tree, and I ate it."[5]

"There is perhaps no feeling in the world more alarming than the feeling you get when you realize that your sin has been exposed."

Truly Adam is coming to reflect the image of Satan, the great accuser, rather than the image of God. Not only is he quick to cast all the blame on his wife, but he actually has the audacity to accuse God, implying that if God hadn't given him the woman in the first place, none of this ever would have happened.

The tragedy of this event cannot possibly be overstated. In his sin and shame, Adam is more than willing to sell out everyone he loves in order to preserve himself. Amazingly, God does not even dignify Adam's accusations with a response. Instead, He turns to Eve and asks, "What is this you have done?" Eve also tries to cast the blame for her actions elsewhere, but she seems to do so with less passion and resolve. "The serpent deceived me, and I ate."[6]

The crime has been reconstructed, and the evidence has been weighed. Now God is ready to pronounce judgment.

Suffering and Hope

When God turns to pronounce His judgment against the woman, something quite remarkable takes place—His judgment against the woman is tempered with hope. By saying to her, "I will greatly increase your pains in childbearing,"[7] God is making it clear that all is not completely lost. She will still be allowed to fulfill her God-given purpose to fill the Earth. Yet because of her sin, this purpose will now be accompanied by great pain.

What's more, Eve also will suffer the consequences of sin with respect to her relationship to her husband. Because she wrongly usurped her husband's authority and led him into sin, she will always desire to control him, continually frustrated by his assigned role of headship. Human sin has upset the delicate balance of agape between husband and wife. The battle of the sexes has now begun.

Having pronounced His judgment upon the woman, the Lord God now turns His attention to Adam, His wayward, disloyal, and recalcitrant son. Once again, God's justice proves to be remarkably poetic. Adam had sinned by eating, so the Lord God decreed that his eating would ever afterward be accompanied with the pain of laboring. In a blistering rebuke, God reminds Adam that he is nothing more than dust from the ground—dust that has been held together and given life by the sheer power of God's will. After serving the stubborn, unyielding, and unfruitful ground all the weary days of his life, Adam must ultimately become consumed by it. In a very real sense, the ground from which he eats will eventually eat him—reabsorbing him so completely as to leave no trace that he was ever anything more than a patch of dirt. And yet, even in the midst of this devastating curse, Adam continues to have a basis for hope.

Taking the High Way means appreciating the agape love God demonstrates toward His wander-prone creation. It is the property of agape to stand against and oppose sin, but it is the prerogative of agape to offer mercy to the sinner by taking the burden of his sin upon itself. God demonstrated both of these aspects of agape by uncompromisingly condemning sin in sinful man and by simultaneously embarking on a program of redemption and restoration ...

FOOTNOTES: 1. Genesis 3:1 (NIV); 2. Genesis 3:2-3 (NIV); 3. Genesis 3:4-5 (NIV); 4. Genesis 3:10 (NIV); 5. Genesis 3:12 (NIV); 6. Genesis 3:13 (NIV); 7. Genesis 3:16 (NIV)

GPS: *God-Positioning Scriptures (to Reorient Your Life)*

For the creation was subjected to frustration, not by its own choice, but by the will of the one who subjected it, in hope. —Romans 8:20 (NIV)

 REST STOP: *Pull Over and Ponder*
Eve and Adam ignored God and yielded to Satan. Where do you see the consequences of their actions affecting your life and relationships today?

Mile 26

Detoured, Part 2

The strength of love becomes most apparent when it refuses to be sidetracked by the failures of its beloved.

The Cost of Redemption

Having pronounced judgment and demonstrated mercy on His children, the Lord God now begins to pick up the pieces of their shattered lives. He has offered them a future hope, but they are in need of a present comfort.

In the aftermath of their sin, Adam's and Eve's nakedness has gone from a blessing to a curse. They had, of course, come up with their own solution, but how pathetic that was! Therefore, God in His grace steps in to provide a more adequate solution: garments of skin. Of course, such clothing necessarily involved the death of some animal—a creature completely innocent of the sin that it was now being sacrificed to cover. Thus, the covering of human sin was made possible only by the shedding of innocent blood.

And who was responsible for shedding this blood? None other than the Lord God Himself! Adam and Eve did not realize it, but this act of shedding innocent blood foreshadowed the entire history of redemption. Scripture makes it clear that "without the shedding of blood there is no forgiveness."[1] Consequently, the Old Testament sacrifices, the ram that God provided in place of Abraham's son, the sacrifice of His own Son as "the Lamb of God, who takes away the sin of the world"[2]—innocent lives were required to atone for the sins of God's people.

In every one of these sacrifices, God allowed one of His cherished creations to be slaughtered on the altar of human sin. It is the prerogative of agape to show mercy, but not by abrogation of justice. Rather, true agape offers mercy to the sinner by taking the burden of his sin upon himself.

To the Third and Fourth Generation

Scripture tells us that the consequences of human sin are not limited to the sinner, but his descendants as well, because God punishes the children "for the sin of the fathers to the third and fourth generation."[3]

"... true agape offers mercy to the sinner by taking the burden of his sin upon himself."

When Adam and Eve chose to sin against God's command, they were not only betraying their Father in heaven, but their future children also. Had they but given a thought to how their sin would affect their descendants, they might have avoided the travesty of the Fall. Instead, they thought only of themselves and their ambition to become equal with God. As a result, their children were never to know the sweet pleasures of the garden, or the joys of open fellowship with God, or the full extent of agape.

Adam and Eve's first son was born with such promise. Eve named him Cain, saying, "With the help of the Lord I have brought forth a man."[4] How she and her husband must have hoped that this would be the promised child who would crush the head of the serpent and once again set the world to right! But, alas, it was not to be.

Not long afterward, Eve gave birth to a second son, whom she named Abel. In the course of time, Cain continued to show promise by bringing an offering to the Lord, and as little brothers often do, Abel followed suit with an offering of his own. Yet, the Lord God, who looks upon the inner workings of the heart, found cause to reject Cain and his offering, while accepting Abel and his. Incensed at being "shown up" by his little brother, Cain begins to nurse a grudge against Abel. Over time that grudge grew to hatred that eventually culminated in murder.

Once again, God must stand in judgment of sinful man. As He had done with Adam, God gives Cain the opportunity to confess his sin without coercion or compulsion, by asking him simply, "Where is your brother Abel?" Once again the question was not a geographical one, but was meant to address the relationship damage. Cain, hiding behind a lie, rather than a fig leaf, replied innocently, "I don't know. ... Am I my brother's keeper?"[5]

See once more how sin is the adversary of agape. For the answer to Cain's rhetorical question was yes. Having given Cain an opportunity to freely confess his sin, God now pours out His wrath and fury on this murderous child. And once again, the pattern of poetic justice is upheld. Cain, a tiller of the soil, has stained the soil with his brother's blood. Therefore, the ground will no longer yield anything for him. He will be left to become a nomad, a "restless wanderer" who must forage for food across the trackless wastes of a fallen world.

Horrified and dismayed at the idea of being driven from God's presence, Cain cries out, "My punishment is more than I can bear."[6] Just as his father before him had done, Cain reveals the shameless self-concern of the sinner. Amazingly, God shows mercy even to this unrepentant killer of a righteous man. Graciously decreeing that Cain must not be slain at the hands of men, lest his death be avenged sevenfold, God puts a mark on him and sends him away into exile.

How Adam's and Eve's hopes for their sons must have been dashed by these tragic events. As for Cain, his sin also becomes multiplied in the lives of his descendants. Thankfully, God enables Adam and Eve to have "other sons and daughters,"[7] the first and most noble of whom is Seth. Seth and his descendants are men who once more begin to call "upon the name of the Lord."[8]

In spite of the devastation and despair that sin wrought among Adam and Eve's descendants, its victory was far from complete. As sin spread across the earth, rapidly increasing both in scope and intensity, there nevertheless remained a faithful remnant among men who continued to call upon the name of the Lord. At various times in the history of mankind, this remnant appeared to be in danger of passing completely from the face of the earth, but Love Himself preserved them, keeping alive the promised hope that a redeemer would one day rise up from among the descendants of Eve. In this way, God demonstrated that although He punishes the children for the sin of the fathers to the third and fourth generation, He shows love "to a thousand generations" of those who love Him and obey His commands.[9]

The amazing truth, which became apparent after all the dust from the Fall had settled, was that Satan's great "triumph" had provided yet another venue for the strength of God's love to be demonstrated. In the midst of betrayal, God's love had proven to be long-suffering, fair, and full of mercy. Taking the High Way means sharing the truth of God's love everywhere, every day.

FOOTNOTES: 1. Hebrews 9:22 (NIV); 2. John 1:29 (NIV); 3. Exodus 20:5 (NIV); 4. Genesis 4:1 (NIV); 5. Genesis 4:9 (NIV); 6. Genesis 4:13 (NIV); 7. Genesis 5:4 (NIV); 8. Genesis 21:33 (NIV); 9. Deuteronomy 5:10 (NIV)

GPS: *God-Positioning Scriptures (to Reorient Your Life)*
For the creation was subjected to frustration, not by its own choice, but by the will of the one who subjected it, in hope. —**Romans 8:20** (NIV)

REST STOP: *Pull Over and Ponder*
Do you sense God's love extended down through the generations? Are you living the kind of life that will create a legacy like Seth's—descendants who instinctually "call upon the name of the Lord"?

Mile 27

Paying the Toll

By His life, death, and resurrection, God's Son paid the toll for our sins. In Christ, Love's Great Redeemer, sinful man can at last know the love that had been lost in the Fall.

LOVE COSTS. ANYONE who has ever loved will tell you that. Love cannot be bought or purchased, but it nevertheless has its price, for true love demands that we place the welfare of our beloved before our own welfare, even to the point of laying down our lives.

Jesus once said, "Greater love has no one than this, that he lay down his life for his friends."[1] Without exception, all of Jesus' friends were sinners—sinners subject to the death and decay that Adam and Eve had brought into the world. They had an awful price to pay for their iniquity, but because of His great love for them, the Lord Jesus made that price His own, taking the cost of their sinfulness upon Himself and laying down His own life that they might live.

To many, Jesus' capture and crucifixion appeared to be a sign of weakness, the final proof of His inability to resist the religious and political powers that be. Clearly, He was just another Messianic pretender stamped out by the Romans. He was no great deliverer, for He couldn't even deliver Himself from the hands of His enemies. Yet, Jesus made it clear well in advance that no one had the power to take His life away from Him. On the contrary, His life was His own to lay down on behalf of those He loved. Jesus also made it clear that He possessed the authority to take His life back up again. He would demonstrate by His resurrection that His death had not been a defeat, but a willing sacrifice of atonement for sin.

As Jesus stood before Herod and Pilate, He was given every opportunity to clear His name, but He refused, answering their questions in such a way as to leave them practically no choice but to condemn Him. With the decision came a flood of vindictive abuse and brutal maltreatment. First, Pilate had Jesus flogged, a form of punishment usually reserved for slaves. Then, it was the soldiers' turn to have Him. In order to make Him look the part of the king of the Jews, they put a scarlet robe on Him, pierced His brow with a painful crown of thorns, and put a staff in His hands. Soon, ripping the staff from His hand, they began beating Him with it.

"Love costs. And for the holy God who loves all of us, in spite of our sin, it cost dearly."

Bloody and disfigured, Jesus was at this point barely able to stand. The soldiers shoved Jesus into the street with the splintered cross-beam of His crucifix across His shoulders to walk the steep road to Golgotha, the place of crucifixion. As Jesus appeared before the crowds lining the street, He was disfigured almost beyond recognition, and the crowds were repulsed by His appearance. The only ones who took pity on Him were the women who had followed Him. To them, Jesus was the man who had healed their sons and daughters of disease, who had treated them with dignity and respect in a day when women were seen as second-class citizens, and who had taught them of a kingdom where love and righteousness reigned supreme. He had been the man they wished all men could be. When others had lost faith in Him, they continued to believe.

Tender and compassionate to the end, Jesus paused in His arduous procession and risked another lashing to speak to these women prophetic words.[2] It is truly amazing how quick agape is to make light of its own sufferings in order to concern itself with the needs of others.

A Cross to Bear

Crucifixion is an excruciating way to die, for it involves a slow, agonizing process of suffocation. Imagine Jesus' anguish as He heard the taunts and jeers of the very people He had come to save.

In the face of all the hostility, Jesus prayed for His persecutors even as He hung on a cross. What an amazing, impossible, unbelievable display of love this was! This was a love with the power to break sin's ancient hold on mankind! True agape cures us of our sin by taking the consequences of that sin upon itself.

Both fully God and fully man, Jesus hung there suspended between the consuming wrath of a holy God and the vile fiendishness of sinful humanity. By taking the consequences of human sin upon Himself, He felt Himself forsaken by God. By acting as the emissary of God to a world that did not want God, He found Himself forsaken by men. For the first time in His life, He experienced the hell of being utterly and completely alone. At that very moment that He cried out to His Father, the temple veil, which symbolized the separation between sinful man and God Almighty, was rent in two. The bloody price of human sin had at last been paid, and there was now no longer any barrier between God and man.

This is how God demonstrated His love for us: He paid for our lives—lives that we had willingly thrown away—with the life of His own Son, the One whose life was really worth preserving. Love costs. And for the holy God who loves all of us, in spite of our sin, it cost dearly.

Love is Stronger Than Death

With Christ's death, the awful toll of sin had been paid in full, but the victory over sin had not yet been won. The destruction of God's own Son had only served to demonstrate the full extent of sin's power to destroy. It would now take the miraculous resurrection of the Son to demonstrate the full extent of love's power to conquer sin and death.

On this side of Easter morning, we sometimes forget the utter finality of Jesus' defeat. To those who had loved Him, who had put their trust in Him and had left everything behind to follow Him, Jesus was dead. For three days, Jesus' followers remained in a state of shock. How could they ever pick up the pieces of their lives now that they had staked everything on this "Messiah" and lost?

Imagine their wonder and astonishment when the risen Christ began to appear to them once more, not as a ghost or a disembodied spirit, but as a Man of flesh and blood, with physical scars to prove that He was the same Man who had been crucified! Even death could not defeat this Messiah, this Son of God.

It was by His resurrection that Jesus Christ was "declared with power to be the Son of God."[3] By taking His life back up again, He proved that no one had taken it from Him in the first place. By conquering death itself, He offered the hope of eternal life to sinful mankind and reversed the devastating effects of the Fall. Now mankind would be able to experience true agape once again—a love with the strength to reach to the grave and back in order to rescue those who want to be near Him from the very jaws of death. In Christ, Love's Great Redeemer, love had at last risen from the ashes of destruction.

Taking the High Way means having "the same attitude that Christ Jesus had,"[4] humbling ourselves and sacrificing for others for love's sake.

FOOTNOTES: 1. John 15:13 (NIV); 2. Luke 23:28-31; 3. Romans 1:4 (NIV); 4. Philippians 2:5 (NLT)

GPS: *God-Positioning Scriptures (to Reorient Your Life)*

You must have the same attitude that Christ Jesus had. Though he was God, he did not think of equality with God as something to cling to. Instead, he gave up his divine privileges; he took the humble position of a slave and was born as a human being. When he appeared in human form, he humbled himself in obedience to God and died a criminal's death on a cross. —Philippians 2:5-8 (NLT)

REST STOP: *Pull Over and Ponder*
In what ways has God's sacrificing and conquering love entered your life and placed you on a new road? Do the choices you make on a day-to-day basis honor Christ's sacrifice for you?

Mile 28

End of the Road

Ultimately, Love's great advance will conclude with Love's great conquest. The time will come when Christ will take back everything that Adam lost. Love will have its day of reckoning when all its enemies will be completely swept away.

HAVE YOU EVER walked outside after a thunderstorm and felt that strange mixture of fear and hope that comes with the passing of nature's fury? The sky is dark and ominous as the mountainous clouds drift away. The air is heavy with mist and still crackling with electricity. On one side, the gloom is pierced with thunderbolts and flashes of lightning. On the other, the sun is struggling to break through the clouds. There the light and mist combine and congeal to form a rainbow, hazy and luminous against the dusky backdrop of the sky. When we look upon such a scene, our hearts are pulled in a thousand different directions at once. The two great powers, the light and the darkness, the peace and the fury, meet to form the rainbow, which fills us with that sense of quiet wonder and hushed amazement so closely akin to worship.

The apostle John must have had a similar sense when he looked upon God's throne, as recorded in the book of Revelation. John's apocalyptic vision of the end times foretells the astonishing climax of the greatest love story ever told. With broad, but brilliant, strokes, it paints a spectacular picture of love's final conquest over sin.

Can you imagine being in John's shoes as He stood before His Maker? He was at once afraid and at peace in God's holy presence. In Him resided both the fearsome power of the thunderstorm and the gentle tranquility of the rainbow. Here was a God of holiness and love, justice and mercy, power and peace, wrath and forgiveness! The only response to such a God must be humble and heartfelt worship.

Yet many of us have such a bland view of heaven that the only reason we want to go there is that it beats the alternative. The passion of heaven is such that all our earthly loves pale in comparison. All our suffering and rejoicing, all our agony and ecstasy, all our deepest longings and most passionate desires fade in significance when we catch a glimpse of heaven. That is why God gave John this vision of heaven before showing Him the things of the future. Only in the context of heaven's passion and glorious hope could we possibly endure to hear of the Earth's turbulent and cataclysmic consummation.

Love's Final Warning

Love is indeed patient and forbearing with sinners, and God's love is perfectly so, but love will not endure sin forever. Ultimately, Love will have its day of reckoning. Ultimately, Love's enemies—those who choose to cling to their sin, turning their backs on Jesus, until the very end—will be consumed by it.

This is justice, for Love, allows personal choice. God invites us to have a personal relationship with Him, but if we decide we want other things instead, God allows us our separation forever; He doesn't force us to spend eternity with Him.

God waits patiently, and His invitation is unwavering, but in John's vision, God made it eminently clear that a final day will come. And then God's invitation will no longer exist and He will unleash His fury against that which opposes His Son and His people. The Bible describes the outpouring of God's wrath in vivid and graphic detail.

Love's Last Battle

Having just witnessed God's war against Satan and sinful humanity from the overarching perspective of heaven, John is then given a closer look at the final battle from the viewpoint of the Earth. Nowhere in Revelation do we find that Love's last battle with sin is much of a contest.

After all this buildup on the part of the forces of darkness, they are swept away with a mere brush of God's hand. Satan and his forces are devoured by fire from heaven.[1] Just like that, the war that has spanned the ages is brought to an end, and God's peace is unshakably established. As promised long ago, the head of the serpent is crushed beneath the foot of Christ, whose heel he had bruised at the

"The passion of heaven is such that all our earthly loves pale in comparison."

cross, and Christ's bride, His church—those who chose to accept His invitation to be their personal Lord and Savior—is delivered, once and for all, to be united with Him forever.

Happily Ever After

Then in the aftermath of the outpouring of God's wrath, as the charred and lifeless remains of a sinful world lay smoldering, a shaft of sunlight pierces the darkest hour of morning, and the Lord of light makes His countenance to shine once more upon the world He had crushed. Out of the smoldering remains of heaven and earth, a new heaven and a new earth are resurrected.

Even in our fallen world, life has a way of conquering death. Life goes on. Even in a fallen world where death so often appears to be triumphant, God's redeeming love, when at last it is poured out upon the world in all its fullness, will instantly bring everything to life, making all things fresh and new once more.

As with the first creation, once God has formed this new environment, He immediately fills it with inhabitants. And the church, Christ's waiting bride, will come to be with her Husband and to live with Him in the place that He has prepared for her.

The coming of God's kingdom is more than just a cosmic victory—it is the consummation of a love affair. The tragic effects of humanity's fall into sin are forever reversed and removed. God will wipe every tear from the eyes of His beloved children. They are His forever, secure in His unfailing love. This is the "happily ever after" of the greatest love story ever told.

Learning to Love

We have relived the greatest love story ever told in all of its passion and romance, tragedy and triumph. This epic tale of God's redemptive love for mankind inspires us to love more completely. If we are to learn to reflect God's love in our own relationships, we have only to look to the example of our Lord Jesus Christ.

We should look at each of our relationships as an opportunity to model the love of Christ. As Christians, we ought to be the most loving husbands, the most caring wives, the best parents, the hardest workers, and the truest friends. At every point, the greatest love story ever told has much to teach us about living out our God-given purpose of love. Taking the High Way means becoming conformed to the image of Christ, the greatest expression and clearest example of divine love the world has ever known.

FOOTNOTES: 1. Revelation 20:9

GPS: *God-Positioning Scriptures (to Reorient Your Life)*

I saw the Holy City, the new Jerusalem, coming down out of heaven from God, prepared as a bride beautifully dressed for her husband. And I heard a loud voice from the throne saying, "Now the dwelling of God is with men, and he will live with them. They will be his people, and God himself will be with them and be their God. He will wipe every tear from their eyes. There will be no more death or mourning or crying or pain, for the old order of things has passed away."
—**Revelation 21:2-4** (NIV)

REST STOP: *Pull Over and Ponder*
Hebrews 10:24-25 says, "Let us consider how to stimulate one another to love and good deeds ... encouraging one another; and all the more as you see the day drawing near." Beginning today, how can you be more encouraging and loving to those God's given you?

EXIT 5: *FAITH LANE*

Mile 29

Heavy Mettle

As you continue on your journey, you are carried forward by a vision of an unseen future. And while you may not know where you're going, you know the One who is leading you there ... and that is enough.

APART FROM ITS religious significance, "faith" is simply an ordinary word we use all the time. "I have faith in you." "Come on, have a little faith." In everyday speech, faith is a synonym for trust, belief, and hope.

Yet somehow, when we start talking about religious faith, things tend to get a little cryptic. We begin to associate faith with all kinds of mystical, miraculous concepts like salvation, grace, redemption, and union with God. There's nothing wrong with that since Scripture teaches us that faith is the means by which we receive all those things. However, as soon as we start to think of faith as something mystical and miraculous in its own right, we begin to lose sight of its true significance. It is when we over-spiritualize faith that we forget what it truly means to have it.

133

Few of us would ever tell a friend that our confidence in him or her was based on a "leap of faith." Yet somehow, we have no qualms about thinking of our faith in God that way! Instead of focusing on how faithful and trustworthy He is, we focus on how strong our own faith is. We stop thinking of faith as something God deserves, and we start thinking of it as something we conjure up within ourselves. Consequently, the more irrational and unthinking our faith becomes, the stronger we believe it to be.

When we start to think of faith as a spiritual quality within ourselves, rather than as hope and trust in someone outside ourselves, we have completely lost sight of its meaning. The issue is not how trusting we are, but how trustworthy God is. There can be no room for confusion or uncertainty, because faith is that which connects us with God.

The Testing of Faith

It's normal for us to find it difficult to turn our backs on the things of this world for the sake of our faith in the unseen God. More difficult still are those moments when God Himself appears to betray the trust we have placed in Him. Whenever our faith seems to have more costs than it has benefits, whenever we experience great suffering or injustice, and whenever following God's will seems to make no sense at all, our faith in Him can become stretched to the breaking point—so much so that we begin to wonder if He can be trusted. It is in such desperate moments as these that the true mettle of our faith is tested. In the book of Matthew, we find encouragement from Jesus for such times: "If you have faith like a grain of mustard seed, you can say to this mountain, 'Move from here to there,' and it will move, and nothing will be impossible for you."

"Scripture is filled with stories that encourage us to remember God is always trustworthy."

Scripture is filled with stories that encourage us to remember God is always trustworthy. In one of those stories, we learn that after a lifetime of hoping against hope for a son, Abraham's wife conceived in her old age and gave birth to Isaac, just as God had promised Abraham years before. Isaac was Abraham's pride and joy, His living proof that the Lord could be trusted. Yet one day, Abraham's God seemed to betray that trust by issuing a horrible command, "Take ... your only son ... Sacrifice him ... as a burnt offering."[1] In that barbarous age of child sacrifice and ritual bloodshed, it was not unusual for a god to demand the life of a child, but this was Abraham's God, the same Lord who detested such abominable practices! What's more, the child whom God was ordering to be sacrificed was the very child He had long promised and miraculously brought into existence. To Abraham, losing his son could well have seemed like losing God's promise to him. But the key to that promise lay in Abraham's relationship with God, not in the life of Isaac. God tested Abraham to clarify the intent and hope of his heart.

Imagine the turmoil Abraham went through as he searched desperately for some way to make sense of it all. Abraham did not understand the reasons for this strange command, but he knew his God could be trusted—even when it came to the life of his beloved son. We see further evidence of this fact as we learn that Abraham looked to God for the solution to his terrifying dilemma, even though it was God who was responsible for bringing it about. The writer of Hebrews tells us that Abraham reasoned that God could raise the dead.[2] Abraham was so confident that God would keep His promise regarding Isaac that he was prepared to look beyond the grave for his son's deliverance.

It is that unshakable trust in God's love, that firm conviction that with God all things are possible, and that steadfast willingness to follow Him wherever He leads that gives us the strength to endure the testing of our faith. And it will be tested. Our personal goals, valued relationships, meaningful jobs, or something else may need to end up on the sacrificial altar.

The Essence of Faith

Strip away all of its outer layers, and the essence of faith is this: a life lived for Jesus Christ. Faith does not consist in merely believing certain theological truths. Even the demons do that![3] Genuine faith consists in building one's life upon the Lord Jesus Christ. It involves placing one's trust in the salvation that He won, and then acting on that trust in the way we live each day of our lives.

To get a picture of what it means to have genuine faith, consider the simple act of sitting in a chair. As you approach a chair, you might look at it and think to yourself, *You know, that chair looks pretty sturdy; I believe that it will hold my weight.* You might even think of a time when you witnessed someone heavier than yourself sit down in that very chair without any mishap. Clearly, the weight of evidence would show that the chair before you was quite capable of bearing your weight. Yet despite your firm and well-reasoned conviction that the chair in question will support you, you have not fully trusted the chair until you have actually sat down on it.

So it is with our faith in Jesus Christ. We may consider all the evidences for Jesus' death and resurrection. We may look at people we believe to be far more "sinful" than ourselves whose faith in Christ made a wonderful difference in their lives. We may look back to times in our own lives when God proved true to His word. But until we depend on Him to hold us up, until we lean on Him to the point that if He lets us go, we will surely fall, until we base our entire lives upon the promises He has made, all our beliefs that He is trustworthy are nothing more than best guesses.

The essence of faith, that thing that distinguishes it from all other forms of belief or cognition, is the willingness to build one's life on the foundation of Jesus Christ and Him alone. If our faith is genuine, then it will make a visible difference in our lives. It will change every aspect of who we are. It will affect everything we do. Taking the High Way means having true faith ... the kind that relies on the One who will change us and change the world.

FOOTNOTES: 1. Genesis 22:2 (NIV); 2. Hebrews 11:19; 3. James 2:19

GPS: *God-Positioning Scriptures (to Reorient Your Life)*

Now faith is the assurance of things hoped for, the conviction of things not seen. And without faith it is impossible to please Him, for he who comes to God must believe that He is and that He is a rewarder of those who seek Him. —**Hebrews 11:1, 6**

REST STOP: *Pull Over and Ponder*

The roller coaster of life often tests our faith. When it tests yours, do you respond like Abraham did—with a steady conviction in God's goodness and sovereignty? With which circumstances do you need to wholeheartedly trust God today?

Mile 30

Looking Ahead

Strength requires an inclination toward the future, an anticipation of life in heaven. To live by faith in this present age, you must keep your eyes fixed on your life in the age to come.

CONVENTIONAL WISDOM OFTEN cautions us not to become so "heavenly minded" that we are "no earthly good." The underlying assumption behind this warning is that if we are too focused on our future life in heaven, we will grow apathetic toward our present life on earth and will no longer be concerned about making the world a better place. In reality, it is those who are the most "heavenly minded" who possess the faith to do the most "earthly good."

C.S. Lewis once wrote, "Because we love something more than this world, we love this world better than those who know no other." Lewis understood that it is only as we view this present age in the light of the age to come that we will ever be able to love this world enough to improve it. After all, if there is nothing beyond this world, we might as well "eat and drink, for tomorrow we die."[1] It is only as we look beyond the uncertainty of this world to the certainty of life in heaven that we will ever find the courage to live for more than ourselves.

The Gravity of Heaven

Albert Einstein once said that there is no such thing as empty space. The nature of any particular space is determined by the strongest "gravitating matter" within that space. Our solar system exists in space, but it is the fact that the sun is the strongest gravitating matter within that space that differentiates our solar system from all other aspects of space. If we wish to understand the nature of any particular space, we must examine the nature of whatever within that space has the strongest pull.

What has the strongest pull in heaven? Around what does everything in heaven revolve? The answer is obvious: God is the central figure and defining presence in heaven. Heaven can simply be defined as that place where God dwells in perfect fullness. It is the supreme throne from which God exercises His sovereign rule over all creation.

In Revelation, the apostle John records a vision in which he is taken up to heaven, one of the most vivid descriptions we have of what heaven will be like.[2] In John's vision of heaven, God stands as the central figure around whom everything revolves. He commands the worship and reverence of all those present, from the greatest to the least. Though surpassingly beautiful, heaven will not be defined by its beauty. Though altogether glorious, it will not be known for its splendor. Rather, heaven is the place where the Lord God Almighty, who was, and is, and is to come, is the focus of all attention and the irresistible center of gravity.

Seeing Him as He Is

Heaven is a place where all eyes are on God in the sense that He is the center of attention and the sole object of worship. Yet there is another, more intimate sense in which all eyes will be on God, for at long last, everyone will be able to see Him face to face. No longer will we behold Him as though He were behind a veil or dimly reflected in a mirror. We will gaze openly upon Him in all His glory, seeing Him as He is and knowing Him as fully as is possible for finite creatures to know an infinite Deity.[3]

Ever since Adam and Eve were driven from the garden of Eden, men have longed to see God face to face once more. In Exodus, we learn that Moses pleads with God, "Show me Your glory!" But God responds, "You cannot see My face, for no man can see Me and live!"[4] In 1 Kings, we learn that Elijah experienced the Lord's presence in only a whisper.[5]

In heaven, every barrier to open communion with God will finally be removed, and the Lord Almighty will shine like the sun upon those who seek His face. He will wipe every tear from their eyes, and they will fall down before Him in worship and adoration.[6]

When at last we behold the unmasked glory of the Lord, we will find it to be so pervasive and all-consuming that all who look upon it will themselves be imbued with a similar glory. While God alone will be the center of gravity and the focus of attention, He will not keep that glory all to Himself, but rather will turn around and share that glory with each one, so that they shine like stars in the celestial firmament.

Serving One Another

I'm not quite sure why, but many people worry that in heaven, we will no longer know or be close to the people we loved on earth. Common caricatures of heaven make it out to be a passionless place where every relationship is serene and cold as marble. Nothing could be further from the truth! If you think you love someone now, think how much closer you will be when you both have been perfected in Christ. The earthly loves we experience today are but a shadow of the profoundly intimate relationships we will enjoy in Paradise. We need not worry about losing touch with our loved ones in the midst of heaven's multitudes.

Christ envisioned His church to be one body made up of many members, each of who love and serve all the others. In heaven, this vision will be a reality, as all the saints find inexpressible joy and perfect fulfillment in serving one another.

Contributing to Perfection

You may ask, "If heaven is a perfect place, what need will there be for us to bless and serve one another?" After all, if we will already enjoy perfect peace and unspeakable joy in heaven, no needs will exist for us to minister to!

But, need is simply not a prerequisite for blessing. Some of life's sweetest blessings are those that do not meet any particular need. Art and music are tremendous blessings, but they are hardly necessary. Their benefit comes not in that they make life possible, but in that they make it beautiful. The very fact that we will have no need of further blessing in heaven is precisely what will give meaning to the blessings we bestow upon each other. It is the fact that we do not have to contribute that will make our contribution a rich and significant blessing.

When I was growing up in Shelby, Ohio, I belonged to a very proper United Methodist church. On occasion, the church would host a potluck dinner. All the ladies would bring in these fabulous dishes, presenting their culinary offerings in their best china with their finest silver utensils. It was all a very fancy affair. Once, into the midst of all this solemnity and refinement, a young mother brought her little boy.

"... need is simply not a prerequisite for blessing."

She had apparently dressed him in his Sunday best too early, because when he came in, he was all rumpled and soiled. It was clear that he didn't want to be there, and to appease him, his mother had bought him a box of animal crackers. As he watched the women place their magnificent dishes on the table, he decided that he, too, would contribute to the spread. He walked up to the table and very solemnly positioned his box of animal crackers—the same box he had stuck a grimy hand into just moments earlier—between two homemade desserts.

As it came time for people to serve themselves, each person in the line scooped from each dish and remarked how wonderful it all was. When the first lady in line came to the box of animal crackers, she reached in, pulled out a cracker, turned to the next person, and said, "I got a lion." One by one, each person got a cracker, held it up to announce his or her animal, and then placed it in the center of his or her plate.

That is the picture I get whenever I think of how we will contribute in heaven. Into the midst of a perfect spread, we will humbly deposit our little boxes of animal crackers, and much to our surprise, we will find that everyone present takes great delight in what we have given. That is the beauty of heaven. Even though it is already perfect, there will always be room for us to contribute and to be a blessing to others. Taking the High Way means looking forward to that day when our journey here ends and our new life in heaven begins.

FOOTNOTES: 1. 1 Corinthians 15:32 (NIV); 2. Revelation 4:2-11; 3. 1 Corinthians 13:12; 4. Exodus 33:18, 20; 5. 1 Kings 19:11-12; 6. Revelation 7:17

GPS: *God-Positioning Scriptures (to Reorient Your Life)*

The city does not need the sun or the moon to shine on it, for the glory of God gives it light, and the Lamb is its lamp. The nations will walk by its light, and the kings of the earth will bring their splendor into it. —**Revelation 21:23-24** (NIV)

REST STOP: *Pull Over and Ponder*
How does understanding that "need is simply not a prerequisite for blessing" give you clarity about ways you could potentially bless others on this side of heaven?

Mile 31

Bridging Heaven and Earth

Just as your weekday commute is more hectic than a Sunday drive ... so the joys of Sunday worship inevitably give way to the hassles and frustration of Monday morning. Faith is that which bridges the disparity between this world and the next.

HEAVEN IS WHERE faith finds its ultimate fulfillment, but it might surprise you to learn that in heaven, faith as we know it will cease to exist. In a manner of speaking, heaven is where we will lose our faith. After all, if faith is being "certain of what we do not see,"[1] and if heaven is the place where we will see God "face to face," then it stands to reason that in heaven, we will no longer believe on the basis of faith. Rather, we will believe on the basis of sight. By definition, therefore, faith belongs to this present age and will be made obsolete in the next.

If this is true, why, then, in our attempt to develop a faith that can change the world, must we spend so much time exploring the nature of heaven? Faith is

143

that which bridges the distance between this world and the next. Its focal point is heaven, but its vantage point is Earth. It is this combination of heavenward focus and earthly stance that gives faith its remarkable power to change the world.

Revolving Around the Son

In heaven, God Almighty is the indisputable "center of gravity," the focus of all attention, and the One around whom everything else revolves. In heaven, everything we see will be identified by its relationship to the One who sits on the throne. It will be perfectly clear that nothing exists apart from God, that every molecule of the universe is indelibly stamped with His signature, and that all things derive their ultimate meaning and significance from Him.

> *"It is this combination of heavenward focus and earthly stance that gives faith its remarkable power to change the world."*

Here on Earth, however, God's absolute centrality, though no less real, is far less visible and apparent. From our limited vantage point, we often fail to recognize our utter dependence on Him, succumbing to the seductive illusion that we are the ones around whom the universe revolves. It is only as we observe things from a truer perspective that we are able to gain a more accurate perception of reality. By looking beyond the limited confines of the earth, astronomers have discovered that the Earth is not, in fact, at the center of the universe. We live on the third planet from a sun that is located on the outskirts of a galaxy that itself lies who knows where in the vast expanse of the universe.

From our limited vantage point here on Earth, it is easy to be mistaken about what is central and what is peripheral in our universe. From where we stand, everything seems to revolve around us, and we are relatively unaware just how much we happen to be on the fringes of a universe that revolves around something else. If this is true of the physical realm, how much more must it be true of the spiritual realm? From where we stand as fallen creatures in a fallen world, a world that only remotely represents the deeper realities of heaven, it is all too easy to be mistaken about what is central and what is not.

In much the same way that our view of the universe was revolutionized by Copernicus' discovery that the earth revolved around the sun, so our view of life in this world will be revolutionized by the realization that everything in creation revolves around God's Son. The things that once seemed so important will now fade in significance, and things we never before took notice of will now take on the greatest meaning. It is this new vision, this heavenly sight, this God-centered perspective that gives us the power to change the world for Christ.

Reflecting His Glory

In this fallen world, God's face remains hidden from our sight, perceptible only through the eyes of faith. Nevertheless, in Christ we can know Him on this side of eternity, and though we as yet behold His face as "in a mirror dimly,"[2] that distant reflection is still bright enough to transform us into the same image "with ever-increasing glory."[3]

Have you ever gazed intently at a blurry photograph or tried to watch a television show in spite of poor reception? At first, it is maddeningly difficult to make out any kind of detail, but miraculously, the longer one stares at these images, the clearer they become, so that after a while, one hardly notices the poor image quality. That is how it is when we gaze upon God's face in faith. At first, He seems distant and painfully difficult to see, but the more we focus on Him, the more we come to see His presence in every aspect of our lives, the easier He becomes to recognize, and the closer He begins to appear.

If we are to have a faith that can change the world, we must, like David, "gaze upon the beauty of the Lord,"[4] pore over His Word, converse with Him in prayer, see Him in everything around us, and praise Him. In these endeavors, we will, as Paul wrote, find that we are being transformed into His likeness "from glory to glory."[5] Faith is not something that can be conjured up out of thin air. It is something that must be built gradually, steadily, and unceasingly, through constant exposure, and strengthened by repeated testing.

For the person who loves Christ, the disparity between this world and the next is at times almost unbearable. The person who has caught a vision of heaven can no longer be content with a world that is dying. His heart is full, and the love he has for Jesus Christ will overflow in blessings to others. When this happens, we glimpse heaven on this earth.

John Knox, the great Reformer of Scotland, had been ousted from his homeland for his Protestant beliefs. For eleven stormy years, he had remained in exile, traveling as a refugee throughout England and Europe. Everywhere he went, he did what he could to build up the church, but his heart never left Scotland. When at last he was able to return, he struggled for years to establish a church that eventually would shine as a light to the rest of the world. When he died at around the age of seventy, Knox had already succeeded in making Scotland one of the most thoroughly Protestant countries in all of Europe. As he lay on his deathbed, he could be heard saying over and over again, "The church! The church!" Even in his last hour, Knox was praying that the church would continue to thrive in a dark, hostile world.

As we come to develop a faith that can bridge the distance between this world and the next, we will become men and women with vision and passion to change the world for Christ. However, we will soon discover that there are many who do not share our desire to see the world remade in the image of heaven— most of us can remember a time in our lives when we were one of them. Taking the High Way means remaining passionate about our faith and, at the same time, remaining compassionate toward those who lack our perspective.

FOOTNOTES: 1. Hebrews 11:1 (NIV); 2. 1 Corinthians 13:12; 3. 2 Corinthians 3:18 (NIV); 4. Psalm 27:4 (NIV); 5. 2 Corinthians 3:18

GPS: *God-Positioning Scriptures (to Reorient Your Life)*

Do everything readily and cheerfully—no bickering, no second-guessing allowed! Go out into the world uncorrupted, a breath of fresh air in this squalid and polluted society. Provide people with a glimpse of good living and of the living God. Carry the light-giving Message into the night so I'll have good cause to be proud of you on the day that Christ returns. You'll be living proof that I didn't go to all this work for nothing. —Philippians 2:14-16 (The Message)

REST STOP: *Pull Over and Ponder*

How does growing to realize that the world doesn't revolve around you change how you view your place and purpose in this world?

Mile 32

Facing Roadblocks, Part 1

As you seek to live a heavenly life in a world corrupted by sin, you will inevitably encounter roadblocks that will test your faith. Don't look for shortcuts! God is using these challenges to perfect you on your journey.

THE GREAT CHALLENGE of faith is that, having caught a vision of what life will be like in heaven, we must continue to dwell here on Earth. It is as if we are caught between two worlds, not yet completely belonging to the one, and no longer quite fitting into the other. It should come as no surprise, therefore, when our faith is continually tested on the road to spiritual maturity.

Roadblock No. 1: Negativity

We will only make a little progress on the High Way before we face discouragement from people who think we have "lost touch with reality." Typically, these naysayers are not our enemies, but our closest friends and family members—the very people we look to for encouragement and support! Our Lord Himself faced such discouragement early in His ministry. The Bible tells us that when Jesus' own family heard about how He was traveling all over the countryside preaching and performing miracles, "they went out to take custody of Him; for they were saying, 'He has lost His senses.'"[1]

People have a natural tendency to try to bring a dreamer back to "reality." All of us started out in life dreaming of doing great things, but many of us, when faced with disappointment, began to give up those dreams as being unrealistic and unattainable. Those who stopped striving for what could be are quick to discourage others. These voices should not be allowed to drown out God's calling. God is ultimately the One each of us must pay attention to. It is His encouragement and perspective that make it possible for us to pursue the greatest possible future.

> *"... the people who will be most ministered to by our faith are usually the ones who seem to be trying to take us down."*

As for the dreamers among us who feel badgered and harassed by discouraging people, we need to remember that their "negativism" often is not caused by any lack of faith on their part, but by their love and concern for us. We need to realize that their constant scrutiny, which may seem intrusive and meddlesome to us, is merely their way of trying to see if what we believe is real. (On a personal note, when I told my stepfather I was going to be a pastor, he said, "This will pass.")

Our focus is on changing the world for Christ, and that is a wonderful goal. But the thing we need to realize is that the people who will be most ministered to by our faith are usually the ones who seem to be trying to take us down. By living out our faith in front of them, and patiently loving them in spite of their pessimism, we may ultimately show them the Reality that can alter their own.

Roadblock No. 2: Hesitation

Yet another roadblock we face comes when we trust God … but only to a certain point. We have already examined the story of Abraham and Isaac. Yet, there is another element of this story that is of particular interest here: Abraham's struggle to deal with the impending destruction of the son he loved. You see, it's one thing to talk about how the Lord was testing Abraham to see if his love for God was greater than his love for Isaac. Thanks in part to the writer of Hebrews, we have the luxury of being able to see the big picture of God's purpose behind the terrible command to sacrifice Isaac. All Abraham could see was that his son was destined to die.

Imagine what Abraham must have been thinking during that three-day journey to the mountain of sacrifice. Perhaps he wondered—as we all wonder when our faith is tested—whether or not this might somehow have been his fault. Had he done something to provoke God to take his promised son away? Were his own failures destined to become the reason for his son's death?

Nevertheless, Abraham remembered—and we, too, must remember—that God is ultimately in control, and that no amount of failure on our part can interfere with His plans or frustrate His purposes. In the final analysis, God is the One responsible for allowing our faith to be tested, and God will be the One to rescue us from it … or carry us through it. Thus, we can take comfort in the fact that none of this is taking place outside the will of God.

Despite his own internal anguish and turmoil, Abraham never gave up hope. When he came in sight of Mount Moriah, he said to his servants, "Stay here with the donkey while I and the boy go over there. We will worship and then we will come back to you."² Somehow, Abraham refused to give up the idea that he and Isaac would return together. He continued to look for God's provision even in the midst of impending disaster.

The great Danish theologian Soren Kierkegaard once wrote about how we should respond to painful and heart-wrenching situations. He called it "infinite resignation," where we resign ourselves to the fact that God is God and that there is nothing we can do to resist His will. While this perspective may be theologically accurate, the response of faith goes one step further by looking at the "impossible" circumstances and fully expecting that God is going to do something great through it all. This involves more than merely "hoping for the best." Rather, it involves resting in the knowledge that our God "causes all things to work together for good" to those who love Him and who are called according to His purpose.³ It means believing that God can redeem any situation, and wanting to be there to see it happen.

Abraham found the strength and the courage to walk with his son all the way down the road to destruction by clinging to the belief that God will ultimately bring good out of every disaster. Rather than abandoning his faith for the sake of the son he loved, he relied on his faith for the hope to believe that God would give his son back to him.

Roadblock No. 3: Narcissism

Another roadblock is our assumption that the testing we are experiencing is all about us when, in reality, it is about God bringing His plans to pass and revealing His Son in us. Consider the ways that Abraham's experience reveals the full magnitude of God's love in Christ.[4] God called Abraham to sacrifice his son, whom he loved. Though in the end He spared Abraham this horrendous assignment, God Himself eventually did the very thing He had asked Abraham to do: He sacrificed His Son, whom He loved.

The terrible sacrifice that God spared Abraham from having to make, He Himself made, thereby showing the full extent of His love for sinful mankind. Naturally, Abraham could not possibly have comprehended the cosmic significance of what he was going through. Whenever we experience trials, we rarely have any concept of any deeper significance to our personal struggles. The painful circumstances we must face appear to be cause for weeping and mourning. When God's provision is clearly seen, we will have cause for rejoicing. As we face struggles and trials, we can rest assured that at just the right moment, God will always provide a way out. Taking the High Way requires us to have confidence in our God. It means having the assurance that He loves us all along the way, even when our faith is tried.

FOOTNOTES: 1. Mark 3:21; 2. Genesis 22:5 (NIV); 3. Romans 8:28; 4. Genesis 22:1-18

GPS: *God-Positioning Scriptures (to Reorient Your Life)*

Therefore we do not lose heart. Though outwardly we are wasting away, yet inwardly we are being renewed day by day. For our light and momentary troubles are achieving for us an eternal glory that far outweighs them all. So we fix our eyes not on what is seen, but on what is unseen. For what is seen is temporary, but what is unseen is eternal. —2 Corinthians 4:16-18 (NIV)

REST STOP: *Pull Over and Ponder*
Hindsight teaches us a lot about God's provision and work in our lives. How might your past experience with roadblocks help you more readily put your faith in God to help you push through the trials you're experiencing right now?

Mile 33

Facing Roadblocks, Part 2

A faith that looks to the future is not afraid to face the challenges looming up ahead. Such confidence comes from knowing God will not fail to keep His promises to His children.

Roadblock No. 4: Conflict

Unfortunately, there are many in this world who will resist our efforts to make this age look a little more like the age to come. To them, we are anything but selfless servants who are laying down our lives to make the world a better place. On the contrary, they see us as troublesome meddlers who are trying to tell them how to run their own lives. From their perspectives, we are an enemy who needs to be stopped.

In all of history, there are few people who have had to face a more intimidating adversary than David faced in Goliath. A mountain of a man standing no less than nine feet tall, Goliath appeared quite comfortable on the battlefield as he stood ridiculing the armies of Israel for their cowardice. David gave no thought to his own weakness or lack of experience as he focused on this man who had positioned himself against God's people and purposes. How can we find the faith to stand against those who would oppose us because of our stance for God and kingdom purposes? We begin by realizing that God is with us as we go about His business, and that He is not the least bit intimidated by the antics of a bully. God is our help and the One who sustains us.[1]

It is interesting to note that before David faced Goliath, he first had to overcome a series of lesser bullies. Among them were his own brother, Eliab, and King Saul. Sadly, it is not unusual for us to be opposed by those who are closest to us. Because they know us best, they can be all too quick to question our motives. The best way to handle such accusations is not to try to justify ourselves, but simply to do as David did—walk away from accusation and continue to progress toward our God-given assignment. Taking the time to defend ourselves and our motives will only distract us from the real task at hand. After all, Eliab's verbal assault on David was all but forgotten after David had slain Goliath.

> *"God is faithful, and He will never fail to deliver His servants from the hands of their enemies."*

While Eliab questioned David's motives, Saul questioned David's ability. His intention was not simply to discourage David, but to protect him from harm. Yet, Saul's pessimism did nothing to change David's firm conviction that God would be on his side. As David faced Goliath, he did not boast in himself. He boasted in his beloved Lord, the living God who fights on behalf of His people. David understood that his own weakness was not a hindrance, but the very thing the Lord would use to demonstrate His glory and strength.

God is faithful, and He will never fail to ultimately deliver His servants from the hands of their enemies. As we are surrounded by enemies from without and accusations from within, we will find that the ancient promise still stands: "Anyone who trusts in him will never be put to shame."[2]

Roadblock No. 5: Inadequacy

Perhaps even more daunting than having to deal with the aggression and hostility of an external enemy is having to face our own moments of weakness, failure, and inadequacy. We live in a nation of strong individualists, where weakness is never to be shown. Why, even our deodorant commercials inform us that we should never let anyone see us sweat, as if such a sign of "weakness" would spell disaster for us in this dog-eat-dog world.

All of us, whether weak or strong, poor or rich, loved or despised depend upon God for our very existence. Yet, so often we deceive ourselves into thinking that we have some control over our own destiny. We need to realize that we are closest to God not when we come to Him offering our best resources, but when we come empty-handed, crying out for His people, His provision, His mercy, and His love. It is when we are "poor in spirit," not when we are at the top of our game, that the "kingdom of heaven" is truly ours.[3]

Of course, our natural tendency is to do everything we can to avoid being "poor in spirit." We grow weary of constantly having to cry out to God for help, and we believe that we have to get our lives together so we won't have to depend on Him so much. We make the mistake of linking success with being less dependent upon God when, in reality, the more we have and the more successful we are, the more we need to depend on God. "From everyone who has been given much, much will be required."[4] At no point can we cease to recognize our poverty of spirit before God our Father.

I've known a certain couple for some time now. Blessed with incredibly high IQs and EQs, they have everything going for them and have built their business into a multimillion-dollar corporation. They are a typical American success story … well, almost. This couple has two children: a son who is an absolute genius, and a daughter who is severely mentally disabled. For more than thirty years, I have watched these people depend on God to help them raise their daughter. At no point in their lives have these enterprising people been able to entertain the illusion that they don't need God. For that reason, I can say of these people that their money made them wealthy, but their daughter made them rich. Because of her and their utter dependence on God, they have learned to love like most of us never do and to have a faith that runs very deep. Blessed are they because through their weakness, God's strength is being perfected in their lives.

The Common Denominator

Although, in many respects, each kind of test we face calls for a slightly different response from us, we are ultimately to respond to every test in the same basic way.

No matter what the circumstances, no matter what the particulars, we can overcome every single challenge we face by doing one simple thing: focusing on future promises rather than on past failures or present difficulties. That and that alone will give us the strength we need to endure the testing of our faith.

A faith that looks to the future is not afraid to face the challenges looming up ahead. Such confidence comes from knowing God will not fail to keep His promises to His children. It is His strength that matters, not ours. Taking the High Way means facing challenges head on, knowing that ultimately God will use them—and us—to change the world.

FOOTNOTES: 1. Psalm 54:4b; 2. Romans 10:11 (NIV); 3. Matthew 5:3 (NIV); 4. Luke 12:48

GPS: *God-Positioning Scriptures (to Reorient Your Life)*

Consider it all joy, my brethren, when you encounter various trials, knowing that the testing of your faith produces endurance. And let endurance have its perfect result, so that you may be perfect and complete, lacking in nothing. —James 1:2-4

REST STOP: *Pull Over and Ponder*
Time and time again, hindsight proves God's promises to move mightily through our faith. Practically speaking, how can knowing that God's promises also apply to the unknowns of our future help you take confident steps toward changing the world?

Mile 34

Where the Rubber Meets the Road

Faith looks to the future of life in heaven. It affects the way we live life on earth. It carries us through the trials we face. It transforms our relationships with other people. But the essence of faith is simply this: Jesus Christ, and Him crucified.

SINCE THERE IS nothing quite like a story for giving clarity to a point, let me share one of my favorites: A little boy who had recently been given a bow and some steel-tipped arrows went to visit his grandmother at her farm. The boy shot his arrows at any target he could find—usually without coming close to hitting anything. Then he spotted her prize ducks. Knowing he couldn't possibly hit one of them, he loosed an arrow in the ducks' direction. Imagine his surprise and horror as he watched his arrow skew the lead duck! Panic-stricken, he hid the duck and spent the rest of the day avoiding his grandmother. Eventually, he began to miss his grandmother so much that he went to her and confessed to killing the duck. "Honey," she said to him gently, "I was standing at the kitchen window when you shot my duck. I watched you do it, and I forgave you in that very instant. I just wondered how long you would stay away before you came to me."

In the same way, all of our sins were forgiven at the cross, not just past sins, but our present and future ones as well. We continually stand in that forgiveness, yet in our guilt and shame, we forget and try to avoid God whenever we have sinned. Making spiritual progress is impossible when we are trying to find places to hide from God. It's so much better for us to seek Him out, acknowledge our sin, and get on with life in the forgiveness that He already gave us. Knowing who we are in Christ can revolutionize the way we live our lives.

> *"Making spiritual progress is impossible when we are trying to find places to hide from God."*

Christianity is not primarily a philosophy or some kind of behavior modification program. At its heart, Christianity is a vibrant, loving relationship with Christ. If Christ is not the focus of our faith and the object of our love, we will inevitably interpret the Scriptures as a rule book and Christianity as a dead and worthless religion.

When Jesus came to earth as a man, He lived among a people who were accustomed to trafficking in the trappings of religion, but who were nevertheless spiritually dead. The Scripture had ceased to be thought of as a testimony of God's love for His people and had become, for many, simply a list of duties, a manual for self-improvement, a religious tract. Christ came to extend God's love, to make Himself more personally known to us, and to enable us to have a loving relationship with Him. True Christian faith is established on that simple reality. We must never lose sight of our relationship with Christ. Everything else is based in and springs from that relationship.

When I was a young pastor of a small rural church in southern Indiana, I made a hospital visit to an old, ailing farmer named Nordy. Nordy began our conversation by telling me about a simple, eight-piece puzzle he had gotten out of a box of powdered soap when he was a young boy. Now, Nordy made it clear to me that he was pretty good at puzzles, but he explained that he had worked on this puzzle for weeks, without ever being able to solve it. He came to the conclusion that he had received a faulty puzzle, and he was ready just to give up. But rather than letting him give up, his mother made him write to the soap company to ask if there were any instructions for the puzzle. The trick to this particular puzzle, as Nordy soon found out, was that there were two pieces that had to be put together first, then the rest of the puzzle would eventually come together. But if you did not get those pieces together first, no amount of effort would succeed in making the rest come together.

Nordy paused, and I found myself wondering why he had just gone into such great detail about a childhood puzzle. Nordy said, "You know, preacher, Christianity is a lot like that puzzle. There's you, and there's Christ. You get those two together first, and everything will eventually come together. If not, you can just forget it." I don't believe I've ever come across a better definition of Christianity than that. There's you, and there's Christ, together.

Faith is often thought of as the means by which we receive blessings from God. It is, in most people's minds, one of the mechanisms by which we receive the "good life": prosperity, peace, good health, and happiness. As manipulative and selfish as the "health and wealth" gospel may seem to us, we all have this tendency to think of faith as the means by which we earn God's blessings. What is it about us that makes us want to take credit for God's gifts by chalking them up to our faith?

We all tend to conclude that the good things that happened to us are somehow the result of our faith and that bad things result from its lack. And many have come to regard their personal pleasure as the greatest good. If our jobs, our stations in life, and our relationships do not totally satisfy us, then there must be something wrong with us. In such an environment, it is not surprising that we should think of faith as a means of getting what we want.

Scripture gives another view of faith, however. According to the apostle John, we measure our faith not by the number of blessings we receive, but by the amount of love we show to others.[1] Faith is, therefore, not a mechanism by which blessing comes to us, but the means by which blessings flow through us to others. Christ is the epitome of faith, yet He did not receive health, wealth, and prosperity because of His faith. Jesus' faith in His Father's plan of redemption led Him to lay down His life on our behalf. Shouldn't our faith lead us to do likewise?

My step-father is a good example of the kind of sacrifice the Scriptures talk about. As I was growing up, I saw my step-dad as one of the most boring people alive. For years, I watched him go to work every day at a grim, dirty factory in order to provide for his family. He would come home at the end of the day, watch maybe an hour of TV, and then turn in early out of exhaustion. I can't remember ever seeing him just having a really good time—he simply did what he was supposed to do. Growing up, I swore I would never live like that. I was determined to have a job that I enjoyed, a happy family to come home to, and a life that was personally fulfilling. Today, having been more "successful" at achieving those goals than I ever dreamed I could be, I find myself looking to my step-dad as my hero. Why? Because he didn't have to be fulfilled to love, he didn't have to be happy to give, and he didn't have to achieve all his own dreams before he could sacrifice to help his children achieve theirs.

That's the kind of life that faith in Christ enables us to live. It is without a doubt where the rubber meets the road, because it is a life that makes a difference in this world.

At its heart, choosing the High Way and making a journey to spiritual maturity is a journey of faith, an attempt to find our way from the "now" of earthly existence to the "not yet" of life with God in heaven. The further we continue on this journey of faith, the more our lives will be transformed from present realities into future perfections. Taking the High Way means focusing on Jesus. The more we are remade in the image of Christ, the more we will be able to encourage the world to take the High Way with us.

FOOTNOTES: 1. 1 John 3:14-16

GPS: *God-Positioning Scriptures (to Reorient Your Life)*

And when I came to you, brethren, I did not come with superiority of speech or of wisdom, proclaiming to you the testimony of God. For I determined to know nothing among you except Jesus Christ, and Him crucified. I was with you in weakness and in fear and in much trembling, and my message and my preaching were not in persuasive words of wisdom, but in demonstration of the Spirit and of power, so that your faith would not rest on the wisdom of men, but on the power of God.
—1 Corinthians 2:1-5

REST STOP: *Pull Over and Ponder*
Is your faith about anything other than Jesus Christ and Him crucified out of love for the world? What does your life say about your faith to those with whom you're in relationship?

EXIT 6: REVELATION ROAD

Mile 35

Blind Spots

Sometimes, you will feel alone on your journey. Because you can't see God with your natural eyes, you wonder if He's really there, especially in the midst of a fallen world. It's time to expand your view ...

HOW DO WE learn to see God in the world? I mean to *really* see Him. How clearly do we see Him in the midst of a hectic day at work? Can we find Him in the routine and seemingly insignificant moments of life? Knowing the answers to these questions can mean all the difference between a mature and an immature faith. If we cannot recognize God's presence in, and sovereignty over, every aspect of our lives, we will inevitably wear out, give up, water down, or otherwise compromise our devotion to Christ. It's just that simple. If we cannot see God through the eyes of faith, then we will not serve Him with the passion or perseverance He deserves.

We see this truth dramatically illustrated in the events of 2 Kings. When the prophet Elisha and his servant woke to find themselves surrounded by an army of foreign troops, the servant was terrified, but he found his master surprisingly calm. "Do not fear, for those who are with us are more than those who are with them,"[1] Elisha answered, and he prayed for God to open the servant's eyes. Then the servant saw the hills full of horses and chariots of fire all around Elisha. The difference between the servant's panic and the prophet's courage was accounted for by the difference in their ability to see the spiritual reality behind their apparent situation. Elisha was unmoved by the enemy's show of force because he was able to perceive the presence of God in a circumstance where others didn't notice Him.

"We need never be afraid ... so long as we remember that God is with us, no matter where we are."

When I was a boy growing up in Shelby, Ohio, the only things we had resembling gangs were bands of neighborhood boys who would engage in petty feuds with one another. In these boyhood battles, I benefited greatly from being allied with the biggest, toughest kid around: my neighbor, Red Bricker. One day, Red and I decided to build a treehouse in my backyard. While Red was in the tree, some of our traditional rivals walked up. They didn't notice that Red Bricker was up in the tree, but I was well aware that he was perched on a limb just above me.

"Looks like you're all alone, Hunter," they sneered. With full confidence in who was on my side, I decided to play along. "Yep. Looks that way." "We're gonna tear you limb from limb!" they threatened. "Well," I said smiling, "You just come right ahead." As they made their first move, Red jumped out of the tree right in front of them, and he was roaring! They all turned tail and ran for home (probably to change their pants).

I was able to have confidence in the face of those bigger boys because I knew something they didn't: I knew I wouldn't have to deal with them alone. We need never be afraid to live as salt and light in a sinful world that is often hostile to the things of God, so long as we remember that God is with us, no matter where we are.

I believe that much of our ineffectiveness in reaching the world for Christ is due to our inability to commune with God in the midst of a fallen world, to sense that He is with us in the trenches just as surely as He is with us back at camp, aka church. Our weekday forays into the world are no less under God's protection and superintendency than our weekend gatherings for worship and fellowship. We need to remember that.

Building a Systematic Theology

If we can get past the intimidating terminology, we can see that the process of building a systematic theology is identical to the process of building an intimate relationship. We don't get to know people all at once. Rather, we learn about them bit by bit, as we see them in a variety of settings and circumstances. We grow to know them over time. We then take all these isolated glimpses into their characters and personalities and piece them together into a more complete picture of the kind of person he or she is.

Systematic theology is the process of systematizing our knowledge of God: of taking our various experiences with Him, as well as the insights into His character which we glean from His Word, and putting them together to form a more complete picture of who He is. Why don't we all have the same picture of who God is? One reason is that we all have different experiences of God. The person raised in a Christian home who came to believe at the age of four will likely view God differently than the former atheist who was converted later in life.

As we go through a systematic process, we'll find that some of what we have always believed about God needs to be modified, expanded, or completely thrown out. This can, at times, be painful, making the God we used to feel comfortable with suddenly seem like a stranger. As we grow to appreciate aspects of God that we were never before aware of, we will begin to sense His presence in places and circumstances where we might have missed Him.

Theology from the Bottom Up

Most systematic theologies begin with *how* we know about God and then proceed to *what* we know about God. They then explore the nature of man and his need for redemption before discussing the Redeemer and the process of redemption. Next they examine how we are to live as redeemed people in a fallen world, and conclude by studying the future completion of our redemption in the last day.

This kind of logically deductive approach to systematic theology is not without its limitations. For one thing, it tends to present information about God in a way that seems almost clinical—as if we were looking at Him through a microscope. Another severe limitation of the traditional method is that it can actually obscure some of the ways God has chosen to reveal Himself. After all, God did not begin His revelation of Himself with a treatise on the inerrancy of His Word or a detailed explanation of His eternal self-existence. Instead, He chose to reveal Himself through His interactions with His creatures. God condescended to reveal Himself to us right where we are, rather than demanding that we ascend to where He is. Taking the High Way means developing a systematic theology to see Him better from earth.

FOOTNOTES: 1. 2 Kings 6:16

GPS: *God-Positioning Scriptures (to Reorient Your Life)*

What then shall we say to these things? If God is for us, who is against us? —Romans 8:31

REST STOP: *Pull Over and Ponder*
Can you recall a time when you felt alone in a situation, but looking back you can see that God was present all the while? Is there something so gripping you now that you have forgotten He is in the midst of it with you?

Mile 36

Site Seeing

God fashioned the cosmos for the purpose of making Himself known. Consequently, there is not a single element of the created world that does not bear His signature or reflect His glory.

WHEN I WAS growing up, there was an elderly woman in my hometown who acted as a kind of unofficial town historian. I had to walk past her house on my way home from football practice, and it wasn't unusual for her to call me up to her front porch so she could tell me all about some distant family member. Most days it was absolutely excruciating, and it was all I could do to keep from dozing off. But there was one time she spoke to me that I'll never forget. "Joey, I want to tell you about your father. I knew Bill Hunter—watched him grow up when he was just a little boy. There isn't a time I see you but what I don't think of your father. You walk like him. You talk like him. You act like him. Everything about you reminds me of him."

Now, my father died when I was only four, so I hardly knew him. Nevertheless, my dad continued to live on in me—so much so that people could see him reflected in the way I walked and talked and acted. The moment I learned that lives on in my memory as one of the proudest moments of my life: I am my father's son!

Being created in God's image is not about some attribute we possess in ourselves, but about all the ways God has designed us to reflect His attributes. Being made in His image means that others ought to be able to see Him reflected in the way we walk, talk, and act. Our proudest moments will be the ones that someone looks at us and says, "There isn't a time I see you but what I don't think of your Father."

God created mankind to reflect His character and His attributes. Had He stopped there, He would not have achieved His goal. In order for His revelation of Himself to be complete, He had to make it possible for us to perceive Him. Otherwise, all this evidence of His existence would have fallen on blind eyes and deaf ears.

> "Being made in His image means that others ought to be able to see Him reflected in the way we walk, talk, and act."

God designed our minds in such a way that learning would point us back to Him. The human mind, untainted by sin, cannot help but perceive the reality of God's existence. His signature is absolutely everywhere, whether we look outside of ourselves or within. This is made clear in Romans.[1] God's "invisible qualities" can be "clearly seen" and understood from "what has been made."

Today, many people believe that faith depends on ignorance and blind acceptance, when in fact, the exact opposite is true. It is the unbeliever who must blind himself to the truth of God's existence. Are you suspicious of learning, especially when it comes to so-called "secular" knowledge? Are you afraid that knowing more might lead you to question your faith? If God is the supreme intelligence behind all things, then it stands to reason that all true knowledge should inevitably point us back to Him.

As we pursue all kinds of secular knowledge, we will find that all along we have really been learning about God. The academic disciplines do not contradict belief in God. On the contrary, they will ultimately prepare us for a deeper understanding of who God is. By creating us in His image, God has given us the capacity to think His thoughts after Him, to perceive His reflection in the world that He created.

The Bible reveals God to be a holy Trinity of God the Father, God the Son, and God the Holy Spirit. These three distinct "persons" are each described as being fully God, and God is clearly said to be "one." God's nature is both singular and plural at once, a profound mystery that we see reflected in the way He created the cosmos. Time and time again, He brought order out of chaos by separating two binary opposites and then intertwining them once again into a unified whole. He divided the light from the darkness, then put them together to form a single day. He divided the waters from the heavens, yet in such a way that these two environments constantly interact in an endless cycle of evaporation and precipitation. He separated the land from the seas, yet it is both of these together that comprise our world. Look carefully at the composition of the universe, and you'll see reflected there both God's singularity and His plurality.

Even on a molecular level, we can see numerous ways that God has brought opposites together to form unified wholes. Ironically, the unified whole often displays properties that its component parts do not possess. For example, salt, without which we cannot live, is made up of sodium and chlorine, both of which, singularly, are toxic to us. So also with hydrogen and oxygen — both are highly explosive and flammable gases, but when combined, they form water, with which fires are extinguished. Let's consider a realm other than the molecular: light displays properties of a particle and properties of a wave. Physicists are at a loss for how to explain this, so they simply treat light as somehow both particle and wave! The very fabric of the universe reveals God's nature as both singular and plural at once.

God also created human relationships to reflect His nature of being both singular and plural. God imprinted His nature on human relationships by making men and women identical in substance, yet different in design and function. These two He then called together into a relationship in which they could be "one." Because God has arranged our relationships in this way, the old adage that opposites attract is truer than we might ever have assumed at first blush.

What does all this have to do with God's triune nature? Simply this: by creating us to be in relationship with those who are able to complement and complete us, He has given us a glimpse of the love that eternally exists within the Trinity. Not content for us to simply receive His love, God has designed us in such a way that we may experience His love by reflecting it in our own relationships with one another. By creating a universe that continually displays this pattern of complement and symmetry, God has revealed to us even the most complex and inscrutable aspect of His nature: that He is within Himself a relationship, one God in three Persons.

Taking the High Way means noticing myriad aspects of His creation and remembering Him with gratitude whenever we see them.

FOOTNOTES: 1. Romans 1:20 (NIV)

GPS: *God-Positioning Scriptures (to Reorient Your Life)*

The God who made the world and all things in it, since He is Lord of heaven and earth, does not dwell in temples made with hands; nor is He served by human hands, as though He needed anything, since He Himself gives to all people life and breath and all things. —Acts 17:24-25

REST STOP: *Pull Over and Ponder*

God's existence surrounds us; it radiates from every aspect of creation. Still, it's often too easy to get distracted and miss the breadth of His presence. Where are you most likely to see God in the scenery of life? Consider spending time there today.

Mile 37

A Road of Relationships

Just as God first communicated Himself through the creation of a perfect world, so He continues to reveal Himself through His ongoing relationship with that world. God is intimately and actively involved with His creation, quietly accomplishing His purposes.

WATCHMAKER OR AUTHOR? Disinterested Inventor or Loving Father? Uninvolved Spectator or Sovereign Ruler? These are the questions we must ask ourselves as we contemplate the nature of the God who created everything. The 18th century Deists believed that God created the world much as a watchmaker might fashion a watch: He simply wound up everything and then stepped back to observe how well it would run on its own. To the Deists, God was the consummate Scientist, and the universe was one grand experiment. Having established the experiment's parameters at the beginning of time, it was unthinkable that God might now taint the experiment by actively interfering with His creation!

The Bible, however, paints quite a different picture of God's relationship to the created universe. It is God who supplies the water that sustains life and brings forth the earth's bounty. It is God who sustains His creation. The doctrine that God continues to be present in and involved with the created world is known as the doctrine of God's immanence. If God really did create the universe in order to give Himself in relationships, then it only makes sense that He would continue to sustain, provide for, and reveal Himself to His creatures. God's relationship with the created world is an ongoing relationship—one in which He is actively and continually engaged.

He Relates Through People (Ekklesia)

Ever heard someone say, "Why do I have to come to church on Sunday morning to worship God? I can go out on my bass boat or a golf course and be much closer to God than I would be singing hymns and listening to a sermon." If we can see God in the world around us and commune with Him anywhere we happen to be, what do we need the church for? The answer is that the church is more than just a social organization to which we belong; it is a theological reality to which we subscribe.

"Genuine love must be intimate, exclusive, and personal as defined by the receiver."

From the very beginning, God's activity in the world has centered around building a people for Himself, a people who could know and experience the depths of His love. We see this pattern when Jesus called His first disciples. These men were called to leave behind their earthly dreams and occupations—sometimes even their own families—in order to become part of the church, the people belonging to God through Jesus Christ. We who have become new creatures in Christ need an environment in which we can thrive. The church is that environment. Worshiping, serving and fellowshiping with other Christians who share our beliefs, perspectives, ideals, and practices is critical to sustaining our new life in Christ.

He Relates Through Law (Boundaries)

Whenever God has called people into relationship with Himself, He has, without exception, given them some law or set of laws that they were required to obey. Why would God restrict the people He had chosen to show love to in this way? Because with God, law is far more than a list of dos and don'ts; it is a means of demonstrating love. Time and time again, in Scripture, God makes it clear to His people that their love for Him will be expressed through their obedience to His commands.

Why must our love for God be expressed by keeping His commands? Why isn't it enough just to have an emotional love for God? Because true love is always behaviorally specific. True love seeks to express itself in the proper way, and love that does not express itself in the proper way is foolishness. In Isaiah, God castigates His people for assuming that He is just like them. He is not, for His ways are higher than our ways, and His thoughts higher than our thoughts.[1] He cannot be loved in any way we see fit. Rather, He must be loved in accordance with who He is. Genuine love must be intimate, exclusive, and personal as defined by the receiver.

God's law gives us the boundaries, and we must learn to love Him within those boundaries.

He Relates Through Leaders (Prophets, Priests, Kings)

In building a people for Himself, God has always provided His people with leaders who could point them to Him. God has historically given His people three distinct "offices" of leadership, each of which reveals a certain aspect of His triune nature.

The first office of leadership that God has given us is that of the king. All of us have "kings" in our lives, people who do their best to keep family, office, church, or whatever other "kingdom" they are in charge of, united, and in proper working order. People in such a role most clearly reflect the character and attributes of God the Father, in that they are responsible to meet the demands of justice and order on the one hand, but mercy and protection on the other.

The second office of leadership that God has given us is that of the prophet. Prophets are individuals who speak forth the word of God in no uncertain terms, in order to call God's people to live within the boundaries that He has set for them. We may not like to hear what the prophets in our lives have to say to us, but if we keep them around and listen to them carefully, they will save our hides more times than we can count. God sends us His prophets to help spare us a deeper and more devastating pain.

The third office of leadership that God has given is that of the priest. The priest is the complement to the person who acts as a prophet. Where the prophet speaks boldly for God, the priest speaks on behalf of the people to God. If the prophet is the prosecutor, the priest is the defense attorney. Christ is called our "great high priest,"[2] who by His death and resurrection made atonement for sin once for all. The office of priest foreshadowed the earthly ministry of God the Son, who made peace between God and man through His perfect sacrifice on the cross.

He Relates Through Power (Miracle and Providence)

So often, when we consider how God makes His presence known to us, we focus on miracles: those momentous demonstrations of divine power like the parting of the Red Sea, the ten plagues in Egypt, the virgin birth, and the resurrection of Christ. Consequently, whenever we pray, we tend to ask God to intervene in our lives suddenly, immediately and in dramatic fashion. We expect Him to come to our rescue in a big way. We want miracles so we can know that God is at work, and we can quickly become frustrated or disappointed when they don't come in the way we expect. Yet the problem at times like these is not with God, but with our childish and simplistic understanding of how He operates in the world.

Contrary to popular belief, God does not just wait in the wings until things get so bad that He has no choice but to step in. Such a view implies that God is not actively involved in the world unless there happens to be a major emergency. That view would be tacit denial of God's sovereign control over every event in history.

When we realize that God is providentially directing every detail of His creation, we understand that the miracles we see from time to time are mere snapshots, momentary glimpses of the way God is at work all the time. When God seems absent, it is not because He really is, but because our awareness of His presence is lacking. Therefore, we must pray that God would open our eyes to see His providence, His miraculous orchestration of every detail of our lives. Taking the High Way means learning how God continues to reveal Himself through His ongoing relationship with the world. As we do, we will have the confidence to live in that world—as people who are called by His name and secure in His love.

FOOTNOTES: 1. Isaiah 55:9; 2. Hebrews 4:14 (NIV)

GPS: *God-Positioning Scriptures (to Reorient Your Life)*

But be very careful to keep the commandment and the law that Moses the servant of the LORD gave you: to love the LORD your God, to walk in all his ways, to obey his commands, to hold fast to him and to serve him with all your heart and all your soul. —Joshua 22:5 (NIV)

REST STOP: *Pull Over and Ponder*

Among the various ways God relates to us— through the law, relationships, leaders, and by miracles—where do you see God's presence making a difference in your faith recently?

Mile 38

Wrong Way! Part 1

The world is often cruel, chaotic, senseless, and marked by conflict. It is in a state of disarray because mankind, created in God's image and nurtured in a perfect environment, consistently misses the perfect and drives headlong into sin.

WHEN I WAS a kid I was allowed to play outside until it got dark. Of course, my mother and I would often differ on what "dark" really was! In the evening, she would call me to come in, "Joey, time to come inside." I would protest that I could still see fine and that it wasn't dark yet. A few minutes later she would call me again, "Joel Hunter, it's dark. Come inside." And I would protest that I could still see perfectly fine. But with her very serious and final call, "Joel Carl Hunter, it's dark as pitch out there. Get in this house this instant!" Even though I "could see perfectly fine and it didn't look dark to me," the tone of her voice caused me to give up my best arguments and race toward my house. From inside, I would look out through the picture window and be surprised at just how dark it really was out there.

Just as our eyes grow accustomed to the darkness of a warm summer evening, so our hearts and minds grow accustomed to the dark thoughts, people and activities that tempt us to sin. The longer we remain in the geography of temptation, the more normal sin seems, and the more restrictive and repressive God's boundaries appear to be. It is not until we return into the light of God's presence that we realize just how much darkness we were in.

> *"The longer we remain in the geography of temptation, the more normal sin seems ..."*

Ultimately, the philosophical basis for all sin is the doubt that God is either willing or able to provide for our needs. And once Satan raises this doubt in our minds, he is quick to encourage us to look elsewhere for that provision. He seduces us with the lie that we have to provide for ourselves—that we must be "responsible" and "take initiative." What's more, he always tries to disguise our rebellion (that is, after all, what it is) as being for some good cause. By the time the serpent was through seducing Eve, he had her totally convinced that her act of disobedience and separating from God would lead to greater good for herself and the husband she loved.[1] Once the serpent had convinced Eve that she could not trust God to provide for her and that she needed to provide for herself, all he needed to do was step back and let her make her own decision.

Mankind gradually sank into sin by means of deception, doubt, and the decision to provide for themselves. To this day, Satan continues to pull this bait-and-switch every time he entices us to sin. First, he tries to convince us that God's plan for us is not enough. Then, when we fall into sin and discover that God's provision is far better than anything we can obtain for ourselves, Satan tries to keep us from relying on God by telling us that while God did have a perfect plan for us, we've now blown it, permanently messing it up and putting ourselves beyond the reach of God's love. Although we will certainly have to face the consequences of our sin, our great God's sovereign plan for our lives cannot be messed up by our sins. Even though we have missed the perfect mark, God is able to restore the perfect life after sin by taking the broken pieces of our lives and putting them together again.

Eve, Descartes, Kant, and Warhol

Since the day that Eve decided to seek a source of knowledge apart from God, mankind has tended to miss the connection between knowledge and faith, and it is the division which is responsible for much of the fragmentation and disconnectedness that we experience. Like Eve, many of us have accepted this lie that knowledge and faith are separate. Throughout most of human history, this schism between knowledge and faith has been a subtle one.

During the apostolic age, when the first Christians fanned out across the Roman empire to proclaim the good news of Christ, even pagans were still very aware of the connection between ultimate truth and daily life. Consequently, when they came to put their faith in Christ, it revolutionized their entire view of the world. Augustine, the brilliant fifth-century theologian and philosopher, reflected this early Christian mindset when he said, "I believe that I may know." In the Middle Ages, the church followed Augustine in believing that God is the source of all knowledge. In a time of great change and instability, it was the church that persevered and continued to transmit knowledge of art, literature, law, philosophy, science, and theology.

During the Renaissance and Reformation, the connection between knowledge and faith was both challenged and strengthened. Ultimately, it was the French philosopher Rene' Descartes who introduced the modern schism between knowledge and faith. In his attempt to develop a system of philosophy based on rational certainty, Descartes embarked upon a systematic program of doubt in the hope of finding the one truth that was foundation to all others. His thought was that if he could find a firm foundation for knowledge, then he could reason his way to all truth. Descartes' foundational truth was the famous expression, "I think, therefore I am." While he was able to doubt the existence of God and the physical word, he believed it to be impossible that he could falsely conceive of his own existence.

The problem with Descartes' philosophy was that he no longer saw God as the source of all knowledge (as Augustine had), but had made his own self-awareness the starting point for all true knowledge. Immanuel Kant went even further, arguing that the human mind is incapable of knowing anything that is infinite or that transcends sensory perception. Kant effectively drove a wedge between knowledge and faith, and subsequent thinkers continued to widen the schism between what we can know of the material world and what we can know of God.

Today, many people see religious faith and knowledge of the world as mutually exclusive and completely separate from each day. The pop art of Andy Warhol can be thought of as the visual expression of this schism. In contrast to Medieval and Renaissance art, Warhol's art concentrated only on glorifying the mundane. His countless images of Campbell's soup cans and Marilyn Monroe reflected the underlying belief that the ordinary is all there is. Without any reference back to the Creator, soup cans are just as worthy of immortalization as anything else.

Many of us live lives that reflect this same philosophy. We see no connection between the various spheres of our lives. Our work, our marriage, our friendships, even our religion, are not connected to each other or to God. Such a disconnected, compartmentalized existence is a far cry from the cohesive, meaningful, and abundant life God created us to enjoy.

What can we say in response to all of the thinkers and philosophers who have widened the schism between knowledge and faith? Who can show us how to bring together the fragmentary and disconnected aspects of our lives? I, for one, would like to nominate my seventh-grade English teacher, Mrs. Wolfe. Mind you, at the time I would not have ranked Mrs. Wolfe as being among the great philosophers of our age. Sitting in her class seemed like torture, but looking back I realize that as Mrs. Wolfe taught me how to write a paragraph well, she also taught me how to live a life that made sense. Mrs. Wolfe absolutely hammered into her students the idea that a good paragraph must begin with a topic sentence. As I'm sure you know from the Mrs. Wolfes in your own life, a topic sentence is one which states clearly and succinctly the main point that the paragraph is trying to make. Once you've written a topic sentence, every other sentence in the paragraph must somehow develop or refer back to the thought expressed in that topic sentence. Otherwise, you just end up with a string of disconnected and unrelated thoughts.

I've learned that this kind of coherence of thought is not only characteristic of a good paragraph, but characteristic of a good life as well. We were created to relate every thought, everything we learn, back to a single topic sentence: "Love the Lord your God."[2] Taking the High Way means reflecting in all we think, say and do that we believe we were created to love God, and to be loved by Him.

FOOTNOTES: 1. Genesis 3; 2. Deuteronomy 6:5

GPS: *God-Positioning Scriptures (to Reorient Your Life)*

For the wrath of God is revealed from heaven against all ungodliness and unrighteousness of men who suppress the truth in unrighteousness, because that which is known about God is evident within them; for God made it evident to them. For since the creation of the world His invisible attributes, His eternal power and divine nature, have been clearly seen, being understood through what has been made, so that they are without excuse. —**Romans 1:18-20**

REST STOP: *Pull Over and Ponder*
An abundant life in Christ demands a holistic approach. What areas of your life (relationships, finances, skills, hopes, education, work, etc.) might you have set apart from your relationship with God?

Mile 39

Wrong Way! Part 2

At the very point that we ought to turn back toward God, we often respond by accelerating further into ourselves, making the distance between Him and us even greater. Do we simply want to live our lives on our own terms, with virtually no input or interference from outside ourselves?

"Me" Thinking

You would think that once we see what a mess our lives become when we try to control them ourselves, we would quickly recognize our need for God and begin depending on Him. But as Scripture makes clear, there is virtually no end to the sinful heart's propensity for self-deception. At the very point that we ought to turn back to God, we often respond by accelerating further into ourselves, putting even greater distance between us and God, and shifting down into what I call "me" thinking.

Paul describes people in the last days as "lovers of self."¹ This phrase is not merely the first of a series of descriptions; it is actually the "topic sentence" that every succeeding description serves to amplify. The people described simply want to live their lives on their own terms, with virtually no input or interference from outside themselves.

This kind of "me" thinking is, of course, diametrically opposed to the way God created us to live. God designed us so that we could find fulfillment in the context of relationships. Yet, in our sinful state, we expend a tremendous amount of energy seeking fulfillment apart from relationships. We become "lovers of self" in the hope of finding a love we can manage. We choose comfort over intimacy, and narrow our world by limiting our interactions with other people. Simon and Garfunkel captured this dynamic in their song, "I Am a Rock," sung from the perspective of a man who has unapologetically isolated himself from all human contact.

The early church believed it had received the true revelation of God and was intent on sharing that truth with anyone who would receive it. In direct contrast to the early church's outward focus was that of the ancient heresy known as gnosticism. The gnostics believed themselves to be among a select few who had been given a secret, mystical knowledge that could liberate them from the misery of the created world. Yet they felt no compulsion to share their knowledge with others because they believed it to be beyond the ability of the "worldly" to comprehend. The gnostic belief that only a select few could know the universal and absolute truth evolved into the modern philosophy of pluralism. Pluralism asserts that while there may be a universal truth out there, none of us can possibly know it—at least not all of it. All we can really know is our own opinions of the truth, and we must be careful not to question the opinions and insights of others, since they may be in touch with a part of the truth that we have as yet been unable to perceive.

> "Analysis and observation teach us to see in terms of categories, but relationships teach us to see through the eyes of another."

From the modern era to the postmodern era, pluralism has given birth to a philosophical movement known as deconstructionism. Deconstructionism states that there is no absolute truth or ultimate reality; reality is a social construct that we create ourselves. Rather than a universe, a single, coherent reality, deconstructionists believe we live in a "multiverse," a world composed of many different realities. It is up to each of us to create the "reality" that is perfectly suited to us.

Today we are philosophically encouraged and technologically enabled to create our own "reality." Of course, what we're really doing is not creating our own reality. On the contrary, we're merely reinforcing our belief in the avatar illusions that we have concocted. The end result of this kind of "me" thinking is that our "personal reality" will become increasingly separated from the ultimate reality that God alone has established.

Jeremiah, Aristotle, and Asimov

Perhaps the most subtle way in which we can lose sight of God is by getting too caught up in the very things He uses to reveal Himself to us. Even as we try to live our lives for God, we can slowly lose our focus on Him. There is no detail, no aspect, no facet of the created world that does not reflect Jesus Christ. The people with whom we come in contact, the circumstances in which we live, the joys we experience, and even the problems we face have all been given to us by God. He is right there in the midst of it all.

To the extent that we begin to see all the details in the light of who He is, we make progress toward spiritual maturity. It is this very approach to life that allowed Mother Theresa to minister to people most of us would cross to the other side of the street to avoid. She did what she did because, as she put it, "I see Christ in every one of their faces." This degree of spiritual perception comes not through careful analysis and observation, but through spending enough time with Christ that you begin to see things from a different perspective. Analysis and observation teach us to see in terms of categories, but relationships teach us to see through the eyes of another.

The prophet Jeremiah is an excellent example of someone whose relationship with God prompted him to see God in every detail of life. Jeremiah speaks of God's presence in the earth and in the heavens, in the clouds and in the rain, in the lightning and in the thunder, and in every detail of creation.[2] Jeremiah viewed God as central to everything else. Unfortunately, it is all too easy for people to go from seeing God as central to seeing Him as primary. This is how Aristotle saw God: not as present and active in every circumstance or detail of creation, but as its ultimate cause, its source of origin, and its reason for being.

Many of us see God this way: He is important, and we have a theoretical sense that He is ultimately behind it all. We're glad about that, but we remain determined to live life on our own terms.

An even further step away from seeing God as central is to see Him as over all. Isaac Asimov's view of God is that God and religion are important, but nonessential parts of life that can be chosen from among a smorgasbord of ideas and opinions. While few of us would align ourselves theologically with Asimov, or Aristotle, we will slip into their ways of thinking about God if we value the mechanics and the particulars of living for God more than we prize God Himself. That is how a seminary student can get so busy trying to learn about God that he lets his devotional life suffer. This is how a minister can allow the demands of ministry to get in the way of his relationship with God.

Mankind was created for the express purpose of knowing God. As the Westminster Shorter Catechism puts it, "Man's chief end is to glorify God and to enjoy Him forever." Taking the High Way means valuing our relationship with God enough to consistently extend the effort required to keep Him our central focus—and making sure, along the way, that the effort itself doesn't become our central focus.

FOOTNOTES: 1. 2 Timothy 3:2; 2. Jeremiah 51:15-16

GPS: *God-Positioning Scriptures (to Reorient Your Life)*

Don't be naive. There are difficult times ahead. As the end approaches, people are going to be self-absorbed, money-hungry, self-promoting, stuck-up, profane, contemptuous of parents, crude, coarse, dog-eat-dog, unbending, slanderers, impulsively wild, savage, cynical, treacherous, ruthless, bloated windbags, addicted to lust, and allergic to God. They'll make a show of religion, but behind the scenes they're animals. Stay clear of these people. —2 **Timothy 3:1-5 (The Message)**

REST STOP: *Pull Over and Ponder*

The irony of self-deception is that we don't recognize it, so we don't often think to pray against it. Spend a moment asking God to reveal where you've lost sight of Him. Do you feel driven by a hope "to glorify God and to enjoy Him forever"?

Mile 40

Breakdown

Whenever we lose sight of God's presence and activity in our lives, we live as though He is absent. Casting about for some new source of security and hope, we begin to use the people we love for our own selfish ends, to depend on the world around us for the things that we need, to look for new gods to worship and some way to earn salvation.

NO MATTER WHAT our religious beliefs or theological perspectives, when we fail to see God's presence and participation in every aspect of our lives, we inevitably begin living like practical atheists. In this Mile, we will discover that our ignorance of that is *not* bliss. Only when we understand the extent to which we have missed the perfect, will we fully appreciate the lengths to which God has gone to restore to us the perfect life after sin.

Infidelity

Infidelity is more than the act of adultery; it is a sin of the heart, a spirit of betrayal, selfishness, and greed that is present within us all. This is why when Jesus spoke of infidelity He addressed the desire of the heart rather than just the physical act. Infidelity can take many forms, but it all boils down to using or betraying the ones we love rather than serving them and remaining loyal. Whenever we belittle our spouse in order to receive approval from someone else, we are betraying the one we love in order to get something from someone else. The same is true when we complain about our children in order to get sympathy from other parents, or when we downplay our friendship with one person in order to "get in good" with another.

"Infidelity ... is a sin of the heart, a spirit of betrayal, selfishness, and greed that is present within us all."

The tendency to "sell out" the ones we love in order to get what we want is a stark reminder of how far we have fallen. When we live our lives moving away from God rather than toward Him, the purpose for which we were created gets turned on its head, and we become takers rather than givers, adulterers rather than lovers, and greedy beggars rather than generous kingdom builders.

Worldliness

God calls individuals to leave the cultures and communities that they have always known in order to form a new community of faith. The people of God are paradoxically called to live in the world but not to be of the world. It is perhaps little wonder that God's people have often slipped into opposing, but equally dangerous, mindsets with respect to their relationship with the world around them.

One of these mindsets sees the world as completely profane. People who hold this view regard the world as an utterly corrupting influence, and they try to separate themselves from it as much as possible. At best, these people see the world as something that doesn't fit into the equation of their relationship with God, a "remainder" which is best ignored altogether.

The problem with this perspective is that God Himself made the world and declared it to be "very good."[1] Even though it has since become marred and made ugly by sin, we have nevertheless been commissioned to look after it and to take care of it. If we neglect this calling and withdraw from the world, we may eventually find that it has grown more wild and sinful in our absence, to the point that it is more capable of causing us and others more pain than we ever anticipated it could be when we deserted it.

An opposing and even more common mindset than withdrawal from the world is the tendency Christians have to become overly consumed with the world: to look to it, rather than to God, as the source for everything we need and the remedy for all of our problems. In Scripture, we see how the Israelites did this time and time again. Enamored with the pagan cultures of neighboring kingdoms, the people of Israel "imitated the nations around them,"[2] following their gods and engaging in their wicked practices. As Christians, if we're honest with ourselves, it soon becomes clear that we have just as many ways that we try to "hedge our bets," looking to the world around us rather than to God for the satisfaction of our desires. We may not worship at the feet of an idol, but we often depend upon our material possessions, our reputation with others, our personal comfort, our social prominence, or the people who care about us to give us what we need. We must never underestimate the hold that the world continues to have on those of us who are consumed with it.

Idolatry

Whenever we lose sight of God and begin focusing too much of our attention on the world around us, we slip into the sin of idolatry. We tend to associate idolatry with ancient statue-worshiping pagans rather than with ourselves. In truth, we are no less susceptible to idolatry than the Israelites, who while waiting on Moses to finish commanding mountaintop conversation with God, built and worshiped the golden calf.[3] John Calvin, a French theologian said, "Man's mind is like a store of idolatry and superstition; so much so that if a man believes his own mind it is certain that he will forsake God and forge some idol in his own brain." The times when people are most likely to fall into sin and unfaithfulness to God are when they grow bored with life's mundane details and become anxious to experience the next big thing. It is during such times that we fall into idolatry by trying to create our own solutions to the pettiness and monotony of life. We don't build golden calves, but we do use our gold cards to buy temporary relief and satisfaction.

We do these things not in active rebellion against God, but because we have ever so subtly and gradually turned away from Him to seek our own way in the world. Such a shift of allegiance is the essence of idolatry.

Earning Salvation

Infidelity, worldliness, and idolatry: these are the sins that inevitably manifest themselves whenever we lose sight of God's presence and begin to live as though He were absent. Yet, there is one other sin that accompanies our attempts to live in God's absence. One of the gravest of sins consists of the belief that what God has provided for us is not quite enough; that there is something left that we must do if we are to be completely accepted by Him.

This was the very sin that Adam and Eve committed in the garden. Believing that God had not given them all the wisdom and knowledge that they really needed, they foolishly turned elsewhere for it. Scripture tells us that we are saved from sin solely by God's grace: our salvation is a gift which is completely free and unmerited.[4] There is simply no way that we could ever earn or deserve salvation. Scripture makes it clear that while we are responsible to repent of our sins, trust Christ as our Savior, and submit to Him as our Lord; we could do none of these things unless we were first enabled to do so by God Himself.

This notion that it is God who is completely responsible for human salvation is absolutely unique to Christianity. All other religions agree that man is ultimately responsible for his own salvation; that his fate depends on something that he does rather than something that God does. Some religions may affirm that man is totally responsible for his salvation, others that he is only partially responsible and that God helps him along the way; but in the final analysis, all of them agree that man must do something in order to merit heaven and to escape hell. This belief that we ultimately determine our eternal destiny has an impact on how we see ourselves. On the one hand, it leads to a tremendous sense of pride and self-reliance. On the other hand, this belief is also a tremendous source of insecurity and anxiety. Before long, we catch a glimpse of our complete inability to become righteous by our own efforts, and we realize that if our righteousness is the criteria for salvation, then we have absolutely no hope of obtaining it.

Only Christianity offers the hope that we can find acceptance in Christ no matter how far short of God's righteousness we have fallen. Only Christianity is realistic enough in its appraisal of human ability to declare categorically that there is no way we can earn God's favor and acceptance. Only Christianity holds out the promise that in spite of our inability, God has done everything necessary to reconcile us with Himself. Taking the High Way means leaning completely on Him. Faith alone allows us to experience His acceptance.

FOOTNOTES: 1. Genesis 1:31 (NIV); 2. 2 Kings 17:15 (NIV); 3. Exodus 32:1-6; 4. Ephesians 2:8

GPS: *God-Positioning Scriptures (to Reorient Your Life)*

[Jesus said] Let me tell you why you are here. You're here to be salt-seasoning that brings out the God-flavors of this earth. If you lose your saltiness, how will people taste godliness? You've lost your usefulness and will end up in the garbage. —Matthew 5:13 (The Message)

REST STOP: *Pull Over and Ponder*

The thought of worshiping at the feet of a golden calf may seem silly ... but what do you turn to when God seems absent?

Mile 41

Cross Roads, Part 1

We were created to know perfect fellowship with God, to live a perfect life in a perfect world. But our sin has separated us from God, shattering our lives and bringing the world to ruin. So God sent His Son into the world, to bring us back to God, and to restore the perfect life after sin.

WHY IS THE cross, a symbol of torment and death, the primary symbol of Christianity? Why would we adorn our necks and crown our churches with one of the cruelest instruments of execution ever devised by man?

Other religions use much more positive and triumphant symbols. Judaism has the Star of David, a six-pointed star which Israel's most militarily successful king used to adorn the shields of his soldiers. Islam has the crescent moon and star, which appears originally to have been the battle standard of the powerful Ottoman Empire. Eastern religions have the yin and yang symbol, which represents the harmonious interplay of heaven and earth, male and female, light and darkness, activity and passivity. Why would Christians choose to identify themselves with a symbol of death and defeat?

One reason is that Jesus Himself defined His role as the Christ in terms of the cross. Jesus made it clear that "the Son of Man must suffer many things and be rejected by the elders and the chief priests and the scribes, and be killed, and after three days rise again."[1] Jesus did not say that such a thing *might* happen, or even that it definitely *would* happen, but that it absolutely *must* happen. Why all this emphasis on the cross? Through His crucifixion and resurrection, Jesus did more than just satisfy God's justice so that we, the sinners, could receive mercy; He completely reversed our history.

> "Through His crucifixion and resurrection, Jesus did more than just satisfy God's justice ... He completely reversed our history."

God's plan of redemption was meant to do more for us than simply to let us walk away from our sins, hurts, frustrations, and failures. It was meant to take those very same sins, hurts, frustrations, and failures and use them for our ultimate triumph. Jesus accomplished this incredible reversal by descending lower than any sin, failure, or hurt we could ever have experienced, and He did this by means of the cross. He chose to put to good use all of those very things that we would prefer to overlook, scoot by, or forget. The issues and interruptions that can so easily trip up, or delay our progress don't need to prevent our climb to the ultimate triumph.

One of my favorite analogies is about the little boy leading his youngest sister up a steep mountain path. The climbing was difficult, for there were many rocks in the way. Finally, the little girl, exasperated by the hard climb, said to her brother, "This isn't a path at all. It's rocky and bumpy." "I know," her brother replied, "but the bumps are what you climb on." Likewise, we can step up to life from death, to victory from failure, to healing from hurt.

Redemption: Bought with a Price

In most systematic theologies, the redemptive work of Christ is simply one among many different theological topics that receive attention. However, it is not the way the Bible treats the story of redemption. In the Bible, redemption is the primary subject, the central theme, the scarlet thread that ties all 66 books of the Scripture together into a single, unified whole. Redemption is Scripture's primary theme, because it is history's primary theme. Ever since Adam and Eve sank their teeth into the forbidden fruit, God's central activity in history has been the redemption of fallen man and His fallen world.

Consider for a moment what Christ accomplished by His death and resurrection. Through His death on the cross, He has accomplished our redemption, purchasing our freedom by His very own blood. By His resurrection and ascension, He has entered the heavenly tabernacle as our great high priest, where He is now the mediator of a new and more perfect covenant between God and man. This redemption that He established was accomplished once for all, and is now completely secure, so that it can never be taken away. Consequently, we have gone from owing a debt that we could not hope to pay, to receiving the promise of an eternal inheritance that we could not possibly have earned.

There was once a wealthy American businessman traveling in the Middle East who came upon a slave market. There he saw a beautiful, young girl for sale. Weeping uncontrollably, she had obviously not been a slave all her life, because she had not yet become hardened to her situation. The businessman guessed that she had probably already been violated and abused, and that she was dreading the fact that it was about to happen all over again. So he waited for her to be auctioned off, and he bid enough to purchase her from the slave market. When he received his papers of ownership, he went and gave them to her, telling her that he had purchased her freedom. Then he just smiled and walked away. The girl just stood there for a moment, dumbfounded, looking down at the papers in her hand. When at last what he had done for her finally sank in, she began to jump and shout, saying, "He redeemed me! He redeemed me!" Then she ran after him, pleading with him to make her his servant. Our redemption in Christ is just like the redemption of this slave girl by this man. As Christians, we have been "bought with a price" and we are therefore not our own.[2] Where once we were in miserable bondage to sin, in Christ we have now become the willing servants of God, reaping the eternal benefits of His boundless generosity.

God's Process of Redemption

Theologians talk about two distinct aspects of Christ's redemption: "redemption accomplished" and "redemption applied." When they speak of redemption accomplished, they are referring to what Christ won through His crucifixion and resurrection to make our redemption possible. When they speak of redemption applied, however, they are talking about our part in the process—that is, how Christ's redemption actually becomes applied to our own individual lives. When it comes to the question of how we personally receive Christ's redemption into our own lives, many of us make the mistake of seeing this process only from a human perspective. We look back on our own experience and see that we made a conscious decision to follow Christ: we "trusted in Him for salvation" or "asked Him into our heart" or otherwise "came to faith." This moment of decision was then followed by a series of changes in our lives: changes in attitude, changes in perspective, changes in values, and changes in behavior. But, Scripture makes it clear that things are not quite that one-sided.

In the Gospel of John, Jesus explains to a Pharisee named Nicodemus how a person actually enters the kingdom of God. He begins with the startling assertion that "unless one is born again he cannot see the kingdom of God."[3] In the Greek, this phrase "born again" can also be translated, "born from above." According to Jesus, unless someone is born in this manner, he cannot even see the kingdom, much less enter it. Can the blind suddenly "decide" to see? Can the dead one day "choose" to live? The Bible makes it clear that unless God first gives us new birth from above, unless He gives us eyes to see and breathes life into our dead bodies, it is impossible for us to see Him or turn to Him.

To help understand this dynamic, look at the scientific field of genetics. Although we do not believe in genetic determinism, which states that everything we do is predetermined by our genes, it is certainly true that our genetic makeup predisposes us toward certain things and makes other things impossible for us. No matter how hard I might work to become a professional basketball player, my particular genetic makeup—the fact that I am "vertically challenged"—would undoubtedly prevent me from ever reaching that goal. Because we are all born into sin, our sinful nature invariably prevents us from ever receiving the things of God. We need, in effect, a gene transplant, a new nature, one that is capable of recognizing and accepting the gospel of Christ. It is only after God changes our hearts that we become able to respond to the gospel in faith.

This does not mean that we had no part in the process of our own redemption. Although we do not actively participate in our regeneration—just as we do not actively participate in our physical birth—we *do* participate in our conversion.

In fact, by giving us a new heart and a new nature, God makes our conversion possible by making us capable of cooperating with His work of redemption.

Too many Christians today find themselves either doubting the certainty of their salvation, or taking pride in the fact that they had enough sense to believe and be saved. Both of these responses rest on the notion that we are ultimately responsible for making the decision to come to Christ. If we understand that our conversion is something we do because God is already at work in us, then we can view our conversion with great confidence and great humility, knowing that our faith in Christ proceeds from a nature that has been forever changed. Taking the High Way means being "born again" to a new life of righteousness and communion with God. Our hope in a perfect life, after sin, rests securely on this truth!

FOOTNOTES: 1. Mark 8:31; 2. 1 Corinthians 6:19-20; 3. John 3:3

GPS: *God-Positioning Scriptures (to Reorient Your Life)*

And when I came to you, brethren, I did not come with superiority of speech or of wisdom, proclaiming to you the testimony of God. For I determined to know nothing among you except Jesus Christ, and Him crucified. —**1 Corinthians 2:1-2**

 REST STOP: *Pull Over and Ponder*
Think back on your moment of salvation and God's redemptive work as it pertains to you. Have you fully grasped what it means to be "born again"? If you have yet to commit your life to Christ, I encourage you, I invite you, to tell Him today that you want to do life forever with Him.

Mile 42

Cross Roads, Part 2

In spite of all the centuries of sin and corruption that have ensued, Christ has come—and will come again—to restore all that we have lost.

Justification, Adoption, and Sanctification

Through the process of justification, Christ redeems us from the penalty for sin. By His adoption of us into the family of God, He redeems us from the alienation of sin. And by our continued growth in righteousness, known as sanctification, He redeems us from the ongoing power of sin.

Justification is a legal term. Through justification, Christ redeems us from the penalty for sin. To be justified is to be pardoned of some crime, to be declared righteous even though one is really guilty. God Himself satisfied the demands of His justice by allowing Christ to bear the penalty for sin that we deserved. The justification that Christ bestows is more than a pardon of guilt and release from punishment. It is not that we are still guilty of sin and God is simply looking the other way; on the contrary, Christ has justified us by taking away our guilt altogether! Christ makes it "just-as-if-I'd" never sinned.

As if this weren't amazing enough, God also redeems us from the isolation, loneliness and alienation of sin by adopting us into His family. Through Christ, God once again made it possible for us to approach Him without fear, to crawl up in His lap and call Him "Abba," "Daddy." It is through this intimacy of relationship that God also sanctifies us, setting us apart for Himself and making us holy.

The process of their sanctification is not an exercise in self-improvement, but you might think it is just that if you know Christians who have those two things confused. Sanctification isn't being holy by our own efforts, doing our best to increase our virtues and to eradicate our vices. If we try that route to perfection, we will become discouraged and slip back into some oft-repeated sin. Whenever we despair of our own efforts at holiness we need to ask ourselves, "Would God have justified us and adopted us into His family only to leave us to become holy on our own?" Of course not! We must realize that holiness is not so much about living up to a set of rules and regulations, but about growing in our relationship with the Father who loves us. Sin will lose its power in our lives when our lives become so consumed with God and His goodness that sin no longer has any place to gain a foothold.

Through our justification, we are made right before God, and our sins are washed away. By our adoption, we are brought into intimate fellowship with our heavenly Father. And through the ongoing process of our sanctification, we more consistently reflect the image of Christ in our thoughts, words, and deeds.

Perseverance, Death, and Glorification

How can you know that you are secure and won't lose your salvation? Two things: God loves each one of us just as much as He loves Jesus Christ, and therefore doesn't want to let us go. Second, He has the power to hang on to us. So with the combination of absolute power and absolute love, anyone who has accepted Jesus Christ as personal Savior has absolute security. If He loved us when we hated Him, and sent Jesus to secure our salvation when we hated Him, then surely He loves us enough to keep us now that we love Him, even though we fail Him. He loves us enough to make us His children and then keep us as

His children—and has the power to do it. What love! In John 10:28-29 we are told that no one can snatch us from God.

Our role is to persevere, and He will never let us fall away completely. He has adopted us, and He calls us to press forward toward spiritual maturity.

If our eternal destiny is already secured, why does God require us to persevere? There are at least two reasons: on the one hand, it teaches us to depend on Him for our strength, and to find peace in the knowledge that no matter what trials we face, our salvation is secure. On the other hand, our striving to remain faithful to God and to grow in holiness teaches us to choose life over death.

For the Christian, death is always an enemy—he recognizes that as long as God leaves him on this earth, he has an eternally significant purpose to fulfill. Think about it: if God's only purpose for us during our time on earth is for us to be saved, wouldn't He bring an end to our earthly existence and take us to heaven at the moment we acknowledge Him as our personal Lord and Savior? He doesn't do that, because our purpose here is not limited to our personal salvation. We are to live as a witness of His grace. We are to live in ways that others can see Him in our words and actions. We ought never to lay aside our God-given purpose, no matter how difficult or painful our circumstances become.

> *"We ought never to lay aside our God-given purpose, no matter how difficult or painful our circumstances become."*

Physical death is the final consequence of our lives as sinful creatures. The resurrection of our bodies from physical death, an event that theologians refer to as our glorification, marks the completion of our redemption in Christ. But if our glorification takes place at the Second Coming of Christ, what happens to us during the interval between our physical deaths and the resurrection of our bodies? After all, there are believers who died approximately 2,000 years ago.

Although there have been a few theologians throughout the history of the church that have taught that when we die we experience a kind of "soul sleep" of unconscious state until the resurrection, the Bible clearly teaches that we are united with the Lord immediately after our physical death. Jesus promised the thief on the cross, "Today you will be with me in paradise."[1] When we die, we enter immediately into eternal life in the presence of God.

Our inability to imagine what heaven is like has been reasonably compared to the inability of a child in the womb to understand what life beyond that environment will be like.

But we do wonder what our glorified bodies be like. The Bible does not give us a detailed description, but it does say that our bodies will resemble the glorified body of Jesus Christ. All our weakness, immorality, and corruption will be taken away, and there will no longer be any barrier to knowing God.

Paradise Regained

Christ's redemption did not only affect us individually, it affected the world entirely. Mankind's fall into sin subjected all of creation to corruption and death. In order to restore the perfect life after sin, Christ's redemption must liberate not only the sinners themselves, but everything that their sin has touched and tainted.

Through His Second Coming, Christ will finally redeem us from our partial fellowship with Him. In this present age, we know Him only in part, seeing Him no more clearly than if we were looking at a dim reflection in a tarnished mirror. For millennia, Christians have been making frenzied attempts to predict exactly when Christ will return. But the important thing to remember is that the Second Coming in not about when, it is about Who. We look forward to it as the day when we will see our Savior face to face.

When Christ returns, not only will He redeem us from our partial fellowship with Him, He will also redeem us from the injustice of this world. Most of us learned a long time ago that life in this world is not always fair, that sometimes the bad guys prosper while the good guys suffer. Yet somehow, we never seem to be able to just accept that life's not fair. Why is that? Because God has placed in us an innate desire for perfect justice. It is in our nature to want life to be fair, and on the Day of Judgment, when Christ metes out justice to all mankind, that desire will be perfectly satisfied at last. The Bible makes it clear that all people, both believers and unbelievers, will have their deeds acknowledged one day. Even the believer whom Christ has set free from the judgment of condemnation for sin is still subject to the judgment of his works.

We were created to have fellowship with God in the midst of a perfect world, but we lost both that fellowship and that world when we chose to abandon God and to seek our own way. For those who have been redeemed, Christ's coming holds the promise of a return to Paradise, of an eternity in the presence of God, and of a second chance to live the perfect life after sin. Taking the High Way means living this life while keeping the next in mind ... knowing that what we do today will have an effect on how we spend eternity.

FOOTNOTES: 1. Luke 23:43 (NIV)

GPS: *God-Positioning Scriptures (to Reorient Your Life)*

Beloved, now we are children of God, and it has not appeared as yet what we will be We know that when He appears, we will be like Him, because we will see Him just as He is. And everyone who has this hope fixed on Him purifies himself, just as He is pure. —1 John 3:2-3

 REST STOP: *Pull Over and Ponder*
Read James 1:2-4. The process of sanctification relies occasionally on moments in which we must persevere through trial and confusion. How does 2 Corinthians 4:17 help you stay hopeful today in light of eternity?

Mile 43

Low Fuel?

Do not wait until you are mature to love broadly. Maturity grows as your love for others outweighs your love for yourself. And feeling that way about others turns your whole life around. Even "running on fumes" at the end of a day is worth it if you are making the effort for those who seem beyond your reach.

IF WE ARE ever to become like Jesus, we must begin with His heart, with the central motivation that drove Him to live and die and live again as He did. We are to honor and serve others. That may or may not make us happy and comfortable. Doesn't matter, our journey has a purpose greater than that.

Dietrich Bonhoeffer, the German pastor and theologian who was put to death for conspiring against Adolf Hitler, put it this way: "The cross erased the equation that religion equals happiness." In other words, our faith does not necessarily guarantee our happiness here on earth, because our love demands that we give ourselves away, sacrificing in order to benefit others. Such a love is focused outward, continually looking for someone to whom it can give. Genuine love's greatest desire is to bless others, and it matters little whether or not that blessing is ever reciprocated. Such love is not safe, and it is not given safely.

Yet, is this kind of love realistic? Can we ever hope to sustain such a love, particularly if it is never reciprocated? If we continually give ourselves away, won't we eventually reach the point where we have nothing left to give? If we really tried to live this way all the time, isn't it inevitable that we would eventually burn out? No. If we run out of "fuel," it is not because we have given too much away, but because we have lost our original passion and focus.

Whenever we love as Jesus loved, laying down our own lives for the sake of others, there inevitably comes a point where we hesitate and think about just how much we are actually giving away. For just a moment, our focus shifts from the needs we are working to meet to the work we are doing in order to meet them. We start to mull over just how much it costs to give sacrificial love, and we begin to wonder how long we can keep it up. We begin to look for ways that we can hold back in our giving, ways that we can conserve our energy and protect ourselves from possible hurt or disappointment; but when we do that, we find that the burnout we fear is all too close at hand. However, if regarding the cost of our sacrifice drives us to depend on God to supply all our needs so that we can continue concerning ourselves with the needs of others, then we will never run out of fuel, since we can never give away more than He can provide.

"Genuine love's greatest desire is to bless others ... Such love is not safe, and it is not given safely."

Reviving His Perspective

So, who are these "others" we are supposed to be loving and serving? Jesus Himself was asked this question. When Jesus confirmed to a Jewish scribe that in order to gain eternal life, he needed to love God with all his heart and love his neighbor as himself, the scribe then asked Him, "And who is my neighbor?"[1] Jesus answered with the parable of the Good Samaritan in which a Jewish man, robbed, beaten and left for dead, is ignored by a passing priest and Levite, but is helped by a man from Samaria. We cannot underestimate how shocking this story must have been to its original listeners, because at the time, the Jews and the Samaritans absolutely despised one another. It was unthinkable that a Samaritan would show such kindness to a Jew.

Whom did Jesus say we are to regard as our neighbor? The answer implied in the parable is anyone who is in need of mercy, no matter who he or she might be, or what barriers we might need to cross in order to reach them. Basically, Jesus made it clear that we should regard everyone as a neighbor; there is no one whom we can legitimately ignore.

Jesus' perspective was clearly one of reaching out to those who were far off and loving those who were least like Himself. He had, after all, left the company of the saints and angels in heaven who adored Him in order to reach out to those who did not yet know Him as God. He did not reach out to the religious people who were looking for His coming, but to those who would never dare to darken the door of a temple or synagogue.

Sadly, the church has lacked this perspective for quite some time. We need to experience a paradigm shift in our thinking. Many of us think of love as proceeding outward in an ever-expanding series of concentric circles. We see it as our duty to love our families first, followed by our immediate neighbors, then our church, then our town, then our country, and finally the rest of the world. We think that we must first learn to give perfect love to those we're closest to before we can even begin trying to love those who are far off. The problem with this kind of thinking is that we never get beyond the walls of our own homes.

As Christians, we have been called upon to love broadly, to follow Christ in seeking out those who are in need of grace, no matter how far that might require us to go. The nature of love is such that the more broadly we love, the better equipped we will be to love those who are already close to us. We cannot wait to begin reaching out to others until we have become mature. On the contrary, the only way we will ever become mature is through the process of reaching out to others.

Does this mean that all Christians need to serve as foreign missionaries? Of course not. But it does mean that every one of us needs to revive Christ's perspective of compassion for those who are still far off—those who don't yet know Him because, for whatever reason, they remain just out of reach of the gospel. As we are going through the little corner of the world God has placed us in, we need to reach out in love to those we come across.

Reviving His Posture

How did Christ show His love to the people He came to serve? This is an important question, because the church today seems to have forgotten how to serve other people in Christ-like love. The only remedy for this situation is for us to revive the posture that Jesus assumed when He Himself served others.

Nowhere is this posture more clearly portrayed than in the Gospel of John when Jesus washes his disciples' feet.[2] The first thing to notice about this passage is that it tells us why Jesus was able to serve in such a humble way—it was because He had complete confidence in the strength of His position. He was able to get up from the table and begin washing the disciples' feet because He "knew that the Father had put all things under his power, and that he had come from God and was returning to God."[3] He had absolutely nothing to lose.

As Christians, we have been called upon to serve others not out of some kind of "worm theology" or "slave mentality" that says that we are worthless. On the contrary, it is because we are the children of God and have complete security in Christ that we are able to humble ourselves and serve other people. In Christ, as we reach higher levels of spiritual maturity, we are most willing and able to reach deep into destructive and despairing circumstances for the sake of helping others.

The second thing to notice about this passage is that Jesus served His disciples by doing that which obviously needed to be done—something that was right in front of Him to do. He didn't go looking for "ministry opportunities" or follow some predetermined schedule of events, He simply walked along, responding to the needs of whomever He happened to run across. It was just that simple. The way His kindness might eventually be received was not even a consideration for Jesus. He simply acted to meet the needs that He saw in front of Him. Perhaps the most remarkable aspect of this passage is that Jesus also washed Judas' feet, in spite of the fact that He knew Judas was about to betray Him.

Most of us serve only in situations where we think our efforts will do some lasting good. We work hard to distinguish those who are really in need from those who would try to take advantage of our kindness. Jesus, however, did not just serve those who were worthy, but those who were unworthy as well. He simply acted to meet the needs that He saw before Him. When Jesus got up from washing His disciples' feet, He made it clear to them that they (and we) must now assume the servant's posture that He had so vividly demonstrated. Our Lord left little doubt as to the importance of our posture before one another and the world. Taking the High Way means demonstrating the love of Christ by laying aside our pride, humbling ourselves before others, and getting our hands dirty as we serve in His name.

FOOTNOTES: 1. Luke 10:29 (NIV); 2. John 13:5-20; 3. John 13:3 (NIV)

GPS: *God-Positioning Scriptures (to Reorient Your Life)*

In this is love, not that we loved God, but that He loved us and sent His Son to be the propitiation for our sins. Beloved, if God so loved us, we also ought to love one another. No one has seen God at any time; if we love one another, God abides in us, and His love is perfected in us.
—1 John 4:10-12

 REST STOP: *Pull Over and Ponder*
Examine who you are expressing love toward and how you are doing it. Where do you see room for improvement? Who can you practically love better today? In which new way could you extend a hand of service and acceptance?

Mile 44

Service Stations

As the Body of Christ, the church is to serve as a visible expression of Jesus to the world. How can you model Christ for the world? By following Christ's example of ministry to others.

BISHOP WELLINGTON BOONE has a wonderful saying: "If the devil can't push you over backwards, he'll try to pull you over forwards." In other words, if he can't beat us down with failure, he'll try to trip us up with success. We must be careful that our success does not blind us to the needs of the people around us. We must never accept the illusion that poverty, sickness, sadness, and helplessness are all things that only exist on the other side of the world. We need to be aware of and responsive to the needs of our neighbors if we hope to make a difference in the world. There are many stations in life where we can be of service ...

In Education

Jesus Christ came into the world at a time when Roman rule and Roman roads were bringing together people who had vastly different cultural backgrounds, philosophical views, political ideologies, and religious beliefs. New ideas abounded and were circulated widely by a seemingly endless procession of charismatic teachers and their followers. With so many people having such ready access to this multiplicity of voices, learning began to be prized like never before; yet, somehow, truth began to seem more elusive than ever.

"If we do not start with God, our knowledge of the world is certain to become fragmented and distorted."

The intellectual world that Jesus and the early church had to face bears a striking resemblance to the world we live in today. We are currently experiencing a communications revolution in which we are being inundated with new information as never before. We are drinking from the data stream as from a fire hose, and the result is a kind of intellectual tension similar to that experienced by the people of Jesus' day. As the information overload inevitably increases, people will begin to look around for someone who can help them to make sense of it all. I believe that the church is uniquely suited to fill this vacuum.

If we do not start with God, our knowledge of the world is certain to become fragmented and distorted. Think of a puzzle. If a puzzle had no picture on the front, it would be virtually impossible to solve. What's more, at no point would you have any sense of the puzzle's larger pattern. That is precisely how polytheistic pagans of old tried to understand the world. It is also how many people today, overloaded with random pieces of information from a wide variety of sources, are trying to understand the world.

The church must give people the big picture that will enable them to piece together their own personal puzzles. By teaching them that in Christ all the pieces of their lives can be brought together into a unified and meaningful whole, the church distinguishes itself from all the other voices out there clamoring for attention and claiming to have the truth. Jesus had a way of cutting through the endless political and theological debates with which the Jews of His day were so preoccupied, in order to reveal a clarity and simplicity which can only be found in God.

In Art

Another area where the church can minister to people's emotional needs is through the medium of art. I know what you're thinking. When did Jesus ever pursue any kind of ministry through art? Nowhere in the Bible does it speak of Jesus painting, sculpting, or building something in order to point people to God. Well, it's a little more subtle than that. Jesus was not the artist; He was the work of art, the visual representation of the invisible God.[1] The incarnation of the eternal Son was the ultimate expression of God's artistry.

The church, as Christ's Body, is now a visible representation of Christ. We are God's portrait of what life in Christ can be. We represent the One who appeals to the heart and moves the soul in addition to satisfying the mind. If God has gone to such great lengths to reveal Himself through the visible imagery of the created world, mankind, Jesus Christ, and His church, doesn't it stand to reason that we also ought to communicate the gospel not only through the written and spoken word, but also through various forms of expression?

It used to be the case that the church was at the center of the arts. The church has often surrendered the arts to people in the world, which has only served to strengthen the belief that the arts are somehow dangerous, or anti-Christian. Today, the church needs to reengage the arts, to use them once more to bring Christian truth to a culture that is becoming increasingly non-literate.

As Christians, I believe we are all called to be artists. This does not mean that each of us needs to begin painting, singing, or acting; rather, it means that each one of us should consider how we can communicate Christ in ways that will touch people's hearts as well as their minds. Everything we do has the potential to reveal Christ to the people around us. As Saint Frances of Assisi put it, we should "preach Jesus, and only if necessary, use words." When we strive to communicate the gospel in a way that touches people on an emotional and visual level, we will help them to sense God's presence and activity not just in "religious" settings, but in every dimension of the world in which they live. We also need to encourage the efforts of Christian artists, who can point people to Christ through the creation of visual images, beautiful music, powerful dramas, and other modes of artistic expression. For too long the church has looked on these endeavors with ambivalence, rather than recognizing that they can serve as a vital expression of the gospel message.

To Future Leaders

Jesus' ministry perspective centered around the multitudes of people who had not yet come to know Him. Yet they definitely were not at the center of His ministry activity. It was really a very select few who received the bulk of His attention. The twelve disciples whom He had designated as His "apostles" were invited to walk and talk with Him, to watch His every move, to ask Him the questions everyone else was afraid to ask, to share in His ministry, and to glimpse the true nature of His kingdom.

If Jesus wanted so much to reach the many, why did He spend so much time with so few? If He knew how much the crowds needed Him, why did He so frequently withdraw from them in order to spend time with a mere handful of followers? The answer is clear. The crowds were like sheep in need of a shepherd, so Jesus spent vast amounts of time training shepherds that could care for His flock.

As Christians, we need to revive Jesus' ministry to future generations of believers by pouring our lives into leaders that can carry the flame of the gospel long after we are gone. We need to withdraw from the crowds long enough to teach our children how to live out the substance of Christianity before the multitudes. Taking the High Way means demonstrating our love for Jesus by taking good care of His "lambs," just as He asked Peter to do for us.

FOOTNOTES: 1. Colossians 1:15 (NIV)

GPS: *God-Positioning Scriptures (to Reorient Your Life)*

Everything in the world is about to be wrapped up, so take nothing for granted. Stay wide-awake in prayer. Most of all, love each other as if your life depended on it. Love makes up for practically anything. Be quick to give a meal to the hungry, a bed to the homeless—cheerfully. Be generous with the different things God gave you, passing them around so all get in on it: if words, let it be God's words; if help, let it be God's hearty help. That way, God's bright presence will be evident in every-thing through Jesus, and he'll get all the credit as the One mighty in everything—encores to the end of time. Oh, yes! —1 Peter 4:7-11 (The Message)

REST STOP: *Pull Over and Ponder*
How have you seen God work through various forms of educa-tion, art, and leadership within your local church community?

EXIT 7: *RIGHT TRACK*

Mile 45

Positive Traction

Waiting until you're stranded in the middle of nowhere is not the best time to decide that you need to get serious about maintenance. Similarly, waiting until you're in the midst of a trial is not the best time to get serious about holiness.

MOST OF US cruise along in our day-to-day lives with "holiness on hold." Then when we tragically fail in a relationship, face big temptation, or reap the rotten fruits of a poor choice, we begin to desire holiness. To expect that we can put holiness on hold and still become spiritually mature is a misconception. True holiness is more than a conviction brought on by painful experiences or an immediate solution to a crisis. Unlike the instant effect of salvation, holiness is a progressive work of God in man in which we aspire to sin less and less—stop spinning out of control—and become more and more like Christ. The theological term for this process is *sanctification*. God can and will expand the capacity that each of us has for being holy.

In our personal attempts to clean up our acts to try to avoid the effects and pains caused by our sins, we may believe that doing the right things, the godly things, can make us holy and happy. That's a false assumption. Hidden in such assumptions are beliefs that stem from a "works" mentality. These beliefs suggest that there are degrees to holiness, degrees to goodness, and degrees to success as Christians. The truth is, there is only one measurement of holiness, and that is our closeness to God—and in many ways even that is up to God.

> *"God can and will expand the capacity that each of us has for being holy."*

Coming to terms with our inadequacy and our depravity is a considerable challenge for us if we struggle with a "works" mentality. We live in a world where comparing and competing with one another is practically a pastime. The fact is we are all unholy without God. With God, we are holy. There are no degrees of measurement, and there is no middle ground. If we have been given a "new life" in Christ,[1] we cannot be a little bit holy, just like we cannot be a little bit pregnant or a little bit human. Holiness is not dependent on who we are; holiness depends on God's nature entering us.

Improving behavior doesn't make us holy or place us a notch above others. There is no amount of Scripture we can understand well enough, no quantity of wisdom we can gain, and no number of kind acts we can perform that will make us holy. There is only one way to become holy and that is for God to make us holy.

That's a difficult concept to grasp because we live in a society that seems to have drawn the conclusion that man is the center of the universe, that we are the ones who are high and lifted up. Even the church has been susceptible to such misdirected focus.

The aim of God's holiness, though endearing and transforming to us as individuals, focuses less on the needs and desires of individuals and more on the unity of His children. You see, God loves us personally. He loves us as individuals. He saves us as individuals. Nevertheless, when we become Christians, we are members of His family. God, the Father, has always been interested in the family. God is a family man.

Understanding Holiness

Hopefully, all of us who call God our Father offer the world a glimpse of His holiness. Personal holiness requires that we trust and hope in the One who is truly holy. Holiness is not available through that which the world offers every day. In fact, the word "holy" actually means separate or set apart for God's service. Holiness is out of the ordinary.

Close Call

Years ago, I made a quick trip to Ohio to visit my ailing stepfather. Before I left Florida, I called my son, Isaac, who was a college student in Indiana at the time, and let him know that I would be in nearby Ohio. Isaac mentioned that he had a big test and couldn't get away. "No problem," I said. To my surprise, on Friday, Valentine's Day, Isaac knocked on the door of my sister's house. He stepped inside and gave me a big hug. "I borrowed a car," he said as he noted the expression on my face. "Come on, Dad, you were only a couple of hours away, and I just wanted to be with you, that's all."

Why would he do something like that? Because he could not find anything better to do? Yeah, right—it was Valentine's night, and he could have been on a date. I just took him at his word—he wanted to be with me. Imagine that.

The primary reason that God desires for us to seek holiness is potentially the most liberating truth of all: God just wants to be with us! It's that simple and that pure. Our pursuit of holiness is not a case of need or a case of His expectations, but a case of relationship.

God is not a distant being in heaven coaching us along by yelling, "I know you trust in Me, but if you want something, you're going to have to make it happen by your own effort." Holiness doesn't say, "Be busy in order to accomplish." It doesn't say, "Try harder. Burn out for God!" Those are lies. They create bondage and inhibit the freedom God has given us. It's in the process of being with Him that perfection comes. We, like God, have the natural desire for relationships and intimacy. He is our Father. We're His children. Taking the High Way means welcoming the desires of God's heart as our own and reflecting His goodness as a result.

FOOTNOTES: 1. Romans 6:4 (NIV)

GPS: *God-Positioning Scriptures (to Reorient Your Life)*

For it is God who works in you to will and to act according to his good purpose.
—Philippians 2:13 (NIV)

REST STOP: *Pull Over and Ponder*
"Holiness is out of the ordinary." Where do you see God's sanctifying work in your life setting you apart from the world for His purposes? Is your relationship with God the driving force in your sanctification, or are you trying to obtain holiness by other means?

Mile 46

On Solid Ground

Even in our pursuit of God, He is actually the One who's working. However, our commitment, obedience, and knowledge can enhance our relationship with Him.

VENTURING OUT TO pursue a relationship with God requires extraordinary courage and humility on our part. It requires a willingness to allow Him to reveal areas in our lives that need His intervention. Like wounds, there are areas painful to expose and even more agonizing to touch, and there are scars, places that have hardened so, that we no longer have any feeling at all. God knows from personal experience all about pain and all about scars. We can trust Him with ours.

Even so, many of us would rather live hiding in a spiritual "no man's land" than risk going out. Our fears may make us miserable, but at least they are familiar. So each of us has a decision to make: We can endure the useless pain of our inaction and fear, or we can move toward God with purpose.

We'll never qualify for a relationship with God. We can never do enough or be enough to impress Him. In fact, taking into account our sinful nature, we're not qualified for any good service. However, God is, and His qualified Spirit is in us. In Christ, we qualify. In Christ, we are ready. God is totally and completely responsible for changing us and making us ready. If it were up to us, we would choose ourselves over God. God draws us, changes us, and prepares us even when we are not searching for Him.

A member of my congregation, who was formerly an exotic dancer, told me the amazing story of how she became a Christian. One night, while she was on stage at an adult nightclub, she saw someone she had never expected to see—Jesus Christ was standing about fifteen feet from her in the middle of the audience. She heard Him say, with absolutely no condemnation, "I want you for something better than this. I have got something far better for you." That night, she walked out of that place and never returned. She hadn't prepared for a visit from Christ, but God came to her and requested a commitment regardless of her lack of readiness, and she yielded to Him.

> "God draws us, changes us, and prepares us even when we are not searching for Him."

Many of us are caught unprepared when a powerful and loving God enters our lives. We may be accustomed to experiencing His blessing, but the concept of a relational and intimate God is quite foreign to us. We settle for pursuing His provisions, comfort, and instruction instead of actively seeking intimacy and closeness with Him. Thankfully, God doesn't wait for us to get ready for Him. Behind the scenes, He pulls us closer and makes us ready. To respond, we must attune our ears to His gentle calling and we must surrender.

When we were teenagers going out with friends for the evening, our parents would say, "Now, be good." They never said, "Be holy!" Yet God, as our eternal and perfect Parent, commands us to be holy. For sinful people (that would be us) that's a phenomenal and formidable calling. It's far beyond our ability to achieve, yet it's a command of God.[1]

In this society, we're not well-equipped to answer commands. In fact, most of us view God's law as the basis for discussion and interpretation, rather than as the basis for action. We talk about God so that we can understand Him better;

then if we understand, we may act. The problem is that we never come to a full understanding of God. Until we come to terms with our limitations in that area, we'll be bound by our own conceptions of Him. God's law, while it's His perfect will that we follow it, was also designed to bring into light our total depravity and need for Him. Seeking His calling to be holy is both His command and our acknowledgement of our desperate condition. Our reaction to God's command needs to be to trust Him enough to act on it.

Years ago, I had the opportunity to watch as a father taught his little girl how to swim. She clung to his neck in absolute terror. Patiently, he said to her, "Look at me, Honey." Her large round eyes darted from his face to the water. Trying to calm her, he hugged her tightly and said, "I'm not going to let you go. I'm not going to drop you. I want you to trust me." She was too frightened to hear his words. Finally, he said, "Honey, the water is not your enemy. If you do what I say, the water is what will hold you up."

Reflecting on the father's words, I thought about how the same truth applies to us. If we have a relationship with our heavenly Father, clinging and trusting are what gives us confidence to do His commandments, and His words will hold us up. When we choose to ignore His commands and willfully do things on our own, we struggle with our fears and encounter difficulties. More importantly, we end up delaying His work in our lives. Like the words of the father to his little girl, God's commandments are designed to provide hope and help to give us courage.

The world equates following God's commands with less freedom. In reality, obeying His commands draws us closer to Him and provides us with more freedom, more understanding, and less discouragement. Holiness and obedience to His commands are all about His connection with us. Relationship is the goal; blessings are the consequences.

Knowing God

Do you feel like you are living life merely by practicing the formulas? You have learned the details of "how to make it," but you've failed to capture the big picture. Your life seems like a series of mechanical decisions. You've been trained. You know the facts. You have the information, but you still do not quite get it.

A French author, Sebastien-Roch Nicolas de Chamfort, once wrote, "A man is not necessarily intelligent because he has plenty of ideas, any more than he is a good general because he has plenty of soldiers." In other words, what's important is not how much you have learned, but what you have learned—and to what end. We really need to shake off the mentality of just learning the facts for facts' sake. That's not learning; that's data entry. Our minds can become cluttered and unproductive with too much useless knowledge. We may amass hordes of information on a variety of subjects, feel intelligent, and even apply our knowledge, but to what end?

The pursuit of knowledge for knowledge's sake can distract us from relationships with others and from the most important relationship of our lives: our closeness with God. Ultimately, knowledge holds value when it challenges and equips us for worship and service. God has always intended knowledge to link people to Him. Jesus linked intellectual knowledge to a relationship with His Father. As Christians, our attainment of knowledge should always have a personal aspect of intensifying our relationship with God.

A Christian's goal is not simply to learn about the world, but also to learn about the Creator of the world. Our pursuit of knowledge must focus on the things that will encourage the work of God in us. Taking the High Way means gaining knowledge about God's character and His ways, expanding our confidence in Him.

FOOTNOTES: 1. Leviticus 11:45

GPS: *God-Positioning Scriptures (to Reorient Your Life)*

But whatever was to my profit I now consider loss for the sake of Christ. What is more, I consider everything a loss compared to the surpassing greatness of knowing Christ Jesus my Lord, for whose sake I have lost all things. I consider them rubbish, that I may gain Christ. —**Philippians 3:7-8** (NIV)

REST STOP: *Pull Over and Ponder*
What knowledge gained throughout your life has proved to be most valuable? Read John 17:3. If, through Christ, we are blessed with eternal life, and the reality of eternal life is knowing God, how can you more abundantly experience eternal life today?

Mile 47

Tuning Him In, Part 1

Hearing His voice is a matter of both "reception" and "frequency"— stay tuned in all circumstances. Actively seek ways to commune with God because you desire to know Him.

THE GREEK PHILOSOPHER Plato believed that life could be viewed from two perspectives: the sensible and the intelligible. According to Plato, most of us believe only in one type of reality—sensible reality experienced through our physical senses—seeing, hearing, touching, smelling, or tasting. Thoughts, ideas, and beliefs not experienced in the material world, intelligible reality, are deemed nonexistent or unimportant. In *The Republic*, Plato created an allegory for his theory by describing a group of individuals trapped inside a large cave. Their view of life was confined to what they could experience within the cave. Trapped since birth and never able to comprehend that there could be anything beyond their situation, even flickering shadows on the walls were real and significant. Then one day someone ventured out of the cave, encountered the light of day, and began to recognize the stark difference between the illusions of the cave and the truth of life outside.

The cave symbolizes the material world in which we live. Plato thought that believing only in that kind of reality welcomes ignorance. Outside of the cave is a world of ideas and revelation. Perceiving the world through ideas, inner meditation, and theories helps to set us free from the prison of ignorance. The Christian view, though similar to Plato's belief in intelligible reality, involves so much more than the stoic pursuit of ideas through inner meditation. It says we need to be trained to listen "beyond the cave," beyond our common perceptions of reality. Such training is a formidable challenge, especially when our ability to recognize God's guidance is not yet mature.

Even the prophet Samuel had some difficulty recognizing God's voice. While sleeping in the temple, he heard a voice speak to him.[1] He ran to Eli, the high priest, and said, "Here I am, for you called me." But Eli said, "No, I did not" and told him to go back to sleep. As with most people, Samuel had become so acquainted with things "inside the cave" that he never considered the call could have originated from the Lord. Finally, after God called him for the third time, Samuel understood what was happening. By training his mind and heart to hear God, Samuel began to yield to God and eventually became a faithful prophet to His people. Like Samuel, we must actively seek ways to commune with God if we truly desire to know Him.

In order to hear Him, we must have the correct frequency (i.e., reference point), which is not inside the cave. Perhaps the most unique, separate, and distinct aspect of our relationship with God is the way He uses prayer. Instead of prayer being something we are supposed to do, God sees it as something we are. He wants our lives to become heartfelt prayers to Him, and the practice of praying is the beginning of this. Yet to "cave dwellers," praying is foolish and worthless, and we, like they, have been bathed in such ideology. To us, it is peculiar and frightening to trust in something outside of our experience. At times, we may believe "praying is a waste of time, and we can accomplish more through action than through praying." "God already knows what we need—so it is not necessary to pray." "Praying is simply a feel-good psychological exercise."

We must begin praying if we desire to seek holiness through a deep relationship with God. Praying requires trusting in Someone else, being vulnerable, relying on that which is unseen, and waiting patiently. Praying is more than laying our requests before Him. It involves getting to know Him. It involves

God's revealing to us who we are to Him. We begin to see what's valuable in our lives and what's holding us back. Praying is our primary avenue to holiness.

Before We Pray

Praying is an act of intimacy rooted in faith. As Oswald Chambers said, "Prayer is not monologue, but dialogue. God's voice in response to mine is its most essential part." Even though praying appears to be a simple act of talking to God and listening to His voice, it's amazing how many of us look to the recitation of a prayer only as a means to get God to do what we want done, on a the timeline we've given Him. In this fast-paced world, we don't like waiting when there's so much to do. And we are accustomed to getting immediate responses to almost any question we have about anything, simply by employing our favorite search engine. So we find it frustrating when we don't sense God's immediate response to the questions or needs we communicate in our prayers. We expect God's response to our prayers to be like an ATM's response to our debit card: fast and accurate.

"We must begin praying if we desire to seek holiness through a deep relationship with God."

The point has often been made that there is a vast difference between saying prayers and praying. Praying is an act of intimacy. It comes from a faithful heart and offers the perfect opportunity for praising God and building our relationship with Him. While God expects us to tell Him our needs and request His help, the faithful preparation of our hearts will make all the difference in the maturity and inimacy of our relationship with Him and in our expectations of Him, as well.

Praying to Discover

It's through praying that we acknowledge God's divine presence in our lives. As we pray, we openly recognize our inadequacy and His supremacy. Then God helps us discover those things in our lives that we need to give to Him. As we mature in our connection with God, He will begin to consume those parts of us that need to die. Eventually, God's holiness will remove the moral decay from our being.

A while ago, I read a scientific article that provided me with a graphic analogy of how God works in our lives. During the Civil War, maggots were used in the healing of certain types of open wounds. They were called "surgical maggots." Even today, the medical community uses them occasionally because these kinds of maggots will only eat dead or decaying flesh. They don't damage healthy flesh. Even though it's a rather revolting depiction, it provides us with a striking illustration of what holiness does within us. In time, God somehow consumes those parts of us that are dead and rotting away, removing those sins from our hearts that could destroy us. We may think of praying as an invitation to God to perform surgery. While He is doing the work, He helps us to discover what He's doing in our lives.

Praying Continually

Bobby Knight, a former coach of the Indiana Hoosiers basketball team, was once interviewed on "60 Minutes" and asked, "What does it take to be a team that's continually in the top rankings and continually winning? It must certainly take the will to win." Bobby Knight replied, "It does. It takes the will to win. However, it primarily takes something even more important than that—it takes the will to prepare. It takes the will to go out every day and practice the fundamentals over and over until they become second nature, and then first nature to you."

Even though prayer is not basketball, the well-made point is transferable. By drilling the fundamentals of praying—praise, confession, thanksgiving, and request—into our daily routine, praying can become second nature, even first nature to us. The Bible admonishes us to "seek the Lord and His strength; seek His face continually."[2] Paul instructed us to "pray without ceasing."[3] We can have that kind of closeness with God. Taking the High Way means staying in close communication with God every day.

FOOTNOTES: 1. 1 Samuel 3; 2. Psalm 105:4; 3. 1 Thessalonians 5:17

GPS: *God-Positioning Scriptures (to Reorient Your Life)*

Always be joyful. Never stop praying. Be thankful in all circumstances, for this is God's will for you who belong to Christ Jesus. —1 Thessalonians 5:16-18 (NLT)

REST STOP: *Pull Over and Ponder*
Praying is the key to holiness and truly knowing God. Consider your prayer life; what do you expect from God when you pray? How do you pray? How often? What more can you do to ensure that your life is lived as a heartfelt prayer to Him?

Mile 48

Tuning Him In, Part 2

When you begin to live a prayerful life, something wonderful starts to happen. Your life becomes so in tune with God that you recognize His answer ... even when it's not what you expected.

A Fast Fix

Another way we can experience prayer-filled lives is by fasting. Jesus practiced fasting. Many of the founding church fathers practiced fasting. Fasting is a way of putting behind, just briefly, the daily responsibilities that fill our lives so that we can realize the greatest offer that has ever been made: God's love. Fasting is an important practice in our Christian walk because most of us have become reasonably successful at satisfying ourselves with the things of the world. Somewhere along the line, instead of relying on God for our satisfaction, we began to rely on the world.

The primary reason for fasting is to remind us to rely on God and to value what is eternal. It forces our bodies and hearts to depend upon Him. It also demonstrates a sobering truth: that we don't need the world as desperately as we need God. Through fasting, our pain is transformed into praying. Experiencing the pain of denying our wants draws us closer into relationship with God.

When it comes to choosing something from which to fast, there are four categories. The first is **fasting from striving**. God said, "Be still, and know that I am God."[1] He issues that command because He loves us and wants us to hear from Him. He knows our tendencies to fill our lives with excitement, accomplishments, and possessions so as to forget our sorrows, worries, and frustrations. Being still before God means turning to Him to be made content.

The second category is **fasting from habits**. This is a tough one because habits comfort us, at least partially, by the familiarity of the routines themselves. We can, though, purpose to fast from habits that are not building our relationship with God.

The third category is **fasting from certain types of substances** in our lives. The most common of all substance fasts is the fast from food. However, some other substances to consider fasting from are nicotine, caffeine, alcohol, or other select pleasures that over time become addictions to us. We use substances in an attempt to fill needs that can only be filled by God. We need to figure out what we are really looking for and ask God to lead us toward that.

The last category involves **fasting from impulsive emotions**. Many of us have default emotions that we return to when things get tough. For some of us, the impulsive default is to worry. When we worry our thoughts travel into an imaginary world where we speculate on various scenarios. In doing so, we leave reality behind. There's a problem with that. Our God is very real, so when we worry, we go without Him to a place that doesn't exist and try to address circumstances that may never materialize. The Message says this about that in Matthew 6:34, "Give your entire attention to what God is doing right now, and don't get worked up about what may or may not happen tomorrow. God will help you deal with whatever hard things come up when the time comes." Another impulsive emotion is anger. Anger issues tend to progress unresolved for years. By fasting, we can take a couple of days to purpose change and say, "God, I am going to fast from anger. I am not going to be angry with anybody today because You said, 'Vengeance is Mine.' Instead of becoming angry, I am going to let You have the control."

The final impulsive emotion is very common and powerful—self-pity. With it we experience a range of feelings—remorse, shame, sadness, despair, and hopelessness. Instead of allowing such emotions to take over, we can choose to spend a whole day thanking God for all He has done. And rather than wallow in a self-centered emotional cesspool, we can pray for and serve others. Fasting invites God to take control of our lives.

Praying Expectantly

Years ago, there was an old church located in a rural region of the Western prairies. During what was typically the rainy season, there had been a tremendous drought. The farmers and sharecroppers in the area suffered greatly. The idea spread throughout the community to pray for rain. As the people crowded their way into the small church, they waited restlessly for the preacher to begin the meeting. When he arrived at the pulpit, he stood silently while surveying the people before him. Then he said, "Brothers and sisters, you know we came to pray. Before we begin, I've got just one question for you: Where are your umbrellas?"

When we pray to God for something, we need to live as if we are going to receive it. Praying expectantly demands that we act accordingly because He who promised is faithful. Jesus said, "Therefore I tell you, whatever you ask for in prayer, believe that you have received it, and it will be yours."[2] If we want new jobs, then praying expectantly demands that we keep our eyes open for the opportunities that God will bring to us. If we desire to be more patient with our children, then praying expectantly demands that we seek ways to practice patience in our daily routines.

"When we pray to God for something, we need to live as if we are going to receive it."

Like most people, we pray for something and then continue to build our lives on the basis of not getting it. If we've been praying for financial freedom to get out of debt or at least be able to pay the bills, what choices are we making to live up to those prayers? A poor (in every sense of the word) choice is to continue charging everything to credit cards. Believing that God will provide and taking prudent corrective actions involves wise stewardship and faithful tithing on our part.

When we begin to live a prayerful life, something wonderful starts to happen. Our lives become so in tune with God that we recognize His answer even when it's not what we expected. Taking the High Way means learning to become satisfied and sensitized to God's responses to our prayers. By acting on our prayers, we respond to God's work in our lives even when we cannot see the end result.

FOOTNOTES: 1. Psalm 46:10 (NIV); 2. Mark 11:24 (NIV)

GPS: *God-Positioning Scriptures (to Reorient Your Life)*

And Jesus answered saying to them, "Have faith in God. Truly I say to you, whoever says to this mountain, 'Be taken up and cast into the sea,' and does not doubt in his heart, but believes that what he says is going to happen, it will be granted him. Therefore I say to you, all things for which you pray and ask, believe that you have received them, and they will be granted you." —**Mark 11:22-24**

REST STOP: *Pull Over and Ponder*
Both fasting and praying expectantly are actions that require us to trust God. What would truly living as though your prayers will be answered look like in your life? Consider fasting in one of the four categories as you seek to move forward on the path to holiness.

Mile 49

Boundaries, Part 1

Unless you purposely allow God to test your heart throughout the process of holiness, you will simply cruise along ... convinced that your successes are fueled by the consistency of your hard work, rather than the work He's performing in you.

So, WE NEED to consider whether or not we're on the right track toward holiness. Are we doing this in our own strength, with our own goals, and on our own timetable? Are we "being still" and truly worshiping Him, or are we trying to gain control again? God is the One who draws and changes us. Striving to forge goodness of character on our own is inadequate. For example, we may be successful at avoiding tempting materials or people, but without God, over time, we'll be unable to contain either the desire we are suppressing or the pride growing within us.

We have a God who's in control of the sanctification process. The freedom that comes from knowing that is nothing short of spectacular. It sets us free from a works mentality and makes us grateful. Even now, God is forming us and changing us through His love, discipline, and gentle prodding. Nature offers us a powerful example of this spiritual principle ...

The emperor moth is one of the most beautiful and largest of all moths, with a wingspan of about four inches. The process of hatching from its cocoon proceeds very slowly. First, the moth chews out a narrow opening in the cocoon. Then, the moth struggles for hours to squeeze its gelatinous body through the hole. If we were to witness an emperor moth emerging from its cocoon, we might be tempted to help it and thereby make its struggle less hideous. Our assistance, though, would cause irreparable damage to the moth. If we enlarged the hole of the cocoon by merely a fraction of a centimeter, the creature would emerge with a large gelatinous body and very tiny wings. God designed the emperor moth to struggle through the narrow opening in the cocoon in order to redistribute fluids throughout its body. The struggle of emerging is what fills the potential wings with all the moth needs to be ready to fly.

"Boundaries are intended to keep out what could ruin us."

As God's children, we are governed by a similar principle. Like the moths, we have certain limits that are necessary to our success and abundance. Unless we struggle through them and do what's necessary to stay within those boundaries, we'll remain earth-bound, underdeveloped creations of God. Just as the lines guide us on the roads we drive and keep us from going into the ditch, we will only make spiritual progress within certain boundaries. Boundaries are intended to keep out what could ruin us. If we choose to stay within the boundaries, then we'll benefit and move forward. If we choose to break the boundaries, then we'll struggle and suffer setbacks.

Boundaries in Relationships

One boundary that God addressed involves the relationships we choose to cultivate. Although we would like to believe that our behavior is governed by our values, all too often we will willingly sacrifice our values in an attempt to gain human approval. In time, our relationships—whether positive or negative—will begin to reflect who we are and how we act. Scripture admonishes us to select friends and mates who have similar values, and this has nothing to do with exclusivity or favoritism. Developing relationships with people of different backgrounds, races, nationalities, and even different religions can be an immensely rewarding experience. If we only associate with people who share our opinions, experiences, perceptions, or prejudices, then the work of God in our lives is severely limited along with our impact on others. However, surrounding ourselves with people who continually compromise or disrespect our values can be devastating to our spiritual growth and intimacy with God. Likewise, it can markedly influence our actions.

Just as children must be taught how to read, write, pray, practice good manners, make wise decisions, and drive a car, they must also be taught how to choose friends and relate to people. We need to seek to cultivate healthy friendships of our own, and we must provide our children with instruction that can help them make wise decisions when choosing their friends.

Boundaries in Anger

In my local newspaper, there was a designated "Ticked-Off" section. People wrote in and described various conflicts that made them angry throughout the week. It started out as a single section, once a week. Later, there were additional "Ticked-Off" sections on pages covering sports and teen interests.

People get enjoyment out of reading what makes others mad. They can identify with it. We all probably can identify with it. However, anger is a serious issue to God. Anger destroys relationships.

We all experience occasional bursts of anger as a natural reaction to disturbances in our lives. But there is another level of anger—a rage that smolders. Fed by our bitterness, lack of forgiveness, and pride, this nurtured anger is the type of rage that Jesus warned about.[1] It's an anger that's like a virus running rampant throughout our bodies. Over time it takes over our lives. By refusing to forgive another or confess our hurtful actions, we end up making prisoners of ourselves. When we fail to forgive another person or apologize for our actions, we prevent a link with God and leave a space between us and Him.

Taking the High Way means forgiving others. When we experience an impasse with anger, we should act on the prayer of Jesus, when He prayed, "Forgive us our sins as we forgive those who have sinned against us."

FOOTNOTES: 1. Matthew 5:21-24

GPS: *God-Positioning Scriptures (to Reorient Your Life)*

And "don't sin by letting anger control you." Don't let the sun go down while you are still angry, for anger gives a foothold to the devil. —Ephesians 4:26-27 (NLT)

REST STOP: *Pull Over and Ponder*

Do you have a clear concept of God's boundaries for you? How might staying within those boundaries help you fulfill God's purposes for you not only in your immediate future, but in the scope of eternity, as well?

Mile 50

Boundaries, Part 2

There are all kinds of tempting places and things that you need to steer clear of. Keep your eyes on the road, watching for the subtleties of sin, and guard yourself from the more obvious temptations.

Boundaries in Quarrels

In addition to our battle with anger, we also have a tendency to be quarrelsome. Scripture tells us to avoid quarrels. That is easier said than done. It's easy to get caught up in the debate over words, ideas, and theories. Paul instructed us to avoid such discussions no matter how important they may seem to us, because God is in control. "But refuse foolish and ignorant speculations, knowing that they produce quarrels."[1] The word "refuse" in this passage literally means "just say no." In other words, it's totally within our power to do something about these situations.

In his letter to Timothy, Paul not only instructed him to avoid quarrels, but he also tried to prepare Timothy for the inevitable development of them. Like a wise grandfather, Paul explained that regardless of our good actions, there will often be misunderstanding or opposition. Paul's strategy for Timothy was to plan reasoned responses for disputes ahead of time and by doing so, avoid the unreasoned passions that spring from within. We, too, have to plan ahead of time to avoid foolish arguments. God's plans are not dependent on our successful arguments, but Proverbs 15:1 assures us that a gentle answer turns away wrath.

Boundaries in Vengeance

If we disregard the far-reaching effects that revenge has on our lives and on the lives of others, we perpetuate the problem. Intense anger and a vengeful spirit will keep us from considering the reason for other people's actions. There's always more to our conflicts with others than that which is readily apparent. And maturity requires that we try to understand the situation from their perspective, not just our own. Their actions are often deeply rooted in their own life experiences, hurt, and pain. If we respond in love and humility, we'll be able to see that the consequences of blessing someone who has done us harm far outweigh the repercussions of vengeful actions.

"There's always more to our conflicts with others than that which is readily apparent."

In the 1970s, the Berlin Wall divided that German city. Communities on the east side of the wall were under a Communist government, and those in the West were living in a democracy. The tension between the two was often palpable. One such day, a group of East Berliners gathered all of the rancid garbage they could find and loaded it on a large truck. In the middle of the night, they backed the truck to the wall and dumped the garbage onto the Western side. In the morning, many West Berliners awoke to a hideous smell. Upon seeing the garbage, they cleaned it up and then planned their response. Three days later, the West Berliners gathered at the wall. Using ropes, they lowered, into East Berlin, baskets filled with loaves of freshly baked bread, utensils, clean garments, and other goods that were necessary for a wonderful daily life. Also, in each basket they had placed a note that said, "You can only give what you have." Eventually, the wall between the two sides was removed—literally.

As followers of Christ, we have more than enough to give. We have been given more than enough to simply cope. We don't have to respond "eye for eye" or "tooth for tooth."[2] We can respond as Jesus Christ has to us—with mercy and love.

Boundaries in Our Thought Lives

What resides in our hearts is every bit as important as what comes out of our mouths or what we do with our bodies. In the greatest sermon ever preached, the Sermon on the Mount,[3] Jesus pointed out that it's not just our actions that count, but our motivation behind those actions. Often, I have heard people say, "Since the Bible says it's wrong to even think bad thoughts, I might as well go ahead and take action anyway." That's ridiculous reasoning. Certainly God holds us accountable when we entertain evil thoughts, but when we actually perform them, the effect on other people's lives—as well as on our own life—is devastating. I have seen marriages and families torn apart by one person's decision to act on private evil thoughts. The sobering truth is, our evil thoughts will not remain in the thought realm forever; if we continue to entertain them, eventually they lead us to action.

By refusing to nurse lustful thoughts, we can successfully avoid falling into temptation. Often, this requires drastic action like Odysseus in Homer's *The Odyssey*. He traveled beyond the island of the Sirens where sea nymphs sang enchanting songs. Many seafarers who heard the songs were lured toward them, only to crash onto the island rocks. To avoid the possibility of heeding their call and grounding his boat on the rocks, Odysseus had his crew strap him to the mast of the ship so he could not respond to the Sirens' calls. He also had the crew put wax in their own ears so that they could not hear the Sirens' songs. His actions demonstrated remarkable self-control and foresight. We, too, must be willing to take steps to avoid temptation, but always be aware that God is the One who gives us the power to overcome.

Sweet Surrender!

The more intimate our relationship with Christ, the more readily we will recognize every counterfeit gift Satan has to offer us: lust isn't love; greed isn't need; a dare isn't an opportunity; ego isn't confidence, and anger isn't inherently righteous. We relinquish the former for the later, knowing that He asks us to do it because He has something much better for us.

Years ago I heard a story that has this point at its heart: A precious little girl begged her father for pop beads after seeing them in a store window. The plastic beads, popular in the 1950s, could be snapped together to make bracelets or necklace. Her father, hoping to help her grow up a bit, told her she could earn the money to buy them herself by doing some additional chores for her mom. She diligently accomplished each task assigned, and in two weeks she had earned all she needed to buy the pop beads. What a great day it was when she made that long-awaited purchase. As soon as she got home, she made a pop bead necklace, put it on, and wore it all day. That evening when she walked out to give her Father a hug before bedtime, the pop beads encircled her neck and lay in full display on her pajama top. Her Father, seated in a big chair beside a crackling fire he'd built earlier in the evening, pulled her up to sit with him, just as he did every evening. He told her he was proud of her for all she had done to earn those beads and that he thought they were beautiful. Then he said, "Sweetie, give me your pop beads." She laughed, climbed down, and went to bed. The next night, same scenario, except she didn't laugh before she climbed down. The next night, the little girl didn't get close enough to the chair for her father to pull her close, but she heard him ask again for her pop beads as she walked slowly toward her bedroom. She didn't get there before she turned around, ran back to him, climbed into his lap, and whispered, "Daddy, I love my pop beads, but I love you more. If you want them you can have them." He smiled, unsnapped the beads, and without hesitation, he flung the strand into the flaming fireplace. Before she could even think about what had just happened, He pulled a beautiful strand of real pearls from his pocket and draped them around her neck.

Thankfully, we have a Father in heaven who will not ask us to sacrifice anything that He's not ready to replace countless times over. Unlike the bait of Satan, God's gift is real and eternal. It completely fulfills us. Taking the High Way means relinquishing our worldly treasures and idols, and sometimes that means relinquishing what is good for what is best.

FOOTNOTES: 1. 2 Timothy 2:23; 2. Exodus 21:24; 3. Matthew 5-7

GPS: *God-Positioning Scriptures (to Reorient Your Life)*

No temptation has seized you except what is common to man. And God is faithful; he will not let you be tempted beyond what you can bear. ... He will also provide a way out so that you can stand up under it. —1 Corinthians 10:13 (NIV)

REST STOP: *Pull Over and Ponder*

Are there any areas in your life where you're tempted to overstep God's established boundaries? Let the promise in 1 Corinthians 10:13 help you in fulfilling His hopes for your life.

Mile 51

Communication Pathway

By reflecting on the prayer of Jesus, you can increase your understanding of God, His sovereignty, and your position as His child.

IN MATTHEW 6, Jesus provided us with His prayer—the Lord's Prayer. As Jesus said, we must learn to "pray, then, in this way."[1] The Lord's Prayer is the ideal example for us. Prayer is simple and the communication pathway to God, Jesus said: "And when you are praying, do not use meaningless repetition as the Gentiles do, for they suppose that they will be heard for their many words."[2] Jesus knew that it doesn't take very long for the right activities and even the right motivations to get lost in human self-centeredness. He knew that as we talk with God, it's only a matter of time before we start to fall in love with our own voices. So, Jesus' instruction to us was to keep it short! The longer the prayer, the tougher it is to concentrate on the original purpose: to have a conversation with God instead of a monologue to Him.

Throughout history, it has been the human tendency in every religion to have lengthy prayers. For some reason, we view long prayers as sacrificial, powerful, and persuasive. God does not—He values the state of our hearts. We don't need to convince God of anything. He already knows what we need, and we can't change His perfect will for us. He not only has the correct answer; He has the best answer.

There's an old principle in scientific theory called Ockham's Razor. It asserts that when we are faced with more than one alternative, the correct answer is usually the simplest explanation. The principle not only applies to science but to prayer as well. When we use unnecessary verbiage in our prayers, we end up complicating our requests. Neither our actions nor our words will ever force God to consider us. Instead, His perfect love is the reason for His intervention in our lives. Whenever we pray, we're communicating with our real Father. We're responding to a relationship—not a tradition or religious practice. Like our search for holiness, prayer involves an intimate relationship with God. Whenever we launch into long prayer times with God, filling the silence with creative and persuasive words, we're avoiding a deep relationship, dodging His questions, and ignoring His voice. Only our intimate relationship with God, not the quantity of our words, makes our prayers effective.

> "Only our intimate relationship with God, not the quantity of our words, makes our prayers effective."

The first few words of the Lord's Prayer establish an incredible connection: "Our Father who is in heaven, Hallowed be Your name."[3] What a vast contrast: Our Father—so close, who art in heaven—so far. Hallowed be Your name— sacred, honored, and untouchable. These contrasting elements are also the basis of our hope.

It's very important to understand that when we say to God, "Hallowed be Your name," we're connecting to Him in accordance with His nature and love, not our own. God is our Father in heaven, and He loves us more than we can imagine, but His standards never change. He is high and lifted up, so a large part of prayer is seeking to know Him for who He really is.

When Jesus prayed, "Your kingdom come, Your will be done, on earth as it is in heaven,"[4] He was well aware of the difference between what's done in heaven and what's done on earth. In heaven, everyone is pleased to conform to God's will. On earth, that's not the case. In an attempt to make His will happen on earth, the church continually creates rules. Then it finds abounding frustration when it tries to hold everyone accountable to the rules it creates. Doing God's will is more than obeying a command or adhering to a regulation. His will focuses on heart issues—having a godly attitude—that result in godly actions.

The second component of the Lord's Prayer is the opportunity to voice our needs to our Father. God knows our needs before we talk to Him about them. Providing us with good gifts is a natural and wonderful aspect of His character, but that is not His primary focus. God prioritizes our relationship with Him.

In addition, the Lord's Prayer teaches us that we must always remember what God did for us. He forgave us, despite the fact that we were the ones who owed Him. "And forgive us our debts, as we also have forgiven our debtors"[5] communicates the fact that we owed God. Through Jesus Christ, the price for each Christian's debt to God was paid. Our gratefulness can and should be reflected in how we respond to others—we must forgive them.

The third and final part of the Lord's Prayer involves understanding that life is an ongoing battle. Many of us believe that if we simply accept Christ, all our troubles will go away. They don't. We only have the final victory and healing in heaven. On earth, we have it dispensed in bits. Jesus finished the Lord's Prayer with these words, "And do not lead us into temptation, but deliver us from evil. [For Yours is the kingdom and the power and the glory forever.]"[6] We will experience temptation because we face testing. Therefore, we need to ask God to deliver us.

I think that all of us want to come to a place in life where we can coast—where we can say, "This is the place where everything is going to be all right." But it will never happen. Life is challenging all the way along. We need God every day and every hour. Fortunately, God has chosen not to build weak people. He has chosen to build strong champions. And He knows how to do it in us. Our main job is simply to get up in the morning and get going. It's not about trying harder; it's about letting God work. It's not about working harder; it's about showing up. It's about taking each next step in God's direction.

We can't deliver ourselves through our own hard work and deeds. We're not the ones overcoming the odds and achieving victory. God is doing that through us. He's the One who delivers us from evil. We're in His kingdom—it's by His power and to His glory that He frees us. Taking the High Way means believing in the faithfulness of God and persevering.

FOOTNOTES: 1. Matthew 6:9; 2. Matthew 6:7; 3. Matthew 6:9; 4. Matthew 6:10; 5. Matthew 6:12; 6. Matthew 6:13

GPS: *God-Positioning Scriptures (to Reorient Your Life)*

[Jesus said:] "And when you come before God, don't turn that into a theatrical production either. All these people making a regular show out of their prayers, hoping for stardom! Do you think God sits in a box seat? Here's what I want you to do: Find a quiet, secluded place so you won't be tempted to role-play before God. Just be there as simply and honestly as you can manage. The focus will shift from you to God, and you will begin to sense his grace. The world is full of so-called prayer warriors who are prayer-ignorant. They're full of formulas and programs and advice, peddling techniques for getting what you want from God. Don't fall for that nonsense. This is your Father you are dealing with, and he knows better than you what you need. With a God like this loving you, you can pray very simply." —Matthew 6:5-13 (The Message)

REST STOP: *Pull Over and Ponder*
The Lord's Prayer gives us the components that our prayers should contain. Reexamine Matthew 6 and personalize the prayer for where you are at this time in your life.

Mile 52

The Road to (True) Riches

God's desire for you is to acquire true wealth, far more important than accumulating material riches because it's eternal and intimately linked to your relationship with God.

IN THE SERMON on the Mount, Jesus said, "Do not store up for yourselves treasures on earth."[1] Having worldly possessions is not evil, but our shoddy management of them, along with our failure to understand their effect on our lives, can easily divert us from the High Way. We need to ask ourselves this question: How much of what we own owns us? The type of wealth we seek exposes what's in our hearts. The treasures to die for are His heavenly blessings.

Most of us do a great deal of our financing by credit card. We hold to the notion "Buy now; pay later!" and discover over time that a very significant cost of material goods comes in the maintenance. Our worldly possessions continue to drain us even after we obtain them, and we often don't realize the bondage they create. Those of us who treasure our wealth are bound to the practice of maintaining it. It can require so much time and energy from us that we actually sacrifice the things we love (our family, our friends, our relationship with God, and even our morals). And when we sacrifice those things for material wealth, we're prisoners of our greed. True wealth is freeing. True wealth focuses our attention and energy on what is of eternal importance.

As our sons headed for college, Becky and I knew we were entering a prolonged, difficult financial period. We joyfully and willingly placed ourselves under some important financial obligations that would affect us for years to come. Living on a very tight budget, we sold our house and moved into an apartment—neither gated nor fancy—just an apartment. It's certainly not more or less holy to live in an apartment than to live in a house. However, simplicity can be freeing. We lived in that apartment for seven years and found it to be a place filled with the surprises of simplicity: less to maintain and clean meant we had more energy and time for things that mattered more for kingdom purposes.

Jesus described our tendency to allow "the worries of the world, and the deceitfulness of riches, and the desires for other things"[2] to choke us and make us unfruitful. As a nation that takes pride in wealth, we believe that our riches will satisfy us, but instead they cost us dearly—robbing us of time and focus. When we choose to live a simpler life, we are much more likely to find the treasures that bring joy both now and forever.

There's a distinction between our playthings of earth and the treasures of God. We need to understand what Jesus said when He admonished us to "store up for yourselves treasures in heaven."[3] In the Greek, the verb tense and mood involves a continual and repeated action. It's not a one-time thing. Jesus' words were an instruction to us, rather than a request. We should never feel greedy about wanting heavenly treasures. God wants us to pursue Him and to share His wealth.

Before we came to Christ, we were in debt. According to Romans 2:5, we were storing up wrath for ourselves—like a credit card stores up debt. However, when we came to Christ, the balance sheet shifted. We were no longer in debt because all of our debt was paid in Christ, all of it. Now, as Christians, we have an account in heaven, where we can store up treasures.

Throughout Scripture, we're provided with many illustrations of how to obtain these treasures. God's treasures are not gained by our pursuits, but as by-products of our relationship with Him. In a way, His treasures naturally accumulate as He draws us nearer to Him and as we seek to love Him more. Often, the act of being faithful in good works is actually what God uses to change our hearts. The Bible explains that throughout our lives, there are three "driving skills" that can keep us on the right track and help us to store up the treasures of heaven:

Skill No. 1: Steering Money

The first way we can accumulate the treasures of God is by wise management of our material goods. In the book of Malachi, God literally says to test Him by giving Him the first 10 percent of everything we get—that is tithing. This is the only thing God says to test Him on in all of Scripture. He wants us to give, and He instructed us to do so. A tithe is usually given to the church. Offerings are anything given beyond that amount. We should strive to use the other 90 percent of our income in responsible ways that have a positive eternal influence on our lives and the lives of others.

"Getting our bodies in the right places— just showing up— matters."

Our tithes and offerings make a difference for Christ in the lives of others. In churches across this country, people accept Jesus Christ into their lives. Every week marriages are put back together. Every week the hungry are clothed and fed—and the list goes on and on. Through our giving—our money, time, and service—we are participating in the work of God to honor Him and help people, many of whom we will never know.

Skill No. 2: Steering Yourself

Another way to lay up treasures in heaven is through proper conduct. Somebody once said that 90 percent of success in life is just showing up. Getting our bodies in the right places—just showing up—matters. Whether it is to work, volunteer, minister, listen, encourage, support, or simply to be just another warm body in the room, we need to show up. We may not feel like being there, but our feelings aren't the most important reference point for our decisions. Maturity comes from placing ourselves in the right places, doing the next right thing, and being willing to learn and grow.

Skill No. 3: Steering Relationships

The final way we can capture the treasures of God is by building relationships and investing in the lives of people. After all, God has always been about relationships.

Investing our lives in people is messy. It's complicated and painful. Jesus knew that before He came to earth as a man. However, He knew the significance of His investment would far outweigh the cost. To discover the treasures of God, you can't choose to overlook people. Taking the High Way means praying, loving, serving, exercising patience, and demonstrating daily how important others are to us and to God.

FOOTNOTES: 1. Matthew 6:19; 2. Mark 4:19; 3. Matthew 6:20

GPS: *God-Positioning Scriptures (to Reorient Your Life)*

For the love of money is a root of all sorts of evil, and some by longing for it have wandered away from the faith and pierced themselves with many griefs. —1 Timothy 6:10

REST STOP: *Pull Over and Ponder*
What specific steps can you take this week to better live out the three "driving skills" and discover the true treasures of God?

Mile 53

What's Under the Hood?

If you haven't become more joyful, giving, loving, patient, gentle, or wise toward others since you have become a Christian ... then it's time to lift the hood. Chances are you are missing something crucial.

HUDSON TAYLOR, ONE of the founders of the modern missionary movement, said this: "If your mother and father, or if your husband and wife, or if your brother and sister, or if your children, or even if your dog is not happier because you've become a Christian, chances are you haven't become a Christian."

In Matthew 5, Jesus described the character of a maturing Christian—actually the character of His indwelling Spirit. These character traits are popularly known as the beatitudes, and they represent the inner blessings of God. Bear in mind, the beatitudes should not be confused with happiness, because happiness is based on circumstances. These are the blessed and developing inner qualities that drive every true believer.

"Blessed are the poor in spirit, for theirs is the kingdom of heaven."[1] Jesus took the concept of material wealth and explained it on a spiritual level. "Poor in spirit" could be translated as those who realize that they need God in every area of their lives. Jesus told us that we are blessed when we realize our inadequacy, blessed because our poverty makes us profoundly aware of the truth of our nature.

"Blessed are those who mourn, for they shall be comforted."[2] Jesus referred to a different type of mourning, something deeper—our awareness of sin. There's a sharp contrast between mourning from the pain of a difficult circumstance and mourning over the cause of that painful circumstance. Jesus said that we are blessed when we recognize how our sin has damaged us and caused hurt to God and those around us. When we mourn over the fact that we will always have the tendency to make mistakes and mess up, we'll be comforted and blessed by God.

> "... those of us who are gentle are able to remain so because we have an inner strength."

"Blessed are the gentle [meek], for they shall inherit the earth."[3] Gentle does not mean weak. In fact, those of us who are gentle are able to remain so because we have an inner strength. We understand that we don't have to run the universe and win every battle. God's running it just fine, and He's already won the war.

"Blessed are those who hunger and thirst for righteousness, for they shall be satisfied."[4] Jesus Christ told us that if we want to be truly satisfied, we must seek after His righteousness, and if we truly do this, then we will live satisfied, no matter what our lot in life.

"Blessed are the merciful, for they shall receive mercy."[5] In a world that seems to lack mercy, what does it take to be truly merciful? Most importantly, it takes an understanding that God is merciful. Unless we believe in His mercy, it will be extremely difficult for us to extend mercy.

"Blessed are the pure in heart, for they shall see God."[6] The pure in heart never have ulterior motives. They assume that God has a purpose for every circumstance.

"Blessed are the peacemakers, for they shall be called sons of God."[7] As we pursue peace and allow God's qualities to fill our lives, we will remind others of God and demonstrate that we are His children. Still, the price of being peacemakers is sacrifice. It may require us to get in the middle of conflicts and perhaps even forego our own safety. Jesus was the model peacemaker. While He never sided with sin, He always sided with sinners—including you and me!

The tendency of so many of us is to attempt to look as if we are better than we actually are—to create a more appealing image of ourselves to others. But our created illusions of holiness, like a mirage, disappear upon close examination. Only by surrendering to God and establishing an intimate relationship with Him will we become holy. That's because holiness is a by-product of that kind of relationship with God.

His love is great enough for us to rest in each day. His love is great enough that we can relinquish control and yield to Him. His love is great enough that we can love others deeply. His love is great enough that we can love Him in return. His love is enough that we are compelled to kneel before Him—for He is holy. Taking the High Way means letting our justification only come from Jesus Christ.

FOOTNOTES: 1. Matthew 5:3; 2. Matthew 5:4; 3. Matthew 5:5; 4. Matthew 5:6; 5. Matthew 5:7; 6. Matthew 5:8; 7. Matthew 5:9

GPS: *God-Positioning Scriptures (to Reorient Your Life)*

It is not this way among you, but whoever wishes to become great among you shall be your servant, and whoever wishes to be first among you shall be your slave; just as the Son of Man did not come to be served, but to serve, and to give His life a ransom for many. —**Matthew 20:26-28**

REST STOP: *Pull Over and Ponder*
After reading through the beatitudes in Matthew 5, how is your understanding of what it means to be "blessed" as a child of God altered?

EXIT 8: *SALT AND LIGHT TRAIL*

Mile 54

Lighting the Road

You are the light of the world. As you continue along the road to spiritual maturity—loving God and serving people—others will be able to see Christ better, because of you.

WHEN BENJAMIN FRANKLIN wanted Philadelphia to consider streetlights for the first time, he did not go to the city fathers and debate the merits of his idea. Instead, he placed a lantern outside his house near his porch area and kept it shining all night. As people walked past his house after dark, for a brief moment, they could see where they were walking. His neighbors loved the idea so much that they also began leaving lanterns outside their own houses. Before long, the city of Philadelphia was lit up with street lamps. No one argued them into it. Ben Franklin did a good work; others saw it, liked it, and imitated it.

Jesus proclaimed, "You are the light of the world."[1] We can make a tremendous difference and be beneficial to the world—we can bring out the best in others.

Light makes everything it touches visible. Therefore, if we are the light of the world, it isn't about our being seen, it is about helping others see. If we are doing what we need to do—loving God and serving people—others will be able to see Christ better as a result of our good works, which flow from a heart of worship.

Worship is the difference between just doing good works and doing ministry. Christian ministry can be defined as a good work that begins in worship, ends in worship, and gives glory to God. Ministry and worship are integral to each other. We can't separate them. Our chief purpose in life is to glorify God and enjoy Him forever. Worship is not something we are to do occasionally; it's the perspective with which we are to do everything.

"Worship is the difference between just doing good works and doing ministry."

Entangled in the details of ministry, Christians forget the reasons we became involved in the first place. But we can't forget them and be effective in ministry. If we go out and try to win the world for Christ with a hard heart, we are only going through the motions. It's sort of like rocking in a rocking chair. There's a lot going on, but we're not getting anywhere. If we attempt to do things for God without worshiping Him, our personal relationship with Him will suffer in the process. Worship is very simple. It's adoring God for who He is. It's the daily practice of expressing reverence to God.

We should worship God, but we are also to love our neighbor as ourselves.[2] Note the triune nature in this verse: God, neighbor, self. We cannot separate them. We can't have our own worshipful, emotional relationship with God and think that it's complete. Completion comes by extension—extending ourselves to our neighbors. That's the character of God, the character of Jesus Christ. We cannot separate worship from ministry.

My brother-in-law, Mark Beeson, is the pastor of a mega-church in Indiana, and even with the busy schedule that requires of him, he has taken a couple of weeks every summer for more than thirty-five years to oversee a Junior High Summer Camp. One of my favorite stories that he tells makes this point well. Mark says he was standing in the midst of the camp's worship service, lost in the adoration of our Savior. Eyes closed, hands raised in praise, he was tearing up as they sang Hillsong's, "You came and rescued me. I want to be where You are ..." Then came a tap—a slight tug that jolted him from heaven's gates. A small camper was at his side—tapping his back, tugging his shirt. Assuming the boy had something very important to say, something so crucial it warranted the interruption of sacred worship, Mark bent down to hear the boy's small voice over the singing. "Hey Poppa B," he began, "In the boys' restroom, in the second stall on the right when you come in, the toilet paper ran out. It was all gone, but I replaced it. I put on some new toilet paper so you wouldn't have to." Then the seventh grader smiled one of those beaming "I'm so happy I could help" smiles. Mark wasn't sure why the boy felt it necessary to tell him what he'd done as he was trying to worship, but said, "Thank you. I'm proud of you. You did a good job." Then Mark turned back to face the band and resume singing and God struck him with this thought: Worship is more than singing songs with your hands in the air. Worship is serving too. Mark says God tugged on him with the hand of a student and interrupted his praises. With one hand lifted to God as we sing and the other busy with the tasks of devoted service (even if it means putting on a new roll of toilet paper), we all, Mark concludes, should practice ambidextrous worship.

Proverbs says, "To do what is right and just is more acceptable to the Lord than sacrifice."

Faith is incomplete without extension. Until Christ's nature of being salt and light seasons and brightens the places where we spend our time—workplaces, restaurants, schools—our faith is not complete. True faith is completed by extension—extension according to God's nature, not man's. Taking the High Way means understanding that loving God is not only a matter of how we treat Him; it is how we treat other people because of Him.

FOOTNOTES: 1. Matthew 5:14; 2. Matthew 22:39

GPS: *God-Positioning Scriptures (to Reorient Your Life)*

*Then Jesus again spoke to them, saying, "I am the Light of the world; he who follows Me will not walk in the darkness, but will have the Light of life." —*John 8:12

REST STOP: *Pull Over and Ponder*
Do your daily actions and words shed light on not only your devotion to Christ, but His work in the world? What is a practical step you can take today to shine brighter?

Mile 55

Your Spiritual Wiring, Part 1

You were not created to make this journey by yourself. The body of believers not only needs your gifts and abilities; it needs you ... who you are and who you were made to be.

I N ORDER TO serve more effectively, each of us is given a spiritual gift when the Holy Spirit enters our hearts. Paul tells us in 1 Corinthians 12 not to be ignorant of our spiritual gifts.

God has given us our place in this world and our gifts to share. He has wired each of us for the contribution we are going to make.

It's good to understand what our spiritual giftedness is and how God has uniquely wired us, but in discovering those things, we must remember God has given *us*, not just our gifts, to the world so that we can reveal how great He is.

As we begin to understand how important it is that we share our God-given gifts to strengthen the church and to serve the world, we must also recognize that God has placed limitations on us. One of the absolute killer foibles of mankind is not to admit our limitations. Our culture today is rife with echoes of Eastern religions that tell us man is not really limited; he is simply an expression of the universe. Yet our salvation depends on an admission of our limitations. We need to realize we are only *a part* of the body of Christ and can't go to God except in our limitations.

If we don't recognize and admit our limitations, then we become prideful and our theology gets confused. A valuable aspect of personal limitations is that what we can't accomplish individually, others united with us in the body of Christ *will* accomplish. Their accomplishment in Christ becomes our accomplishment as well. Still, a human tendency is to compare our God-given gifts to the gifts of others. We might say, "I wish I could do that. That's what a real Christian is!" Where do we get that idea? God has made us so that even the members who are least obvious and those who are weakest are absolutely vital to the body.

> *"Jesus embodied the essence of ministry by simply ministering to anyone who crossed His path ..."*

If I compared my evangelistic skills to Dr. Billy Graham's, I would not get out of bed in the morning. Should I feel badly because when I witness to people, my eyes still twitch and I get nervous? No! I witness out of obedience even though it's not natural for me. Should I despise God for not making me more like Mother Teresa? My job is to be merciful, but Mother Teresa was mercy incarnate. I can't compare myself to her or anyone else. But I can give what I've got—that which God has provided—when opportunities arise. When you get right down to it, that's really what "ministry" is.

When we accept Jesus into our lives, God's holiness becomes our holiness and the practical result is always "ministry." The character of God, which dwells in all believers, offers ministry to everyone. Jesus embodied the essence of ministry by simply ministering to anyone who crossed His path—whether the person accepted it or not. We see an example of this when a lawyer stood up to challenge Jesus about eternal life.[1]

"Who is my neighbor?" the lawyer asked. Jesus knew where the man was headed with his questions, and He answered him with a story we examined in Mile 43, the parable of the Good Samaritan. From the beginning, Jesus was setting up an absolute non-categorical command as to whom we are to help and love. Describing the man in the story, Jesus said, "And he fell among robbers and they stripped him." If a person is stripped, all marks of identification are taken away. Was the man a Jew or a Gentile? Was he wealthy or poor? Did he live in the territory? What was his status in life? No one would know.

Both a priest and a Levite in the story avoided the injured man, fearing that connecting with him in any way would generate an inherent obligation to help. This is a profound irony that applies directly to us. As long as we keep from acknowledging individuals who are in need, we are giving ourselves permission to avoid responsibility. The priest and the Levite decided to confine their godly activities to an institutional structure, the temple, instead of helping those whom God put in their paths. There are church people who are just like that. If we confine our definition of a godly activity to the institutional church, we are just like the priest and Levite—limiting God's ministry through us.

The Samaritan ministered exactly what was appropriate to the injured man—a simple response to a simple need. Some people don't want to get involved in other people's lives because they fear the possibility of forever being held hostage emotionally by ongoing needs of someone they wouldn't mind helping out for a time. It's important to note that ministry to others doesn't mean taking responsibility for their entire lives; it means giving them what they need at the moment—love does not wait!

At the conclusion of the story, Jesus asked the lawyer which of the three men proved to be a "neighbor." The lawyer was asking for a categorical definition; Jesus answered with a responsibility. This is profound. Our neighbor is anyone who is nearby or in close proximity at any given time—not just he who lives near, but he who is near and needs, us. Jesus made the definition of neighbor coexistent with all of humanity. Taking the High Way means using our God-given gifts to minister to our "neighbors." It's not just an activity; it's exemplifying the character of Jesus.

FOOTNOTES: 1. Luke 10:25-29

GPS: *God-Positioning Scriptures (to Reorient Your Life)*

Jesus … said, "A man was going down from Jerusalem to Jericho, and fell among robbers, and they stripped him and beat him, and went away leaving him half dead. And by chance a priest was going down on that road, and when he saw him, he passed by on the other side. Likewise a Levite also, when he came to the place and saw him, passed by on the other side. But a Samaritan, who was on a journey, came upon him; and when he saw him, he felt compassion, and came to him and bandaged up his wounds, pouring oil and wine on them; and he put him on his own beast, and brought him to an inn and took care of him. On the next day he took out two denarii and gave them to the innkeeper and said, 'Take care of him; and whatever more you spend, when I return I will repay you.' Which of these three do you think proved to be a neighbor to the man who fell into the robbers' hands? ... Go and do the same." —**Luke 10:30-37**

REST STOP: *Pull Over and Ponder*

If your "neighbor" is anyone you come in contact with, mentally tally those you may have passed by this week. Pray for an opportunity to minister to those *near* you today. What's one thing you can do this week to reach out to those who *live near* you?

Mile 56

Your Spiritual Wiring, Part 2

Don't think less of yourself because of the particular gifts God gives you or think too highly of yourself, believing that it all depends on you. The mission of God does not reside in one, but in many.

NEWSPAPER COLUMNIST AND author George Matthew Adams once said, "There is no such thing as a 'self-made' man. We are made up of thousands of others. Everyone who has ever done a kind deed for us, or spoken one word of encouragement to us, has entered into the make-up of our character and of our thoughts, as well as our success."

The real wealth of the church is not in one or two people in leadership. It's not the elder board, or the senior pastor or worship leader. The vast resources of the church are the people who go about serving and doing the work of Christianity. God has made us interdependent so that cooperating and esteeming one another are necessary for healthy ministries. We are gifted differently by design.

What gifts do you have? What gifts do you see in others? Spiritual gifts fall into directional categories that **lift up**—mercy, service, helps, pastor, healing, exhorter; **look deep**—discernment, wisdom, knowledge, faith; **point up**—prophet, evangelist, miracles, tongues; and **look forward**—leader, apostle, administrator, teacher, giver. One of the simplest ways to determine someone's gift is to understand how a need is perceived in a particular situation. Consider the question "What do you think is wrong with the church today?" Responses to this question differ depending on how the person responding perceives the need. People often view the church through the filter of their spiritual gift. And because they do, they will most readily notice what's wrong in the specific areas where they readily recognize need for their own contribution.

Here are some examples: If someone answers, "We have all these programs, but nobody is getting saved," we would spot that person's gift as evangelism. Another person might answer, "It's the leadership. They don't stand up and tell you the truth." That person's spiritual gift is probably prophecy. "Prophesy" actually means "to speak forth the Word of God." A biblical prophet isn't necessarily one who predicts the future, but rather one who understands things from God's perspective and has clarity on what is morally right or wrong.

Those motivated by mercy see the church's error as a lack of kindness, people being disenfranchised, hurt, or suffering and no one demonstrating compassion toward them. However, if others perceive that those same broken people require a laying on of hands and anointing with oil, then this may indicate the gift of healing. Others feel the church is failing to teach. They desire to impart understanding and assume that if people know better, they will do better. These are the people with the spiritual gift of teaching. Exhorters feel that the problem with the church is that people are not growing. There is no one to come alongside them and encourage them in their next steps. People with the gift of service see the problem in the church as a lack of willingness to respond to meet the practical needs of others. Those with the gift of leadership see the problem as a lack of vision, or achievable goals. They have an amazing ability to break down the goal into separate tasks and can find the right people to accomplish those tasks.

There is also the gift of discernment, which is more of a cautionary gift. People who have this gift are able to sense when there is something dangerous or not quite right. Wisdom is another gift. People who have this gift perceive things that later cause others to say, "Why didn't I think of that? It seems so evident." Wisdom is different from the gift of knowledge. People with knowledge know facts, and as a result, others are able to draw inspiration because of the knowledge of God. There is the gift of faith. No matter how bad things get, their person with this gift not only understands, but also sees God intervening. Faith-oriented people know that God's plan will be manifested, so they rarely become disturbed or upset.

God has given some a devotional language to praise Him and help them draw closer to Him. These people have the gift of tongues. Still others have the gift of giving, which is not the same thing as generosity. God demands generosity from all of us. The people with the gift of giving are very good with money, and they enjoy finding worthy investments that will be ongoing resources for the

> *"Faith-oriented people know that God's plan will be manifested, so they rarely become disturbed or upset."*

kingdom. There is also the administrator—the organizer. These people have an ability to work through issues in logical sequence and are also very good at maximizing stewardship of people's time.

It's so important to recognize one another's gifts so that we can respond to each other accurately and speak to each other in terms we understand. Every person is necessary and God is exact in putting all of us together.

The Difference Love Makes

After teaching us about God's distribution of spiritual gifts in 1 Corinthians 12, Paul spends the entire next chapter teaching us about the difference love makes. He wanted us to see that even all our abilities from God are nothing without the central ingredient—love.

Paul encourages us to make sure we don't let the world's attitude shape our attitude and we don't react in ways that are unloving. He knew from experience, just as we do, that the world is not a generally affirming place. In fact, it is often quite the opposite. There are at least two very good reasons we should love whether or not that love is returned. One, our Father is watching, and two, we can't be salt and light for the world if we are arrogant or rude. Christ, our model, took wrongs upon Himself and loved anyway. This kind of love is impossible without a relationship with Jesus Christ that lets Him love others through us.

Scripture tells us that there are three great life anchors available for us today: faith, hope, and love. It says the greatest is love.[1] Taking the High Way means demonstrating God's love by taking the time to learn and to use the spiritual gifts He has given us.

FOOTNOTES: 1. 1 Corinthians 13:13

GPS: *God-Positioning Scriptures (to Reorient Your Life)*

There are different kinds of gifts, but the same Spirit. There are different kinds of service, but the same Lord. There are different kinds of working, but the same God works all of them in all men.
—1 Corinthians 12:4-6 (NIV)

REST STOP: *Pull Over and Ponder*
Have you ever complained about a certain weakness you believe is present in the church? What does this tell you about your spiritual gifts?

Mile 57

Giving Directions

It's important to keep in mind that while you have a destination in life, many people around you are lost. Sooner or later, someone's going to ask you for directions. Are you ready?

ONCE WE HAVE committed our lives to Christ, we have the responsibility and wonderful privilege to share the Good News with others. God did not save us only for ourselves; He saved us for others as well. The most loving thing we can do after we come to Jesus ourselves is lead someone else who is "lost" to Him.

Many people associate "being lost" with being disoriented. However, for Christians, the term "lost" means being separated from the God who loves us as nobody else can. So being lost, from a Christian perspective, is a hellish experience. Eternal separation from God is, literally, hell.

So when does a person become "lost"? It happens from the moment we're born into the physical world. Mankind was originally separated from God when humans were kicked out of the Garden of Eden because of sin. That rebellious nature of mankind is part of us. From the moment we are born we want our own way and think everyone and everything should focus on us.

That pretty much describes every person's life until they come to know Jesus. We look for personal satisfaction through appeasing our appetites and by accomplishing what we can. For a short while, we're satisfied, but the thrills the world has to offer eventually don't thrill us, because we were made with an inherent understanding that there's something that *can* fulfill us. It just takes most of us a while to find out that it isn't something after all—it's Someone.

Because every person starts his life journey "lost," those of us who are willing to share our faith "stories" can help others know about Jesus. The greatest arguments that the world throws at us can never dispel the moments of our personal salvation experiences.

> "The greatest arguments that the world throws at us can never dispel the moments of our personal salvation experiences."

I gave my life to Christ on the campus of Ohio University. One night in the '60s, I was discouraged because I had hoped that our country would improve with political reform. I rationalized that if we students could oust the establishment, we could definitely bring about change. Yet, when I looked at my generation, I realized we were just as selfish and self-centered as everybody else. That night, I thought about something my childhood pastor once said to me: "Nothing will ever come right in the world until you take care of the sin in your own heart." His statement made such an impression on me that I never forgot it. I realized that it was not up to anyone else to make the world better. Neither the world nor anything else would ever turn out right in my life unless I dealt with my sin. That night, I gave my life to Jesus Christ.

Once we have explained the necessity of a relationship with Christ from a personal point of view, we can follow up with the biblical explanation of God's plan for all. One way to explain the message of salvation is to turn to passages found in the book of Romans. I've included specific verses below to show you one way to use the Scripture to introduce someone to Jesus.

You can start with Romans 3:23: "for all have sinned and fall short of the glory of God." Most people will agree that they've sinned. But if they don't admit they are sinners, there's no use going any further with the gospel message because their hearts are hardened. Pray for those people because God softens hearts. Never try to argue others into the kingdom. That's not our job. We are to share the gospel, not to argue for salvation. It's the work of the Holy Spirit to bring people to a saving faith.

After explaining the human condition, proceed to Romans 6:23: "For the wages of sin is death, but the free gift of God is eternal life in Christ Jesus our Lord." There is nothing we can do to earn salvation. God is ready to give us His perfect gift if we're ready to receive it. An important verse to share in the witnessing process is Romans 5:8: "But God demonstrates His own love toward us, in that while we were yet sinners, Christ died for us." He died for us! Sometimes people will ask, "Why did Christ have to die to pay for my sins?" Because we have a holy God, and a holy God cannot overlook sin. He knew we couldn't pay for our own sins, so He paid for them Himself through Christ's death on the cross. The only essential and acceptable payment was a "perfect" sacrifice—a sinless Messiah dying in our place.

The next step in leading someone to Jesus is found in Romans 10:9-10: "That if you confess with your mouth, 'Jesus is Lord,' and believe in your heart that God raised him from the dead, you will be saved" (NIV). When God created the world, He spoke it into existence. When we speak our request for Christ to come into our hearts, it is so. We must believe that He died on the cross for our sins and was raised from the dead. If we have accepted Christ as our Savior and Lord, we are a son or daughter of the living God. Taking the High Way means inviting others to join His family.

GPS: *God-Positioning Scriptures (to Reorient Your Life)*

But how can people call for help if they don't know who to trust? And how can they know who to trust if they haven't heard of the One who can be trusted? And how can they hear if nobody tells them? And how is anyone going to tell them, unless someone is sent to do it? ... The point is: Before you trust, you have to listen. But unless Christ's Word is preached, there's nothing to listen to.
—**Romans 10:14-15, 17** (The Message)

REST STOP: *Pull Over and Ponder*
What's your story? Using your own words and Scripture, how would you tell someone about your salvation? Do you have a "lost" friend who may need to hear those words?

Mile 58

Driving the Family, Part 1

The way you handle family situations will draw those around you, leading them toward a decision for Christ ... or pushing them away. Learn to lead in your family, and you will lead others to Him.

Proper Submission

When author-teacher Larry Christenson was young, he got into an argument with his mother. In the heat of the battle, Larry forgot his father was present in the room. Larry lost his head and spoke disrespectfully to his mother by blurting out, "You're a big dummy!" Immediately, his father's giant hand reached over, grabbed Larry by his shirt, and literally lifted him off the floor. Horrified, Larry looked into his father's face as his dad asked, "Who's the dummy?" Larry's natural reaction was to answer, "Me, I'm the dummy!"

Every time we disrespect somebody or call someone a name, we ought to feel the Father's hand lifting us up. While looking into our eyes, He says, "Whom are you talking about?" Our response should be, "I'm the dummy," for we are humiliating the very people God created and for whom He died. We must not cause any of God's people physical or emotional harm.

Why not embrace that attitude in our marriages? Marriage should be a natural place to learn how to come under the mission of another. I often hear spouses say critical things about their partners. That's an immature and foolish way to do marriage. Too often, guys will make little verbal jabs about their wives and say degrading things they think are hilarious. But the end result is the same: reciprocity, conflict, and warfare—a horrible way to live. Since every action has an equal and opposite reaction, these little shots will eventually bring about distance in a marriage, or at least some negative return volley.

> "Submission is not for performance, but for intimacy."

When it comes to an attitude of submission, most of us need an entire attitude adjustment. Submitting seems overwhelming and illogical to us. Americans are not raised with a submissive spirit. But with Christ, we can learn to live in submission to one another.

There was an article in *The New York Times* about an American man who, along with his kindergarten-aged son, moved to Japan. The little boy invited his classmates to an American-style birthday party. The father set up musical chairs, and after explaining the rules, he turned on the music. The Japanese children caught on to the game and immediately sat down in chairs when the music stopped. However, one of the little boy's friends stood in front of her empty chair and noticed that her friend didn't have a chair, so she stepped back and offered her chair to him. He quickly sat down. When the little girl was told that she lost the game, she looked at the dad and retorted, "You mean I lost because I was polite? The object of the game is rudeness?"

Most of us have been raised in a culture where the "object of the game" is rudeness. The goal is "Win, and do whatever is necessary to make that happen." There's a better way to live than trying to climb to the top in all-out competition. The best way is to live like Jesus, who served others. When we look at the life of Christ, we should be taken aback by His example.

Submission literally means "one mission under another." We should make our mission one that comes underneath others and lifts them up, always rendering service as to the Lord. Submission is not for performance, but for intimacy. When we bring our best self into a relationship and come under the mission of the other person, there is a closeness that develops. Christ came under the mission of God. He submitted Himself to God. In some mysterious way, the church, the bride of Christ, every Christian is to submit to Jesus. We are told in Ephesians,[1] marriage becomes a reflection of Christ and the church. Marriage offers a husband and wife a sacred relationship in which to practice the discipline of submitting to one another. Submission is more than an attitude; it's sharing the mission of God while we walk this earth.

Proper Authority

When I was a little boy, one of my neighbors was a war veteran named Francie Simon. Often, Francie would be out working in his garden, and I would offer to help. One thing I observed him doing was carefully tying sticks to his plants. I wondered why he would do that. Was he trying to restrict the plants? Was he punishing them? No, he was giving them the support they needed to grow straight.

Likewise, when parents discipline and exercise godly authority in their home, they aren't merely restricting their children. They're giving them the support they need. This gives their children the best possible chance to produce the fruit God desires to manifest in their lives. Discipline should be a mirror image of what God has done in the Law. The Law imposed enough structure so that a healthy and proper relationship could be formed with God. Proverbs says, "Foolishness is bound up in the heart of a child; the rod of discipline will remove it far from him."[2] Like the stick holding up the plants in the garden, the rod is a stabilizing factor and not just a tool for physically disciplining children. There is an old saying: Discipline is not something you do *to* a child; it is something you do *for* a child.

God has given parents authority over their children to ensure that every effort might be made to provide order, peace, productivity, and great hope for the part each child will play in helping the world be a blessing for all.

The fifth commandment instructs us to honor our fathers and mothers. Consider that the first four commandments are about our relationship with God; commandments six through ten are about relating to people. God intentionally planted the commandment about honoring our parents right in the middle. As we honor our father and mother, we build up a natural reverence for authority—especially the ultimate Authority. How children treat their parents has a lot to do with how they see God and how they reverence Him. This refers to adult children as well because no one outgrows this commandment. The word "honor" implies more than obedience. We begin with obedience because that behavior prevents children from destroying themselves. Honor is actually a matter of the heart; it's an attitude of reverence and respect.

We also need repetitive habits of respect in our lives. Just as in the Old Testament, God established ceremonial laws to give people a way to consistently show Him respect and put reverence into their lives. Today, when we teach our children manners and they learn polite interaction and to say, "thank you," "sir," and "ma'am," we are inculcating respect into them.

Some parents think that if they don't exercise their God-given authority, and interact more on a peer level, their children will love them more. That's a huge mistake. If we love our children, we demand respect because it's a part of our way of showing them respect. If we stand firm, our children may be mad at us for hours or even days, but they will come back to us. They know innately that we are giving them what they need.

I have a plant in my office that sits by a window. I probably have a lot more artificial light in my office than natural light because I often work late at night and early in the morning. However, instead of turning toward the artificial light, every leaf on that plant faces toward the natural sunlight coming through the window. Sunlight best meets the needs of the plant, and so it greatly influences the direction the plant seeks to become heartiest.

Likewise, in a spiritual sense, it is our righteousness that draws our children and all of those we interact with in the direction that invites their best opportunity for maturity. "Righteousness" can be defined as "meeting the demands of a relationship." God is completely righteous because He is always faithful to do His part in every relationship He's in. Righteousness is a requirement of godly authority. Taking the High Way means living righteously and meeting the demands of our relationships appropriately.

FOOTNOTES: 1. Ephesians 5:22-33; 2. Proverbs 22:15

GPS: *God-Positioning Scriptures (to Reorient Your Life)*

But Ruth said, "Do not urge me to leave you or turn back from following you; for where you go, I will go, and where you lodge, I will lodge. Your people shall be my people, and your God, my God."
—Ruth 1:16

REST STOP: *Pull Over and Ponder*

How are you doing currently when it comes to "meeting the demands" of your family relationships?

Mile 59

Driving the Family, Part 2

God made you unique. As you begin to appreciate these differences, ask yourself how you can complement what others are doing ... making part of your ministry supporting the ministry God has given them.

Sibling Rivalry

Although Jesus taught us how to relate to our brothers and sisters, many biblical accounts of sibling behavior showcase the worst of it. Let's revisit the story of the first siblings mentioned in the Scripture. In Genesis 4, we read about the births of Cain and Abel. The first biblical reference concerning these brothers focuses on their differences. Cain was a tiller of the ground, and Abel, a keeper of flocks. God accepted Abel's offering, but not Cain's. Cain was furious about that, but rather than try to figure out what may have caused God to respond in that way and then improve his offering accordingly, Cain lashed out at Abel. Abel's success, though, wasn't really the issue. What was going on inside of Cain was the issue.

Like Cain, sometimes we feel we've been wronged by people. Whether the wrong was imagined or real, bad memories are created when we perceive another's slight of us. Now and then, the thought might cross our mind: *Living an isolated life would be so much easier than living in community with people who may or may not "like" us.* Banish that thought. Instead, choose to do the hard work of staying engaged with people. Ultimately, that will serve you much better than the seemingly easier path of isolation. If you choose life in community, I highly recommend you do yourself a great favor: Set good boundaries.

Boundaries appropriately placed strengthen relationships. Robert Frost puts it like this in his famous poem "Mending Wall": "Good fences make good neighbors." Another saying tells us, "We do not have to change friends if we understand that friends change." Proverbs 25:17 warns, "Seldom set foot in your neighbor's house—too much of you, and he will hate you." Understanding these maxims helps us to draw boundaries or to adjust those boundaries according to the change in the other person or circumstance. We should adjust our boundaries so others can fully be who God made them to be.

> *"Boundaries appropriately placed strengthen relationships."*

As you read this Mile, you may call to mind someone in your life (excluding your spouse) who requires some distance from you. You may be worried that if you give that person distance, you'll lose him or her because the person will no longer need you. The opposite is true. If you let that person go, the relationship will be healthier and the person may discover he or she needs you more.

From the beginning, God made each of us different from the other. As we begin to appreciate our differences, we should then ask how we can complement what others are doing. Make part of your ministry supporting the ministry God has given them!

Extended Respect

Author Alex Haley once said that if we happen to see a turtle on top of a fence post, we can assume the turtle got there with some help. In the same way, all of us are where we are in life because of others' help. God made us to be a part of a rich heritage of people, and them to be a part of us. The influences of our families on us are likely to be the results of mixtures of believers and unbelievers. We all have characters in our families who have done some rather strange or funny things. However, God uses every one of those characteristics and memories—the entire mix—for His greatest good.

When I was little, the people at First Methodist Church in my hometown had a profound effect on my spiritual development long before I came to know the Lord. As I matured, God put other people into my path to teach me great spiritual principles that I would only see in retrospect. My grandparents, Carl and Lena Bashore, who meant the world to me, and Dr. Stanley Shoemaker, my childhood minister, were some of these people.

My seventh-grade English teacher, Mrs. Wolfe, who I already introduced to you, had a far-reaching impact on my life. I thank God for my Uncle Max, who had an incredible knack for telling wonderful stories. I credit my love for the art of storytelling to him. I thank God for my childhood friend "Army." He became a Christian many years before I did, and I saw how Christ took hold of his reprobate life and changed him.

I learned another important lesson from a neighbor named Jerry Kelso, a young, rugged man. My mother was an alcoholic, and once when our family was going through some tough times, Mr. Kelso came over to the house to see me. He said, "Joey, I just want you to know that I have had some very difficult times in my family, too. I love you, and if you ever need to talk, I will be here for you." I never told him what a valuable lesson that was for me. He was so strong and seemed to have it all together. Since I had nothing and was embarrassed because my life was broken, I assumed the first thing he would see when he looked at me was a standard that was not met. How wrong I was. He showed tremendous compassion. Now every time I see people whose lives are broken, instead of approaching them with standards, I approach them with sympathy. Instead of approaching them with condemnation, I approach them with compassion. I feel for them; I love them. I learned that from Jerry Kelso.

Let's be grateful for those in our lives who have taught us and provided us a rich heritage. And let's remember that God blesses us so that we can be a rich heritage to those who come after us. God's gifts and equipping are given not just to you. They are to be passed on—to the next generation and the ones who will follow them as well.

Taking the High Way means honoring Christ every day, adding to a heritage of faith that will be a great gift to those who come after us. What will we leave for our families?

GPS: *God-Positioning Scriptures (to Reorient Your Life)*

"Therefore, since we have so great a cloud of witnesses surrounding us, let us also lay aside every encumbrance and the sin which so easily entangles us, and let us run with endurance the race that is set before us. —Hebrews 12:1

REST STOP: *Pull Over and Ponder*

What lessons have you learned from past relationships (the good and the bad) about yourself, life, and God that you should seek to pass on to the next generation?

Mile 60

Revving Up Your Relationships

When people love you, they will begin to see the God you love. And when you love people, the same is also true. Evangelism naturally follows love.

Your Believing Friends: The Spirit's Nurturing

Many of us have friends who have committed their lives to Jesus Christ. We may take their faith in Christ for granted, seldom considering that their faith, like ours, is often tested. Everyone needs believing friends who come alongside and encourage them.

We live in a world full of temptations. Everyone is tempted, including Christians. Paul knew that and emphasized the importance of and the necessity for believers to be in fellowship with one another because Satan, like a predator, looks for the isolated straggler. Believing friends keep us from isolation and its accompanying dangers.

Not only does the world tempt us, it exhausts us and diminishes our efforts as well. The result is that quite often Christians feel like failures. During

281

troubled times, Christians can come alongside their demoralized brothers and sisters to provide encouragement and prayer support. Believers need to be reminded of God's faithfulness and His promises. In other words, fellow Christians need our faith added to theirs.

Your Nonbelieving Friends: The Spirit's Grafting

The Bible is plain about not putting ourselves into partnerships with unbelievers because partners must have their deepest values in common. Second Corinthians 6:14 specifically states that we are not to be yoked with unbelievers, but does that mean we can't have a friend who is an unbeliever? Does that mean we can't love a non-believer with all our heart? I think the answer to those questions is "no," and I find that answer inherent within the context of the whole text of the Bible.

Jesus truly embraced life. He delighted in the simple things like being filled with food or having His thirst satisfied. He came to be with us and enjoy much of what we enjoy. Of course, Jesus never sinned; however, He did socialize with people who did get drunk and who ate too much, and that reputation was transferred to Him as well. This is a risk we take when we hang out with sinners. Christians must remember that the Bible never gives us an excuse to sin. Instead, it gives us a reason to love and to be near those who do sin. The pattern of Christ's life is clear. He had unbelieving friends who accepted Him and enjoyed being with Him. Jesus hung out with unbelievers so that He could share God's love and show them a better way to live.

"It's important to remember in evangelism that relationships precede theology."

Love always has a purpose but not necessarily an agenda. It's purpose is to do good to the ones we care about. We can't do them good, however, if we're never around them. It is important to spend time with people who don't know God and make some allowances for who they are. Non-Christians try to satisfy their needs on their own because they don't know any other way. We can't expect their standards to be the same ones to which we hold ourselves or other Christians.

The world is not really a "deep" place. People are like children trying to get along and make things work for their benefit. They worry about the basic details of life, but they usually don't consider spiritual matters until tragedy ensues and their worlds fall apart. Jesus taught us to help the lost recognize their condition. Jesus asked, "What do you seek?"[1] He used a simple question to get to a much deeper issue—the condition of the soul. Christians should do the same thing. We can get to the deeper issues by asking questions and becoming interested in the lives of others.

We share the gospel message not because we want to be right and have them be wrong, not because we want to improve them, and not because we want them to be just like us. Instead, we share because we love people and we want them to have what we have. It's important to remember in evangelism that relationships precede theology.

Your Acquaintances: The Spirit's Scattering of Seed

What should our ministry be to our acquaintances—those with whom we associate but have no close relationship? I believe it's a ministry of *reference* and *readiness*. We reference the things of God and stand ready with a response. We are to speak God's Word to others and "scatter" references about Him instead of merely waiting to witness to just the "right" person whom we think is most likely to become a Christian. We have no idea whose heart God has prepared.

Jesus' parable of the sower in Matthew[2] helps us understand and recognize our responsibility. In the parable, as in most of Jesus' parables, we see a definite focus on taking the initiative to do good. The sower scatters the seed abundantly regardless of the soil type. Like the sower, we can't always recognize the best soil, so we must scatter seeds everywhere and let God determine which will sprout.

To witness about God, we must be able to talk about Him in ways that naturally relate to people's lives. We may speak "Christianese" in church, but what we communicate in the world—our references of Him—must make sense and be relevant. We should be ready to give people an account of what we believe because hopefully they will ask us. And when we are asked, responding with, "Because the Bible says so" probably will not satisfy the seeker. While it is the absolute truth, that answer doesn't work by itself unless you are talking to a like-minded believer. We must be willing to engage in the world of ideas and spend time with people.

Paul Harvey told about an archaeological dig in Japan in which a fossilized canoe estimated to be 2,000 years old was discovered. They found a seed in the canoe and immediately took it to a climate-controlled lab to be planted in soil. Four days later, a sprout appeared, and within fourteen weeks, a lovely pink lotus flower bloomed. The seed, which had fallen asleep two millenniums earlier, had awakened. We don't know when the seed we scatter may sprout. Our responsibility is simply to sow the Good News of Jesus Christ.

Your Admitting Enemies: The Spirit's Perfection

All of us have certain people in our lives who oppose us and everything we represent. How should we minister to these admitting enemies? Perhaps we should begin by realizing that God has placed every person in our lives for a good reason. Even Satan can only be used according to the purposes of God, as clearly documented in the book of Job. Likewise, our enemies can only be used according to the purposes of God, or He would not allow them to cross our paths.

We, however, are usually tempted to retaliate against our enemies because we have a strong sense of justice. As children, we learn to say, "That's not fair!" God expects more from those of us who call Him Father than He does from the rest of the world. We are to be perfect.[3] "Perfect" in this context does not mean "sinless"; it means "mature." In other words, we're told to grow up and not retaliate like an immature child. A Christian's normal response to enemies should not be, "I'm hurt, so I'll hurt back." Antisthenes, a Greek philosopher, said: "Always pay attention to your enemies. They will be the first ones to spot your mistakes." We would be wise to take note of his point.

I try to listen to every critical comment that comes my way because I can learn from it. In junior high school, I knew a guy who mocked and jeered everything I did. He made my life miserable until I realized God had put him in my life and I started praying about how to get along with this "mean kid." Once I did that, I became a better person, and over time that mean guy who had made me so miserable became a friend.

Of course, there are some of us who struggle with profound enemies—people who have hurt us so deeply that it's incredibly difficult to be around them. In these cases, we must understand that such pain can only be relieved by God's just intervention.

Columnist Charley Reese once wrote, "If malice were tangible and had a shape, it would look like a boomerang." How true. If we don't release people from our unforgiveness but instead try to pay them back by hurting them, we actually become prisoners to our hurt and anger. "'Vengeance is Mine, I will repay,' says the Lord."[4] That is a promise of justice from God! His justice is exact and appropriate.

Taking the High Way means praying for and honoring our friends, acquaintances, and enemies and trusting God with making all things right. Determine to do good to all men, at all times.

FOOTNOTES: 1. John 1:38; 2. Matthew 13:1-23; 3. Matthew 5:48; 4. Romans 12:19

GPS: *God-Positioning Scriptures (to Reorient Your Life)*

When the scribes of the Pharisees saw that He was eating with the sinners and tax collectors, they said to His disciples, "Why is He eating and drinking with tax collectors and sinners?" And hearing this, Jesus said to them, "It is not those who are healthy who need a physician, but those who are sick; I did not come to call the righteous, but sinners." —**Mark 2:16-17**

REST STOP: *Pull Over and Ponder*
Who are your believing friends? Your non-Christian friends? Your acquaintances? Your enemies? Do good to each by praying for them individually today.

Mile 61

Body Work

If you want your physical body to be used for spiritual good, then you must learn to rest. It's not just good for you, it will help you to be an encourager to others and they will see a much clearer invitation to life with Jesus if you aren't exhausted.

THE PURPOSE OF a Sabbath is to slow down, connect with God, and be refreshed for the work He has given you to do. It's important to rest. It's one of the Ten Commandments ... but honestly, throughout my ministry, it has been the one I've struggled with the most.

The Bible tells us that, while creating the universe, God had regular intervals of evaluation and pleasure. "By the seventh day God completed His work which He had done, and He rested."[1]

Why did God rest? Was it necessary? Of course not. He did it as a model to show us that rest is woven into creation and that we should take time out from our work projects. What God did on the seventh day was part of a pattern that we are to build into our lives. In the midst of our busy schedules, we have more than His *permission* to rest. He *commanded* we rest.

When we are diligent about "taking a Sabbath Day" every week, we will find that we are stronger physically, mentally, emotionally, and spiritually for the work He gives us to do. The first step in getting His agenda accomplished is simply to get our physical bodies into a place where we can be used in a spiritual sense. We just need to show up and offer a hug or a smile, or hold a hand, or look into the eyes of those who hurt. We need to demonstrate the love of God.

I was in my final year of seminary when my mom died. I remember driving to the funeral, feeling absolutely numb. I could not even cry. But after the funeral, when I went to the gravesite and stood next to her casket, I lost it. Someone came up behind me and put strong, loving arms around me and literally held me up as I just sobbed and crumbled. When the service was over and I had regained my composure, I turned to thank whoever comforted me ... but there was no one there. To this day, I don't know if that was an angel or a friend. I do know that at the moment, the strength of the everlasting arms of God was communicated to me more than any words ever could.

> *"The first step in getting His agenda accomplished is simply to get our physical bodies into a place where we can be used in a spiritual sense."*

One of the best ways to communicate God's love is to be an encourager. It's been said that when a parade goes by, someone needs to be sitting on the curb clapping. How true. Encouragement matters. The word literally means "to pour courage into." The Greek word for "encourage," or a derivative of it, is used 109 times in the New Testament. People line up to hear encouraging words. "Pour courage" into someone today.

When I was a freshman at college, I ate in a cafeteria that had two serving lines. After a few weeks, I noticed that one line was always longer than the other. I, of course, would select the shorter line. Each week the longer line continued to grow, and I became curious as to why people would intentionally stand in a longer line. I decided to check it out. I stood in that line for a long time, and as I came closer to one of the servers, named Steve, I noticed that he personally greeted every person as he served them. He would ask them how it was going. If they were discouraged, he would give them specific words of encouragement. He would tell them how he once felt the same way, that they were much too incredible to let this moment defeat them, and that their problems would soon pass. I loved what Steve was doing so much that I got a job as the vegetable server so I could be in the serving line near him.

The words *para caleho* mean "to come alongside and call out." They are the same words used for the Holy Spirit—One who comes alongside and encourages, sustains, and refreshes. We encourage because God is the Encourager.

Never underestimate anyone's insecurities. We all have them. There is an old saying, "Flatter me, and I may not believe you. Criticize me, and I may not like you. Ignore me, and I may not forgive you. Encourage me, and I will not forget you." When I entered seminary, the more I encountered the theological "giants" around me, the more I became unsure of myself and questioned why I was there. I believe what kept me in seminary, instead of quitting in discouragement, was the monthly letter I received from the Trouts, the janitors of my hometown church. Every month this wonderful couple sent me a letter, and occasionally, they sent a five-dollar bill, which they couldn't really afford to part with. They wrote that they believed in me. The Trouts had so much confidence in my abilities that they made me want to stay in school. Encouragers help others in their spiritual battles and give them strength.

Throughout His life, Jesus carried a mission so heavy that no mission had ever been or would ever be as monumental. Yet, while He was on earth, He still took time to celebrate life. He encouraged people, and He allowed them to encourage Him. Weddings, gatherings of friends, and children who loved to be near Him He found tremendously enjoyable. Jesus experienced joy. Jesus laughed. If He could find moments of levity, then surely we can, too! There is a drawing by Willis Wheatley titled "The Laughing Jesus." Maybe you've seen it. When I think about Jesus laughing—when I see evidences of His sense of humor in the Scripture—it makes me smile.

We don't have to be combative or scared or even worn out by the details of life, but if we lack a sense of humor, we will likely be all of the above. When we believe that God is in control, we are likely to have a buoyancy to interact more effectively *with* every person and *in* every situation.

Taking the High Way means honoring the Sabbath, taking the encouragement it brings us, and looking for opportunities God gives us to "pour courage into" others.

FOOTNOTES: 1. Genesis 2:2

GPS: *God-Positioning Scriptures (to Reorient Your Life)*

A joyful heart is good medicine, but a broken spirit dries up the bones. —**Proverbs** 17:22

 REST STOP: *Pull Over and Ponder*
When is the last time you took a Sabbath? Laughed? Just "showed up" to see how God might use you in ministry? What can you do to ensure you're using the body God's given you for spiritual good?

Mile 62

Floor It!, Part 1

God isn't limited by our limitations. Don't choose to live a life of "Whoa!" You can accelerate with confidence when you know what direction to go.

Living Beyond The Expected Limitations

Christians are all called, in no uncertain terms, to give their lives away and to live beyond expected limitations. When we feel like we don't have anything of value to give, God says, "I know—that's the point!" Or maybe we've sensed God asking us to minister to others, and we respond, "I don't know the Scriptures very well." God replies, "Precisely!" When He needs for us to comfort someone and we answer, "I am hanging on by an emotional thread myself," He says, "Exactly!" When we say, "Lord, I haven't got a great deal of faith," God says, "I know! That is the very reason you are just right."

God isn't limited by our limitations. He may ignore them or use them, but they certainly don't hinder Him. Jesus labored in the normal tasks of an ordinary

291

carpenter, yet He saved the world. God has a perfect detailed plan, and He desires to show His power through our limitations.

Giving Ourselves for the Future of Others

Living like Jesus requires us to take on His characteristics. Jesus called Himself "the good shepherd"[1] and sharply distinguished Himself from a hireling.[2] The difference between the shepherd and a hireling is demonstrated when the going gets tough. Although both may be on the job, the good shepherd serves out of love, but the hireling works for money and profit.

> **"God isn't limited by our limitations. He may ignore them or use them, but they certainly don't hinder Him."**

There are a lot of people who are Christian hirelings—in Christianity for what they can get out of it. They come to Christ to escape the punishment they would anticipate finding in hell. Those who come to faith for that reason alone are likely to have minimal interest in maturing in their faith and blessing others. They were seeking only eternal life insurance, and that had little to do, in their minds, with worshiping God and serving others.

We all have to ask ourselves, "Am I a hireling, making sure I get proper benefits for my service, or am I a shepherd, whose greatest concerns are those whom God has placed in my spheres of influence?"

When my father died, leaving my thirty-two-year-old mother with two children, Mom probably could have gone on to pursue a career in music because she had a beautiful voice and used to sing with Tommy Dorsey. Instead, she took care of my sister and me. Out of her love for us, my mother gave up her performance ambitions. Most of us, during our lifetimes, have been cared for by people who have given up sleep or their emotional and financial resources for our well-being. They have been our "shepherds," and that is what Jesus wants us to be for others.

Distribution Point: Sacred Knowledge

We are points of distribution to a world in need of God's power. It is important that we accurately assess our scope and depth of knowledge and not attempt to teach that which we do not know. This is never more important than when we are professing sacred knowledge.

All of us have encountered people who believe they know more than they really do. Jesus gave us an example of such people in Matthew.[3] The Sadducees were very narrow in their focus and their source of authority. Jesus told them they did not understand the Scriptures. Knowing the content of the Scriptures is not the same as believing and acting on God's Word, for even Satan and his host know the printed Word.

When Jesus spoke to the Sadducees, He essentially told them the life of the Scriptures is not in the words alone, but in the power and the demonstration of the Scriptures being lived out in our world. They didn't *know* the Scripture because they weren't searching and didn't understand God's power.

Sacred knowledge is not about the intellectual acumen. Sacred knowledge comes from witnessing and recognizing God's power. It has nothing to do with us, but has everything to do with the faith that God has put into us to recognize His love and provision. God can accomplish anything in our personal lives, and we can totally rely on His power. Knowledge of God will help us to be patient even when we face adversity. And it will help us to be thankful no matter what happens. Nothing can separate us from His faithfulness.

Distribution Point: Christ's Mentoring Love

Christians are to distribute the life of Jesus Christ into the whole world. It is that simple. If we are to live like Jesus, we must give ourselves to others by helping them along the way and pouring our lives into theirs. Jesus specifically chose men to join Him as disciples so He could mentor them. Jesus poured His life and faith into people who were very different from one another, and then He sent them out with a very grand mission.

Our time, attention, and energies are needed today to distribute the truth of Jesus Christ to the entire world. We need to single out people to disciple and help them imitate Jesus as we also imitate Him.

Distribution Point: Family

When Jesus lived on earth, He connected people to God *and* to one another. Our Christian family is huge. More than two billion people worldwide claim to be Christian. Whenever we meet another Christian family member, there is this camaraderie because of our connection through the Holy Spirit.

There are people who attend church today because they see the believing community as a refuge. They sort of "camp out" for Jesus and try to relate to Him without connecting to those around them. It's okay to relate to God personally and to hear Him speak, but let me caution you: The church should *not* be a place to hide us from the world and enable us to selfishly retreat from potential believers. Many of us don't like to hear that we need to "go out as salt and light" to witness to a lost world because it makes us uncomfortable. As a result, we become what I, somewhat sympathetically, refer to as "pew gum"— stuck in the church and unable to develop relationships outside of it.

Jesus, though, prayed that all believers would extend themselves and include others.[4] What we're talking about here is future family members, because the character of the kingdom is always extending a hand and offering them a way up—giving them a reason to reach out. There are people we have not yet connected with who are already in God's plan for our journey. Taking the High Way means distributing our resources and ourselves to reach those who are not yet included.

FOOTNOTES: 1. John 10:11; 2. John 10:12; 3. Matthew 22:23-29; 4. John 10:16

GPS: *God-Positioning Scriptures (to Reorient Your Life)*

Those who have insight will shine brightly like the brightness of the expanse of heaven, and those who lead the many to righteousness, like the stars forever and ever. —Daniel 12:3

REST STOP: *Pull Over and Ponder*
Consider your spiritual and social comfort zones. If God is not limited by our limitations—those we imagine or those we construct—in which ways could He stretch you to impact others?

Mile 63

Floor It!, Part 2

Jesus didn't hold back. He gave all of Himself for the sake of the kingdom. You, too, are called to make investments that will last throughout eternity ... giving your time, effort, and resources for the sake of Christ and the purposes of God.

THE WORLD CAN imitate much that the church offers in counseling, fellowship, the teaching of the principles of life, and even some wise ways of living. However, one teaching is exclusive to the church: the storing up of treasures in heaven.

What are treasures in heaven? The Bible mentions at least three. Treasure No. 1 is our relationship with God. We will be in the presence of the One who loves us.

Treasure No. 2 is the people whom we have helped come to know Jesus Christ. Parents will be eternally grateful if they take the time to pray for their children and to read and teach the Word of God to them. Knowing our loved ones will be forever with us in heaven is one of the most meaningful gifts we will ever have.

Treasure No. 3 is the eternal rewards for the things we have done. As we stand in God's presence, we won't be disappointed for those moments when we were Christlike—when we loved people who could not love themselves. People who give up a Saturday morning to paint a widow's house are not going to get to heaven and say, "I wish I'd watched that football game instead." People who teach Sunday school will not lament, "I wish I'd gone to work and earned some more money so I could buy some more stuff." Christians are the ones looking for ways to give, not ways to get.

> "Christians are the ones looking for ways to give, not ways to get."

Living like Jesus is also about stewardship—the investment of God's resources for His glory. Jesus gave all of Himself to increase the kingdom of God, and He expects us to do the same with our resources. All of our resources are meant to honor God. A good and faithful steward will continually ask these questions: "How large a portion of my resources can I put toward that which will never vanish? How can the money the Lord gives me count for all of eternity? How can I use the spiritual gifts and talents He gives me? How can I use my resources for the kingdom of God?" God gives us our answers in His time.

Often, giving of ourselves and our resources takes us completely out of our comfort zones. When the early church began, it had a multicultural base and one characteristic in common—faith. There was a sense that, despite all their differences, they needed each other to be complete.

I love the missionary movements that have their roots in America—they truly are taking Christianity one step forward. But there is an attitude filtering through some of these movements that is taking Christianity two steps back! "Let's go out there and give them our cultural way of worshiping Christ" is not how the church started, and that's not where it needs to be headed. Did you know that even today, there are Christian tribal groups that dress exactly like the missionaries who shared the faith with their ancestors generations ago? It's true. They believe it is part of what is required to be a Christian.

There have been, though, multiple hundreds of mission-focused men and women who have taken the gospel message, minus their personal cultural preferences, into the world. In the 1600s, John Eliot heard Jesus whisper in his ear that there were other sheep not yet part of the flock. As a result, he felt compelled to minister to the Algonquin Indians. Similarly, David Brainerd heard the Lord whisper to him to help bring in sheep from the Susquehanna River Indians. Years later, God whispered the same message to William Carey and Amy Carmichael to evangelize India; to Hudson Taylor, who ministered in China; and to David Livingstone, who spent his life as a missionary to people throughout Africa. In the book of Revelation, we find a wonderful illustration of how all the various cultures will worship together in heaven.[1]

What would it be like if the Lord came to all those who worship every Sunday seated in a church pew and whispered, "I have sheep not yet in the flock"? Our comfort zones must be a painful thing for God to have to deal with when He needs for us to love broader and deeper and more completely.

Go Light Your World

Jesus said, "You are the light of the world. ... Let your light shine before men in such a way that they may see your good works, and glorify your Father who is in heaven.[2] All of us have salt and light opportunities right where we are.

I end this Exit with a story: I grew up in the home of an alcoholic. My mother, whom I loved more than anybody in this entire world, had an addiction to alcohol. As a child, I thought I could fix that problem, so I worked at it throughout my childhood. Sometimes I thought that I was the one driving her to drink because I was a "boogerhead" kid. If I could just be good enough or if I could talk to her and reason with her, then maybe she would quit. Trying to be good did not work, and neither did the conversations. Then I thought maybe I should just take a firm stand and declare that as long as I was in the house, there would be no booze. So time and time again, I would pour out all of her alcohol. Of course, no matter how hard I tried, none of my attempts succeeded. Why? It was simply that I could not correct the situation because I was neither the problem nor the solution.

As we go out in the world, we need to remember that only the intervention of God in someone's life will change that person. We are not the savior; we can't change lives. Taking the High Way means understanding that our responsibility is to point others toward Him … the only One who can truly save and transform people.

FOOTNOTES: 1. Revelation 7:9-10; 2. Matthew 5:14, 16

GPS: *God-Positioning Scriptures (to Reorient Your Life)*

[Jesus said,] "If you are faithful in little things, you will be faithful in large ones. But if you are dishonest in little things, you won't be honest with greater responsibilities. And if you are untrustworthy about worldly wealth, who will trust you with the true riches of heaven? And if you are not faithful with other people's things, why should you be trusted with things of your own? No one can serve two masters. For you will hate one and love the other; you will be devoted to one and despise the other. You cannot serve both God and money." —Luke 16:10-13 (NLT)

REST STOP: *Pull Over and Ponder*

How does the knowledge that you are "not the savior" influence the way in which you interact with those who need the Savior?

EXIT 9: *WORSHIP WAY*

Mile 64

Meet the Maker

You worship the God who is in the fabric of all creation, the God who is self-existent, who is not created. If you fail to think that through, you will become sidetracked from the journey to spiritual maturity ... because you will create gods to your own liking.

God Is ... Unlimited

Urban legend has it that Eskimos have fifty-two names for snow. That's an exaggeration. They don't have fifty-two names for it, but in fact they do have a number of terms that add clarity when communicating about snow with those who live in a winter wonderland. The bottom line is names matter. When something has a name, we can identify it. And once we recognize what it is, we have to acknowledge that there are things it is not. In Exodus 3 we read an exchange between the Lord and Moses where Moses asked God His name. God said to Moses, "I AM WHO I AM."[1] Why didn't God give Moses a name by which he could distinguish Him? I AM is not a name. I AM is a state of being. It's a derivative of the Hebrew verb *to be*. The term can be interpreted as "I am right now," or "I will become what I will become," or "I will call into being what I will call into being."

Something with a name has inherent limitations or boundaries. So, when God said, "I AM WHO I AM," He put no limits on His loving essence and character. If He had given a name, He also would have indicated He had boundaries. He would have invited comparison to every other god that the people worshiped.

> "Sovereignty
> is not only about
> power and
> influence but also
> God's personal
> relationship
> with us ..."

I'll never forget a conversation I had with a man on the street one day. The conversation had made its way to the subject of God, and I asked, "Do you believe in Him?" He answered, "Oh, sure, I believe in *a* god. I believe in the kind of god that we need in order to make us better people, but I don't believe that he has an existence outside of our belief." Wow! Unfortunately, that's what many people believe. God makes it clear in Scripture that He is the God who *is*, whether we think we need Him or not. Our beliefs are not required for His existence. We don't create Him; He creates us.

"I AM WHO I AM," was what Moses needed to hear in order to trust God. It is what you and I need to know about God, as well. God has created a world without our help and continues to sustain it without our help.

God is ... Sovereign

Years ago, while teaching at a seminary, I preached a sermon on sovereignty. To prepare, I opened *Baker's Evangelical Dictionary of Biblical Theology* for a concise definition of "sovereignty." The entry had this simple notation: "See God." That's all it said. I know that wasn't meant to be a definition, but the truth is that we can't get a better definition of sovereignty—look at God.

Sovereignty, in political terminology, carries the connotation of authority and control. That same association applies when we talk about God's sovereignty; but there's more. God's control is such that He doesn't put into effect His plan merely in a mechanical way but in a personal way.

By design, the Bible always proceeds from objective truth to personal truth. God has been a personal God throughout history. Sovereignty is not only about power and influence but also God's personal relationship with us and our personal response to His love.

God helped clarify His unfathomable sovereignty when He said, "I am God, and there is no one like Me."[2] He is sovereign in the present, the past, and the future. If we want to understand what is going on in our lives right now, taking a look at how God arranged the past can provide clarity and allow us to recognize His personal intervention in our lives. The fact is, God chooses whomever He wants, whenever He wants, however He wants, for whatever He wants. The things in our past that we think will hinder our ability to do work for God actually won't inhibit us *if* we surrender them to God. He can take anything from our past and put it to good use. God can perform a "takeover" in our lives at any time.

God Is ... Incomprehensible

One of God's most perplexing attributes is incomprehensibility. It seems odd that we would worship God for what we can't understand about Him. Yet, our lack of understanding often acts as more of a catalyst to draw us closer to Him than the things we can understand. If our god is limited to the scope of our own mind and understanding, if he is no bigger than we are, eventually we will find him inadequate. The Germans have an applicable saying: *Ein Gott, der begriffen warden kann, ist kein Gott,* or "A god that can be comprehended is no God." The real God is beyond our intellectual limits—He is incomprehensible.

The Bible tells us that Job looked for a theological explanation for the tragic events in his life and that he floundered in his query. Zophar, the youngest of his friends, asked Job: "Can you discover the depths of God? Can you discover the limits of the Almighty?"[3] If we were asked these questions, how would we answer them? We often try to find solutions to our questions about God's behavior that make sense from our limited perspective. Such solutions inevitably leave us dissatisfied.

We have all gone through times in our lives when we sensed something was happening that was far beyond our understanding. Maybe it was a feeling that overwhelmed us as we looked at nature, or maybe it was a foreshadowing of what our life would be like in the future, but at one time or another we have had an acute awareness of God. In those moments, we had the impression that even if we understood it, we would be unable to relate to what was truly going on.

Particle physics and astrophysics indicate that reality doesn't consist solely of three dimensions, yet those are the dimensions we deal with every day. Some scientific minds postulate that in order for the universe we perceive to exist, in order to have a reality that's explained through scientific formulas, the universe must have at least ten dimensions. Some researchers speculate that a moment after the very beginning of creation—a ten millionth of a trillionth of a trillionth of a second to be exact, a mysterious, monumental division in the universe's dimensions occurred. At least six dimensions may have remained as part of reality, but not all of them were incorporated into life as we know it. Those six are still around, scientists say.

Only a limited number of dimensions were needed for human life, so matter and energy began to exist within height, length, width, and time. Our theology is built upon the limitations of those four known dimensions, which amount to the basis for our understanding of the universe. Perhaps the question Zophar was actually asking Job was, "Hey, have you considered all the dimensions? Or are you stuck to your limited understanding?"

Much of the theology we argue over—theology over which churches have split—will be revealed as nonsense on the day we know reality as God knows it. One day we will see Him face to face, but right now we operate with limited sight. Taking the High Way means worshiping fully a God whom we can only partially understand.

FOOTNOTES: 1. Exodus 3:14; 2. Isaiah 46:9; 3. Job 11:7

GPS: *God-Positioning Scriptures (to Reorient Your Life)*

For in this hope we were saved. But hope that is seen is no hope at all. Who hopes for what he already has? But if we hope for what we do not yet have, we wait for it patiently.
—**Romans 8:24-25** (NIV)

REST STOP: *Pull Over and Ponder*
Prayerfully consider the question, "Who am I, and what have I been given to do?" Are you willing to believe God has plans for your life beyond your limited understanding?

Mile 65

Taking the Lead

Sometimes, it's not easy sharing the road. Those around you can get in the way. Before you pass them by, remember that God often puts people in your path ... that you might lead them to Him.

God Is ... Faithful

Faithfulness is the personal side of sovereignty. God's sovereignty is so broad, so deep, and so pervasive, that it has to be personal in order for us to even begin to understand it. God uses ordinary events and objects to help His people recognize His faithfulness. The Bible is filled with stories of regular people who lived ordinary lives, and when God manifested Himself in some personal way, they praised Him for His faithfulness.

Our God is a covenant God. A covenant is a binding relationship, and as the psalmist says, is not only a covenant between God and individuals, but also between people. "To all generations I will make known Your faithfulness with my mouth."[1] This is how God has worked since the beginning, giving

His blessings when His people step out in faith to do what He's asked them to do. God's faithfulness extended through Abraham to Isaac and then to Jacob. By the time the biblical story gets to Joseph, Jacob's son and the great-grandson of Abraham, a pattern seems obvious.

Through Abraham's seed, God confirmed His covenant. He was preparing a people to expand the kingdom of God. God was guiding each one of those relationships, from Abraham to Joseph, as the inherited qualities were being passed down from generation to generation. Now, as was the case then, God works in each person's life to fulfill His divine purposes.

> *"God works in each person's life to fulfill His divine purposes."*

I am fully aware that God constructed my life *for others*. Many times He did so through my family—"so great a cloud of witnesses."[2] Through my family, God gave me a strong sense of His presence. He gave me a strong love for learning. He gave me a desire to see past the ornery streak in people's dispositions and glimpse their potential. Through my family, God gave me a desire to love others well. He gave me a yearning to be faithful to Him and to the work He has given me to do. God didn't put these qualities in my life for me alone, but for the benefit of others as well.

Whom did God put in your life to ensure that you would find your way into His presence? He or she is there by God's design as part of God's faithfulness to you so that you can now benefit others.

God Is ... a Fortress

God is the One who protects us. He watches over us. So when we get scared, whether that fear is due to external or internal provocations, our God is more than capable of keeping us safe.

Psalms 91 uses contrasting metaphors to describe God's protection of our soul. God says that He will cover us with his "pinions," an analogy from nature. A bird will cover her young with her pinions (her wings) to protect them from the elements and give them warmth as they grow. The psalmist then likens God's faithfulness to a shield and bulwark. The reason we can keep on fighting the enemies of our soul is because our fortress will never fail. I thank God for this contrasting imagery that the psalmist uses to explain God's power, as well as His compassionate concern.

God is our protector, but the evidence is overwhelming, that good people, even God's servants, experience danger and tragedy. One such incident happened in India. Australian missionaries, a man and his two young sons, were sitting in their Jeep when a gang of radical Hindus came and doused their Jeep with gasoline and burned it. This story, and others similar in their apparent injustice, make our hearts ache and our minds fill with questions. The fact of the matter is that we aren't going to have all the answers until we're in the presence of God Himself. Still, some answers we do have now: "Your eyes have seen my unformed substance; and in Your book were all written the days that were ordained for me, when as yet there was not one of them."[3] In other words, God knows every day of our lives, and we're not going to die a single day before He permits our death. God is a fortress. He is imminent, right next to us, caring for our every concern.

God Is ... Just

The story of God's justice starts from either accepting justice on the basis of our relationship with Him or vainly trying to make justice of our own devising. Are we willing to accept His version of the story or foolishly insist that our version of the world is as good as His? God's grace removes our sin that deserves the full condemnation of the law. Those who belong to God have a relationship that is safe in Him, and they will appear before the judgment throne as if they had never sinned. That's God's justice.

There are people who believe that they are getting away with sin. They claim to believe in God, but they go through life as if God makes no demands. They sin but believe they won't get caught. And because they're not paying a penalty on earth, they keep on sinning, moving farther away from God. Many other people, though, recognize their sin for what it is. For them, God's justice has very different implications. In spite of their inclination toward sin, faith in God assures them that in the final judgment, God will not see their sin; His focus will be on Christ's payment for it. I am one of the many who humbly and gratefully depend on the forgiveness of Jesus Christ, for my pardon. I hope you do, too!

In 1829, George Wilson held up a post office, and in the midst of that hold-up killed a man. He was caught and sentenced to be hanged. Wilson said he didn't mean to do it—it just happened, and people believed him. Some of George's friends went to President Andrew Johnson to beg for his pardon. Johnson granted it, but Wilson wouldn't accept it. Even though he had not intended to kill the man, he was guilty. He would pay for it on his own, he said. His friends appealed to the Supreme Court, and Chief Justice John Marshall handed down this decision: a pardon that's not accepted is not a pardon. Wilson was hanged.

Jesus Christ died on the cross to pardon us all. But a pardon that is not accepted is no pardon.

God Is ... Merciful

Our God is not only just; He is also merciful. Americans have this mistaken idea that mercy is "being nice." We think of nice people as pleasant or naive. Being a nice person is much better than being a mean person, but the word "nice" isn't in the Bible. Being nice doesn't take courage. Granting mercy, on the other hand, is courageous. The term "mercy" implies that even though we've been hurt, we don't choose to administer payback to the ones who hurt us. "Nice" is the default position of knowing how to act in the absence of provocation. Mercy is specific, purposeful, intentional, and incisive.

The word "mercy" in Hebrew comes from the same root as the word "womb." It implies an intimate, protective relationship. "So the LORD has compassion on those who fear Him. For He himself knows our frame; He is mindful that we are but dust."[4] I'm glad He knows that. If we understood that better, our expectations would be a lot more realistic.

In Scripture, all the notable and powerful people, all the mighty generals, all the heroes of faith were great, not because of their power, but because of their mercy. Think about the parable in Matthew 18 about the ruler who was owed a large amount of money. In those days, not only would a debtor's goods be sold, but also he and his family would be sold as slaves in order to pay back the debt. The debtor in this parable was unable to pay back the ruler, but the ruler graciously forgave the debt. That ruler was a great man, not because he exercised power, but because he exercised mercy. He was mighty, not because he demanded justice, but because he didn't.

God has abundant mercy available for us. As His children, we need to live in it. God's door of mercy is always open for us. If you have been away from Him for a long time, go home. He loves you and wants you to be with Him. Why do we keep beating ourselves up? Who are we to say, "If I hold myself guilty, and if I make myself feel bad, then maybe I will help serve the cause of justice." Our feeling bad is not going to make the world better. Taking the High Way means claiming His forgiveness and helping others do the same.

FOOTNOTES: 1. Psalm 89:1; 2. Hebrews 12:1; 3. Psalm 139:16; 4. Psalm 103:13-14

GPS: *God-Positioning Scriptures (to Reorient Your Life)*

Christ arrives right on time to make this happen. He didn't, and doesn't, wait for us to get ready. He presented himself for this sacrificial death when we were far too weak and rebellious to do anything to get ourselves ready. And even if we hadn't been so weak, we wouldn't have known what to do anyway. We can understand someone dying for a person worth dying for, and we can understand how someone good and noble could inspire us to selfless sacrifice. But God put his love on the line for us by offering his Son in sacrificial death while we were of no use whatever to him. —**Romans 5:8 (The Message)**

REST STOP: *Pull Over and Ponder*
God is ... faithful, protecting, just, and merciful. Where do you see these traits of God working in your life and in the lives of those around you?

Mile 66

Full Coverage, Part 1

Sometimes, you feel alone ... that no one could possibly comprehend what you're going through. Don't believe that for a minute. Even if you have a long road ahead, the One who called you is more than enough to cover you on the journey.

A FEW MILES BACK, we explored how God revealed himself as I AM, which is not a name, but a term of being. However, throughout Scripture, God is actually known by many names. Let's consider some of the various names of God—names that attest to the precise ways He has chosen to reveal Himself throughout the generations.

Jehovah Sabbaoth

Jehovah Sabbaoth is a name that indicates that He is the Lord of hosts. Jehovah Sabbaoth is a military term, but it could pertain to any structured group with a leader or commander such as a team, a business company, a family or a community. We'll stick with the military application, because the meaning in this sense is the epitome of what we're talking about—an organization with the purpose of gaining a victory.

The Lord of hosts is the commander of the armies of heaven, and the whole earth is filled with His glory. When we worship, we stand in awe of the Commander. When we talk about serving the Lord of hosts, we first need to understand what an honor it is to be called at all and then to realize how personal the call is. Consider the vastness of the Body of Christ, the church throughout time, because the call isn't just about us alone. God organizes the armies of heaven as well as the forces of earth, and the heavenly host is there to accomplish God's will in the Spirit and in the flesh, to be at His disposal for divine purposes on earth.

> *"... God desires only our love. He wins our battles through a commitment of the heart."*

When you face difficult situations, when you don't have anyone rooting for you, remember that all the armies of heaven are at your disposal for His causes. God desires our love, and He wins our battles through a commitment of your heart. The outcomes of our struggles are the outcomes God has chosen. Abraham Lincoln once said, "I would never pray that God is on my side. I would pray that I am on His side."

Jehovah Jireh

The name Jehovah Jireh indicates that He is the Lord who will provide for all of our needs. This name comes from the story in Genesis 22 of the great trial of Abraham and his son, Isaac. This story illustrates the idea that as we mature in our dependence on Christ, God reveals Himself just in time. God takes us through a series of trials in life because He wants us to mature. God wants to strengthen us, as He did His servants of old.

All through Abraham's life, there was test after test. Some of them he passed; some of them he failed. But he progressed because God was maturing him. In all his sea of troubles, Abraham did not abandon his faith in God. After a lifetime of testing, Abraham was faced with the hardest test that any loving parent can be asked to endure. "Take now your son, your only son, whom you love, Isaac, ... and offer him there as a burnt offering."[1] Can you imagine what he thought? Abraham didn't know the outcome of the test, but he knew his God. Abraham submitted to God and trusted Him to provide for his physical and spiritual needs.

Many people look to God as the supplier of temporal needs. Often the only reason we are disappointed with God is because we want something that we can't have. And we want whatever-it-is because we think somehow we deserve it. But He's told us to get past the physical and develop an eternal perspective. Surprisingly, when we ask Christ to meet our spiritual needs, He often meets our physical and material needs as well.

God comes to us in the nick of time; He's never too late. The breakthrough in our lives will come when we are willing to say, "God, when I consider the most precious thing in my life, I'm willing to sacrifice even that to honor You."

Because we don't know that we believe something totally until our beliefs are challenged, it is a necessity that we be tested. The moment Abraham placed his trust completely in God, the moment that Abraham raised his eyes in surrender to God's will, God provided the sacrifice. Abraham called the name of that place, "the Lord will provide." It's true that God's vision plus our obedience yields God's provision. Taking the High Way means knowing and trusting that God will provide.

FOOTNOTES: 1. Genesis 22:2

GPS: *God-Positioning Scriptures (to Reorient Your Life)*

All those gathered here will know that it is not by sword or spear that the LORD saves; for the battle is the LORD's, and he will give all of you into our hands. —**1 Samuel 17:47 (NIV)**

 REST STOP: *Pull Over and Ponder*
The names of God mentioned in this Mile find their foundation in God's immense power. Call God by these names in prayer this week as you reflect on the potential present in His power.

Mile 67

Full Coverage, Part 2

You will have troubles in an imperfect and fallen world. A sense of fulfillment comes from being in the presence of God ... regardless of your circumstances.

Jehovah Rapha

Of all God's attributes, the one described by the name we find in Exodus 15:26 is one of the most beloved, yet bewildering, aspects of God. "For I, the LORD, am your healer." Jehovah Rapha indicates He is the Lord who heals us. When God heals our infirmities, most of us respond to Him with gratefulness and love. But because sometimes He doesn't heal us or the people we love, we are perplexed by what appears to us to be God's random use of His healing power.

Sadly, there has been a lot of warped teaching concerning healing. Misconception of God's intentions can keep us from worshiping Him fully. Misconception number one is that sickness or disability results from a willful act of disobedience to God. It's true that illness sometimes comes through living a profligate life; it's not true that there's a simple cause-and-effect relationship between sin and sickness. The idea that illness is always caused by sin is a fallacy. If that were true, we'd be sick all the time.

Misconception number two is that all healing is immediate and instantaneous. If someone is ill and has petitioned God, saying, "God, please heal me," and healing doesn't take place right away, the lack of a noticeable, immediate response doesn't mean that God has turned a deaf ear to the petitioner. God chooses when and how to heal.

The third misconception is that if a person has enough faith he/she will be healed. We Christians often "shoot" our wounded by telling them they're not improving because their faith is not strong enough. If only they exercised more faith, things would be different, we tell them. As if we depend on our faith rather than our God for healing! When we understand Jehovah Rapha, the Lord, the One who heals us, we see that it's not the amount of faith that matters, but the One in whom we put our faith.

Misconception number four—we come to Christ and expect Him to heal according to the way we anticipate. We want God to conform to our expectations and overlook the fact that He may work in unpredictable ways. Misconceptions occur when we take what is in the realm of God and try to limit it to the realm of man. Healing is part of God's job description. The nature of Jehovah Rapha is to heal.

> **"We all need healing from God on a daily basis ... spiritually and often physically."**

Although God comes to us as a healer, He does not heal indiscriminately. He chooses His subject, method, time, and place. There are five different means of healing described in the Bible. As we examine them, remember that it's God's option to choose which one He wants to use.

One of the most common ways God heals is easily overlooked. He has created within our bodies immune systems that keep us well and fight illness. It is a credit to God's amazing creativity that most of us are healthy most days while surrounded by viruses and bacteria that have the potential to wreak havoc on our bodies. In addition to the natural process God uses to heal us, on occasion He sometimes will choose to instantaneously and miraculously make us well. This method tends to get the most rave reviews for two reasons:

it fixes the problem immediately, and it reminds us of the incredible awesome power of our God. While you and I might find this to be our favorite of God's methods, percentages of healings that come about this way indicate that it is not likely that this is God's favorite method.

God also heals through medical professionals. When medicine is involved in healing God is not absent. God sometimes opts to allow medicine to effect the cure.

Another of God's healing methods may be a bit more difficult to grasp. God sometimes will heal emotions and attitudes we hold, rather than take the pain away. The apostle Paul cried out to God on at least three occasions to take away "the thorn in my flesh."[1] But each time he pleaded, God said, "No." Jesus told Paul, "My grace is sufficient for you, for my power is perfected in weakness."[2] God had a purpose in Paul's life that involved not taking the disability away. With this "thorn in the flesh," Paul came to experience the power of God as few ever do.

The last form of healing is the one that comes in the resurrection, not on this side of heaven but in the world to come.[3] Many people have expressed anger with God when they asked Him to heal a loved one and He answered in a way they found unsatisfactory. Sometimes healing comes on the other side of death. God always answers prayer in the way He knows will be best. The mode and the timing of the healing are His prerogative. We must trust Him in that process.

The Bible makes the statement that God heals all our diseases. In Isaiah 53, we learn that Jesus Christ heals all our iniquities (sins) as well. Is it "easier" to heal disease or sins? God heals our physical and spiritual weaknesses with equal ease. We've all done some really stupid things in life, haven't we? In fact, we've done some of them quite intentionally, and premeditated stupidity is the worst. Whether we err out of ignorance or intention, we suffer the consequences. But even for the most harmful and sinful of those things, God can provide a remedy. He makes no distinction. God loves every person. He hates our sin, but His character does not let Him hate us.

As we live— and even as we die—Jehovah Rapha, the Lord who Heals, is at work within us, healing our lives, molding our frailty and vulnerability for His purpose.

Jehovah Shalom

Peace is not just an absence of conflict; peace is much deeper than that. It is Jehovah Shalom—the Lord is peace. The Lord is our peace, no matter what storms may come. We fully realize the worth of the Anchor, when we are in the storm.

We all have conflicts in our lives. Often we don't understand the reasons for them because we've never taken the time to examine the underlying causes. When we're in conflict with someone, automatically we think the other person is the problem. A husband fights with his wife, or a wife fights with her husband. Each thinks the other is at fault. We may hope that "straightening out" spouses, friends, coworkers, or family members will result in our happiness, but the truth is that they are neither the real problem, nor the real solution. Until we go to God on our knees, relational problems are likely to grow worse. Taking the High Way means living our life for an audience of One and choosing to honor God with every decision and effort we make. His grace is sufficient to guarantee our final victory.

FOOTNOTES: 1. 2 Corinthians 12:7; 2. 2 Corinthians 12:9; 3. 1 Corinthians 15:42

GPS: *God-Positioning Scriptures (to Reorient Your Life)*

God, our God, will take care of the hidden things but the revealed things are our business. It's up to us and our children to attend to all the terms in this Revelation. —**Deuteronomy 29:29** (The Message)

REST STOP: *Pull Over and Ponder*
Consider the four misconceptions about healing. Keep them in mind as you pray for and support those you know in need of healing.

Mile 68

Service Road

Jesus always observed the people around Him and looked for openings to minister personally to them. You would be wise to follow His lead.

WHO IS THE God we worship? Who is this Creator God who is both singular and plural at once? He is Father, Son, and Holy Spirit, and that triune relationship implies that our God is a relational God. To be in His image is to be in relationship. We must be careful not to isolate ourselves, but to seek to serve one another as individuals and as churches.

The plural nature of relationships in God can be seen in the church. The original church was not a collection of disparate groups with strikingly different belief systems. There was one church uniquely expressed through congregations in many places. That distributed model of church makes so much sense. God is a *sending* God. God *sent* Jesus to us from heaven. At the end of His time on Earth, Jesus *sent* believers into all the world. For the first three centuries, the church was on the go, and the church today should be on the go as well.

I believe that the church has to be structured to work on the move. It has to disperse into the world. Ministry should happen along the way, in our homes, communities, and beyond. Jesus intended for the church to connect with other believers and to *send* people out into the world. He promised that He would be with us through it all.

God's presence was made manifest in a physical sense in Jesus Christ. His strategic mission was to reveal the true character of God the Father, to show the way to salvation, to serve as propitiation for sin, and to establish God's representative body, His church, on earth. The church represents the continued physical presence of Christ to finish the work of preparing a people for the kingdom.

When I look at the relationships that God gives to Northland Church and to me personally, I realize that each relationship is the result of praying. Each one comes through seeking God and asking, "God, where would You have us be? What would You have us do?" No one else can define God's plan for our lives. Only we know how God has wired us, how He has ordered the events of our lives, and it's through consistent and conscientious praying that we can hear what God wants us to do next. Prayer is paramount in God's strategy.

> *"... it's through consistent and conscientious praying that we can hear what God wants us to do next."*

Martin Luther King, Jr., said, "To be a Christian without praying is no more possible than to be alive without breathing."

Our personal purpose and value are revealed as we pray. But also we must recognize God's instruction corporately. Within a church setting, God may show us how we can accomplish His mission through a cooperative effort. As a distributed church, God is calling us to meet people, to develop relationships, and to further develop ministry. Jesus counted every single believer in Christ as a part of the church. Revelation 7 paints a picture of the scene around the throne of the kingdom of God. Throngs of people from all over the globe, from every nation, tribe, and language, worship God. My desire to be in that scene is the primary reason I get out of bed in the morning and take up my duties for the day. I can't wait to witness that heavenly event. If we believe people will worship together in heaven, why don't we do it now? What's stopping us? As distinct groups join in worship together with the help of wireless technology, God's distributed church won't have or need a geographic center. The center, or heart, will be wherever ministry is happening and wherever His people are serving in His name. Case in point: currently, thousands of individuals worldwide participate, live, in the worship services at Northland Church, via their computer or cell phones. They aren't just "watching" the service, they are fully participating—we see their picture, welcome them by name, know their location and how many people are there worshiping with them. This online community is able to meet and greet others online, offer prayers, and ask questions of the online pastor. Certainly Northland isn't the only church embracing wireless ministry opportunities; this is only one aspect of the distributed model of church.

One of the most significant aspects of distributed ministry is the value it places on acts of service. In the 1900's Albert Schweitzer, German-French theologian, musician, philosopher, and physician, once made the comment, "I don't know what your destiny will be, but one thing I do know: the only ones among you who will be really happy are those who have sought and found how to serve." Dr. Schweitzer attributed his inspiration to pursue a life of serving others to Jesus, the ultimate servant. Jesus inspires Christians everywhere yet today to a life of worship and service. When Jesus washed the disciples' feet, He turned a traditional custom upside down. Traditionally, a guest would enter the house from the dusty road and a servant would wash his feet before dinner. When the host did not have a servant, the children washed the adults' feet, and the wife washed the husband's feet. When the disciples entered that room, no servants were present to perform the foot-washing task, so they waited to see who would take on the role of servant. No one made the first move. The meal began. The supper wound down, and the disciples reclined, their feet still unwashed. Jesus stood, removed His robe, and wrapped a towel around His waist. They knew what was coming. Jesus poured water into a basin. What an awful, wonderful moment! Think of it, the God of the Universe washing feet.

By humbling Himself to the role of a servant, Jesus demonstrated to His friends that they had worth in His sight. The disciples, in one moment, suffered the shame of pride and witnessed an amazing affirmation of worth from God.

A member of our congregation once asked me, "What do you think is the most valuable act of service you can render to somebody?" The answer for me was automatic: pay attention to a person's life. Jesus met people's physical and spiritual needs. He was intentionally aware of those around Him. Serving isn't limited to tasks that we perform. Service is the amount of interest and love we convey. Taking the High Way means living a life of service, knowing that God has blessed us in order that we might be a blessing.

GPS: God-Positioning Scriptures (to Reorient Your Life)

It is absolutely clear that God has called you to a free life. Just make sure that you don't use this freedom as an excuse to do whatever you want to do and destroy your freedom. Rather, use your freedom to serve one another in love; that's how freedom grows. For everything we know about God's Word is summed up in a single sentence: Love others as you love yourself. That's an act of true freedom. If you bite and ravage each other, watch out—in no time at all you will be annihilating each other, and where will your precious freedom be then? —**Galatians 5:13-15 (The Message)**

REST STOP: *Pull Over and Ponder*
Purpose to pay attention to the lives of the people God's placed around you this week. What does this intentional observance teach you about how you can best serve each person right where they're at?

322

Mile 69

Guiding the Way

As your Shepherd and Overseer, Christ is guiding you on your journey. And, even though you may not realize it, He is working through you … guiding others unto Himself.

THE BIBLE DESCRIBES two methods God uses to bring about transformation in our lives. One is a personal approach, God as a Shepherd; the other is a corporate approach, God as Overseer.

The image in Isaiah 40 is of a shepherd who gathers a lamb in his arms. But how many lambs can a shepherd gather in his arms? He can only carry one, or two, perhaps even three—if he is very strong. This illustration implies Someone knows us in a deep, personal caring way. Christ nurtures us individually. We're not one in billions, desperately vying for His attention. He knows each one of us.

Christ shepherds us via the small number of people we know best at any one time. Only some of them may be Christian, but Christ is not limited to using only Christians to instruct and encourage us. God uses many people and situations during our lifetime to shape our character. Our growth will come from voices both kind and harsh, administering the kind of pastoral care we need. As Christians, we also have the responsibility to care for and nurture people that we know God has put into our lives.

God also may choose to bring about transformation in our lives using a more corporate approach: God as Overseer. For example, I am more of an *episkopos*—an overseer in our local church—than I am an attentive shepherd. It's my job as a pastor to see that members of the congregation have what they need to become mature in Christ and participate in a personal ministry. I may never know every person by name, but as long as God provides an avenue through Northland for people to grow into the fullness of Christ and develop their gifts for ministry, then the role of overseer has value. Christ is the *episkopos* of our souls. Even now, He is overseeing circumstances in our lives in ways that we could never imagine.

Sheryl, a Northland church member, told a story about her grandfather, a faithful Christian who loved to minister to churches. During the Great Depression he saved and scraped together every penny he could to buy a needed pair of eyeglasses. At about that same time, he'd started participating in a church project that involved building shipping crates in which to send supplies to a Chinese missionary. Sheryl remembers watching him construct the crates by hand. Because he was not yet comfortable with his new glasses, he fumbled with them as he worked, alternately between stuffing them in his shirt pocket and taking them back out. After volunteers had packed all the crates, her grandfather reached into his pocket and discovered that his glasses were gone. They searched the church a dozen times but the glasses never turned up. Sheryl's grandfather was really angry at God over his unfortunate circumstances.

> *"Our acts of kindness or encouragement can change a life."*

The next summer, the missionary from China visited all the churches that had supported his work. Sheryl sat in the back pew by her grandfather, who was still a bit ticked off at God. "I can't thank you enough for what you sent us," the missionary said. "Personally, I want to especially thank you for that pair of glasses. Right before those crates came, Communist soldiers destroyed everything we had, including my glasses. I got terrible headaches, vertigo and nausea every day, so when we opened up those crates, and I saw those glasses, I cried. They fit perfectly, and were exactly my prescription." Everybody in the church looked puzzled, and some murmured, "What glasses?" Sheryl looked at her grandfather, who had tears streaming down his face.

Christ is the great Overseer of circumstances. He uses us to continue His work of ministry on Earth. Our acts of kindness or encouragement can change a life. It's irrelevant whether or not the recipients of our good intentions ever know who we are. We may not know until we go to live in heaven what impact we had on another's life.

Jesus the Shepherd or Overseer is a contrast to another description Scripture gives us of Jesus. Numerous places in the New Testament, we see Him described as the High Priest. Both the shepherd and the overseer relate to horizontal, practical ministries. The shepherd imagery is personal, and the overseer imagery is corporate. The station of high priest, on the other hand, is a picture of a vertical, hierarchical ministry. How is it that Jesus can embody all these roles? Why is it that we need Him to do so?

When the Bible says we have a high priest that can sympathize with us, I can't adequately explain to you how comforting and remarkable that theological statement is. The living God became one of us. Compare that with the Jewish view: God was holy by virtue of His being so different, apart from humankind, and Greek pagan gods were deities not only because of their power, but also because they simply did not care. To be affected by human beings meant conferring on them some degree of power over the gods. The Greek gods, as a consequence, were completely unconcerned with and unmoved by human affairs. But our High Priest is not remote; He sympathizes with us.

Jesus was 30 years old before He began His ministry. And immediately before undertaking His mission, He "... was led up by the Spirit into the wilderness to be tempted by the devil."[1] But the Bible says He never sinned, suggesting two things: He did not encourage temptation and He did not act on Satan's enticements. Temptation is part of human existence. Having rebuffed the Tempter's advances, Jesus understands the trials and tribulations we go through. Everything we think, He thought. He was tempted and could have fallen prey to sin, but He did not. We are tempted, and all too often we fall. But we have a forgiving God who is acquainted with our infirmities.

Taking the High Way means trusting in Jesus: our Shepherd, Overseer and High Priest.

___

FOOTNOTES: 1. Matthew 4:1

GPS: *God-Positioning Scriptures (to Reorient Your Life)*

"Therefore, since we have a great high priest who has passed through the heavens, Jesus the Son of God, let us hold fast our confession. For we do not have a high priest who cannot sympathize with our weaknesses, but One who has been tempted in all things as we are, yet without sin. Therefore let us draw near with confidence to the throne of grace, so that we may receive mercy and find grace to help in time of need." —**Hebrews 4:14-16**

REST STOP: *Pull Over and Ponder*

How do you see God acting as Shepherd, Overseer and High Priest in your current place in life? Take time to commit the following verse to memory. You will be glad you did.

No temptation has seized you except what is common to man. And God is faithful; he will not let you be tempted beyond what you can bear. But when you are tempted, he will also provide a way out so that you can stand up under it. —I Corinthians 10:13 (NIV)

Mile 70

A Spirit-ed Journey

One of the biggest temptations you will face on your journey is this: What you begin in the Spirit, you try to perfect in the flesh. This habit will make progress all but impossible.

AFTER 10 MINUTES in the pool, swimming laps like a seal just below the surface of the water, I realized I was missing a vitally important ingredient found in other sports—air. I must have swallowed half the pool. It reminded me of the way most Christians live their lives. We become fully immersed in the world, initially exercising our best efforts; but as we push past comfort zones, at some point, we sense we are in over our heads. We gulp, panic, and try desperately to get back on top of it all. Problem is, we've swallowed so much of our surroundings we aren't sure what we need anymore to make our best effort truly best.

What happens when we have no energy, no motivation, no love, and no ideal. What can we do then? What can God do? We've learned that God doesn't need to work within our limitations. God doesn't need to make the best out of a bad situation, and He doesn't confine Himself to mere potential. God is not limited to the lesser of two evils. God doesn't need a fresh point of view. He can (and does) bring forth something out of nothing.

If you feel like you are "empty" and that your heart is void, know that your empty heart doesn't hinder God. Some of His greatest miracles have had to do with filling empty spaces. So, when a wife says, "God, I wish I could love my husband, but that love died a long time ago. There is nothing there." Or a sibling says, "God, I wish I could forgive my brother, but I can't even work up the desire to *want* to forgive." We need to remember God can bring something out of nothing. In fact, that is one of His specialties.

Making Nothing Out of Something

When God brings something good out of nothing, Satan will soon show up. It was that way in the Garden of Eden, in the ministry of Jesus, and in our lives today. He will oppose our Christian walk, and he will make every attempt to ruin us. Don't allow him to have anything of value.

Out of experiences with temptation, we learn that something inside us opposes steps of faith we consider taking. We often sabotage our own joy, injure the very relationships we want to strengthen, or destroy the goals we set. Then we berate ourselves for doing the senseless things we hate. Why do we act like this? It is the mystery of lawlessness.[1]

As soon as we acknowledge a moral obligation and avoid it, or recognize something we should not do and proceed to do it, the mystery of lawlessness takes full effect; and its vision of "don't cooperate," mission of "don't submit," and core value of "be independent" turn something wonderful we could have accomplished into nothing. When this happens, repent and direct your efforts back toward God, the One who specializes in bringing something out of nothing.

Birthing a Multicultural Church

The Holy Spirit is personal, and He also moves corporately upon the body of Christ, the church. The story of the Spirit's creation of a multi-dimensional, multicultural church is thrilling.

Can you imagine the variety of people converging on Jerusalem nearly 2,000 years ago for the feast days of Pentecost? The observance of three festivals was mandated for all the Jews within 20 miles of Jerusalem, and visitors from other countries also made the pilgrimage to celebrate.

The biblical narrative centers on the disciples, about 120 believers, meeting in a room. With just so few believers, God's multicultural church began.

"God can bring something out of nothing. In fact that is one of His specialties."

"And they were all filled with the Holy Spirit and began to speak in other languages, as the Spirit was giving them utterance."[2] This was an actual event that the disciples experienced, and because they did, those visitors in Jerusalem who spoke varied languages were all able to hear of God's mighty works from the lips of those who knew Jesus personally. Still today, when believers gather with others to experience worship, the Lord transforms us. We sense His presence, perhaps not by tongues of fire, but He speaks to us in other ways. We are brothers and sisters of Christ all over the world, and as we worship together and proclaim Christ, the world will undergo a transformation.

Never before has a more opportune time come our way to fellowship with believers around the world than now. Their experiences in faith will strengthen us, and we can encourage them as Scripture commands us to.

Gifting Every Believer for the Common Good

I remember reading a quote from Marie Rambert, founder of the first ballet school in England. She said her goal for the school was "to create an environment where creation is possible." I believe that the Holy Spirit has the same goal.

We are endowed from birth with special talents, and when we accept Jesus as our Savior, we receive spiritual gifts as well. The purpose of these gifts is to bring glory to God, not to bring glory to us. We need to do our spiritual training every day. We need to strive for excellence, especially in the area of our giftedness. Then when God calls on us, His Holy Spirit empowers us fully to answer the call. Taking the High Way means acknowledging the Holy Spirit in and looking to the Spirit to impart life, implant hope, and testify of Christ.

FOOTNOTES: 1. 2 Thessalonians 2:7; 2. Acts 2:4

GPS: God-Positioning Scriptures (to Reorient Your Life)

But I tell you the truth, it is to your advantage that I go away; for if I do not go away, the Helper will not come to you; but if I go, I will send Him to you. And He, when He comes, will convict the world concerning sin and righteousness and judgment. —John 16:7-8

REST STOP: *Pull Over and Ponder*

God is more concerned with our reaching our potential than we are. He truly can bring something out of nothing. Confident in those truths, what step can you take today toward becoming what/who He's called you to be?

EXIT 10: *ETERNAL AVENUE*

Mile 71

Out of Sight

Emily Dickinson wrote, "Forever is composed of nows." I like the way she put that, because as much as we are tempted to think of eternity as a destination, it isn't. Eternity is a state of being—not infinite temporal duration, but timelessness, and as such it belongs to those who live in the present.

THE ESSENCE OF eternity is found in the eternal nature of Christ. "In the beginning was the Word, and the Word was with God, and the Word was God. He was in the beginning with God."[1] These brief, yet incredibly profound, verses open the Gospel of John and give us a glimpse of reality before time and before creation. They set the tone for the marvelous revelation to come: Jesus Christ, the eternal One.

In these opening verses, John introduces the concept of the *Logos*, or the "Word." As a Jew, John's use of the term "word" indicates that he was speaking a very personal message—from a very personal God—for a very profound purpose. John focuses on Christ—the Living Word. When Scripture declares, "the Word was God," it is attributing full deity to Jesus. "All things came into being through Him, and apart from Him nothing came into being that has come into being."[2]

Jesus is not merely "a god"; Jesus is fully God: always has been and always will be.

One of the most profound verses in the Bible is John 1:14: "The Word became flesh, and dwelt among us." The Greek word for "dwelt" refers to God's "pitching a tent in our midst," an image that harkens back to the time when God's presence accompanied the Hebrews in their desert wanderings between Egypt and Canaan for forty years. Millennia later, through Jesus, God taught people about the depth of His love, ministered to spiritual ills, and ransomed humankind so that everyone might enjoy, with Him, all the "nows" that together will comprise eternity.

When Jesus was walking around on the earth, rumors were rampant: The Messiah had come. Among those who had accurate information about Jesus was John the Baptist. He was undoubtedly one of Jesus' most recognizable witnesses, and some even wondered if John might be the Messiah himself. John, though, made it quite clear that he himself was not the Messiah. John declared again and again that he was only a witness who was to prepare the way for the greater One to come.

"Jesus is fully God: always has been and always will be."

John the Baptist's role was not unlike that of an ambulance driver, whose job it is to take the patient on a path straight to the one who can heal. In a sense, Christians are spiritual paramedics in that we need to be the ones to rush to come alongside those who are hurt or sick and render immediate care and comfort. If we think we are anyone's savior, though, we are headed for trouble. It's our Christian duty and responsibility to be out there on the scene, helping without pretending we can be the long-term solution.

At the outset of Jesus' ministry, he invited disciples to walk with Him and to learn from Him. Each of the men He chose to spend time with had a unique personality. When Jesus met Simon, He immediately gave him a new name, Peter, which means "rock." Jesus let Peter know that he would be changed because being in the presence of Truth is transformational. He knew Simon was volatile and lived his life on the edge, yet Jesus knew Simon would eventually be as solid as a rock. Today, when Jesus looks at us, He sees not only who we are, but also who we will become. God's truth has the power to transform a life eternally, because His Truth is a Person, not a concept.

"Phase transformation" is a term used by chemists and geologists to refer to one entity of matter being transformed into another entity because of external pressure. Intense pressure over time literally causes the rearrangement of molecules, and the substance becomes something altogether different. For example, coal under intense pressure for a long period of time and with the right circumstances will eventually turn into diamond. It changes from something that can be burned up in a moment to the hardest natural substance on earth.

God transforms lives for eternity. Once we've experienced that eternal transformation, our lives will intrigue those who don't have a personal relationship with Jesus Christ. Following Jesus is an eternal relationship, one that leads to our heavenly reward.

Christ is the bridge between heaven and Earth, between our reality (what is seen) and eternity (what is not seen). Jesus gave His perfect life for our lives of sin. Jesus replaced our inadequacy with what is complete and eternal. Taking the High Way means living now in light of eternity and leading others to the One who is eternal.

FOOTNOTES: 1. John 1:1-2; 2. John 1:3

GPS: *God-Positioning Scriptures (to Reorient Your Life)*

I've told you these things for a purpose: that my joy might be your joy, and your joy wholly mature. This is my command: Love one another the way I loved you. This is the very best way to love. Put your life on the line for your friends. You are my friends when you do the things I command you. I'm no longer calling you servants because servants don't understand what their master is thinking and planning. No, I've named you friends because I've let you in on everything I've heard from the Father. **—John 15:11-15**

REST STOP: *Pull Over and Ponder*
Meditate upon the relationship that you have with Jesus Christ. What changes have been made in your life since you accepted Him as your Savior?

Mile 72

Distracted Driving

It was Christopher Columbus, a navigator of admirable skill, who said, "By prevailing over all obstacles and distractions, one may unfailingly arrive at his chosen goal or destination." His statement wasn't addressing our spiritual journey, but it certainly could have been. Until we get to heaven, many pitfalls and distractions line our way on our journey to spiritual maturity.

Distraction No. 1: Alternate Routes

Each of us has a spiritual thirst to know God. The Bible says that God has set eternity in our hearts.[1] Nicodemus was a Pharisee, a ruler of the Jews. And while nothing was wrong with his brain, something was very wrong with his heart. He knew he needed something more substantial in his life, so one night his curiosity brought him to Jesus. Nicodemus professed to live for God and tried to obey every rule in order to gain His approval as a means of gaining heaven. So when Jesus responded that he must be born again, Nicodemus, who was thinking in physical terms rather than spiritual ones, was confused. So he questioned Jesus further.

Jesus answered, "Truly, truly, I say to you, unless one is born again he cannot see the kingdom of God. That which is born of the flesh is flesh, and that which is born of the Spirit is spirit."[2] Once we accept Jesus as our Lord and Savior, we have a sense of the eternal. There is only one way to get to heaven from where we are, and rather than be frustrated that there is one way, we can praise God that He chose to provide any way at all. Scripture's clarity about the way hasn't stopped some people from taking fruitless treks on alternative routes to try to get to heaven. And still others simply give up the journey altogether, deciding there is no way to get to heaven from where they are.

> "... each of us changes when Christ is our passion."

Jesus continued His response to Nicodemus with some words that are perhaps the most familiar verses in the entire Bible. John 3:16 and 17 summarize God's eternal plan of salvation. This is true love at its best! It is love that reaches out and draws others to Him. God sets the pattern we should follow in all our relationships. God paid dearly for us with the life of His Son—the highest price He could pay. Nicodemus was offered the same life change that God offers us. And like him, our response to that offer for a turn-around is crucial. Jesus told Nicodemus that he couldn't hang back if he wanted to live God's life instead of the life he was living. The impact on Nicodemus must have been significant, because we meet up with him again in chapter 19, when he went to Pilate to get permission to prepare the body of Jesus for the tomb.

More than a thousand years later, Saint Augustine also wrestled with taking a step of faith. He was one of the most profound theologians of his time, but before he came to Christ, he lived a reprobate existence. Augustine's change was remarkable. One day, many years into his journey of faith, he was walking down the road when a woman from his past approached him. Augustine greeted her with kindness, but continued walking. The woman turned and asked him, "Do you not know me? It is I!" Augustine looked at her with warmth, tenderness, and great sincerity. He smiled and replied, "But it is not I." He was different— each of us changes when Christ is our passion.

Distraction No. 2: Following Others Too Closely

Many of the first disciples of Jesus were originally followers of John the Baptist. Curiously, even though John's central purpose was to point others to Christ, not all of John's followers left to join Jesus. Even today, people have a tendency to closely follow the person who points them to Jesus rather than to follow Christ—a decision that will ultimately limit their spiritual maturity. Some of John's disciples stunted their spiritual growth in that way.

The Scriptures indicate that John's disciples expressed a little resentment toward Jesus. There was even a challenge of His spiritual leadership.

We see the disciples in these verses going to John the Baptist with this attitude: "You know, without you, Jesus would still be an unknown." When John the Baptist responded to the disciples, he did so with wisdom and spiritual maturity. "A man can receive nothing unless it has been given him from heaven. You yourselves are my witnesses that I said, 'I am not the Christ,' but, 'I have been sent ahead of Him.'"[3] John remained focused on God's purpose for his life—to point others to the coming Messiah. "He must increase, but I must decrease."[4]

A good practice for all of us as we get up in the morning would be to remind ourselves, "I am not Christ." We're often tempted to play the role of lord in this world and to think that we are its savior. But God is orchestrating whatever is happening in our lives, and He has chosen us to participate in what He's doing. Man can't have anything except what is given to him by God. John the Baptist knew that. When we reflect Christ's humble spirit, others will be able to recognize Him in us.

When I was young, I asked my mom for a sheriff's badge. Of course, play badges were made of plastic and had no authority, but I would pretend my badge was real. Proudly, I'd go into my neighborhood, make a few arrests, and attempt to keep order. When I was old enough to realize the badge was fake, I reacted quite differently. As I stood in the presence of a real sheriff, I hoped he wouldn't see my fake badge. I was humbled because his authority was genuine. A Christian's authority is based on a willingness to recognize that God is in control, not only of an individual's life, but also human history. He must increase, and we must decrease in such a way that the praise, honor, and glory go to Him and Him alone.

Distraction No. 3: White Knuckling

Sometimes, especially when we're in a hurry or the road is treacherous, we grip the wheel so tightly that it literally turns our knuckles white. We would do well to loosen our grip, remembering that God is very capable of intervening and often does intervene in the midst of our daily agenda. Agendas have their place. But if we are overly distracted by our own agendas, we might miss the ways that God will come to us. We see an example of this in John 4, when Jesus met the Samaritan woman at the well. She was not looking for Him, but was on a routine errand. It wasn't a geographical necessity that made Jesus pass through Samaria. In fact, proper Jews generally circumvented Samaria if possible, because of their hatred of the country and her people. So the words "had to pass through Samaria"[5] that we see in the Scripture indicate that there was a divine appointment.

In interacting with the woman, Jesus addressed three huge barriers. First, there was a cultural barrier that existed because Jesus was a Jew, and she was a Samaritan. Second, a social barrier existed because she was a woman and therefore not respected by men. And third, there was a sin barrier, which could have been the ultimate wall between them since she was living an immoral life in contrast to His sinless existence. So how did Jesus break down the barriers? He asked a simple favor of her, and that request gave them an excuse to connect.

The Samaritan woman had been in and out of many relationships, each one an ineffective substitute to fill the void created by pain and loneliness that in reality only Jesus could fill. Jesus did not condemn her; He offered her a remedy for her discontent. He gave her the opportunity to recognize Him as her Savior and submit to His lordship over her life.

Jesus then led the discussion in a direction that would show the woman that He was the Messiah. Among other things, He pointed out to her that worship was not a matter of location, but a condition of the heart.

The capacity to love is essential to worship. The word for worship in John 4:23 literally means "to touch with kisses." It's a very tender, intimate word. Jesus lets us know that we can have intimacy with God wherever we are. Intimate worship of God takes place in our minds and hearts.

Taking the High Way means being willing to accept changes in the mundane and welcome God's redirect of our focus for His purposes. Like the woman at the well, we need to be willing to allow Jesus to change our daily routines. Because she was willing to let Him interrupt her routine, an entire city learned of Jesus. What might happen if we, like she, determined our agenda to be flexible?

FOOTNOTES: 1. Ecclesiastes 3:11; 2. John 3:3,6; 3. John 3:27-28; 4. John 3:30; 5. John 4:4

GPS: *God-Positioning Scriptures (to Reorient Your Life)*
The mind of man plans his way, but the LORD directs his steps. —**Proverbs 16:9**

REST STOP: *Pull Over and Ponder*
What's one thing you could change about your daily routine to glorify God more?

Mile 73

Seeing Signs

*Whether God gives us signs by way of miracles, convictions of the heart,
or by using the relationships, events, and things of the world around us
... He communicates with us all the time.*

AFTER MEETING THE woman at the well in Samaria, Jesus and His disciples continued their journey into Galilee. Jesus did not return to His hometown of Nazareth, where people knew Him only as the carpenter's son. Jesus knew they would not be able to *hear* His voice as the Messiah—His call on their lives would have to come later. So He traveled to Cana. In Cana, however, many people viewed Him as a celebrity of sorts. They only wanted Jesus to perform more *tricks* for them, and as a result, they, too, missed the opportunity to know more of what the Son of God had to offer. How can we keep from making those same mistakes?

We can pay attention to the *regular* ways God communicates and then respond accordingly. God clearly communicates, in the Bible, what He is like

343

and what He wants from His followers. God never contradicts Himself, so if we think we have heard His voice speaking to us personally and that voice is saying something opposing what we read in the Bible, we can know that the Bible has it right. Scripture is our primary source for hearing from God.

One of the significant issues God highlights in His Word is healing. Approximately one-fifth of all the subject matter in the Gospels pertains to healing. The circumstances in which people find healing today are varied, as were the methods that Jesus used to heal the sick. On at least one occasion before Jesus even offered a cure, He asked the patient a surprising question: "Do you wish to get well?"[1] Why in the world would Jesus ask the man if he wanted to get well? After all, the man had been in this condition for thirty-eight years. But that is exactly why Jesus asked him!

A trait all human beings have in common is the ability to adapt. Regardless of what change comes our way, we can almost always adapt to it—and that's good news. The bad news is that regardless of what comes our way, we can almost always adapt to it. We can accept disappointments and adapt to our brokenness so well that we don't want to get better. We can get so used to the way things are that the mere thought of change threatens us.

> *"... we should never be reluctant to go to God and ask Him to heal us."*

When we have physical or emotional needs, we should never be reluctant to go to God and ask Him to heal us. Likewise, we need to have compassion for those around us and pray for them. An incredible level of intimacy results as we come alongside others and allow God to work through us to touch their lives through our prayers, encouragement, and service.

Eternity Standing Strong

As Jesus ministered to those around Him, He continued to generate considerable controversy. His accusers demanded to know who gave Him the authority to act beyond their interpretation of the Law. Jesus neither employed the rules and philosophy of mankind, nor responded with what the world considered to be predictable answers. Rather, His responses were astounding, perplexing, and instructive. Jesus' intimacy with God superseded any need for the approval of men.

344

When the Jews came to Jesus and charged Him with equating Himself with God, Jesus did not respond arrogantly with boastful words concerning His origin. He did not brag about His omnipotence or omniscience. Instead, He took on the nature of a servant so that all could come closer to God. Jesus said a corroborating witness must testify to the truth of His relationship with the Father. In John 5, He mentions at least four witnesses to the truth: John the Baptist, the works Jesus performed, the witness of the Father, and the Scriptures. God's divine words not only constitute objective knowledge or general truth, but they outline the way we can establish a personal relationship with God.

In his book *More Than a Carpenter*, Josh McDowell wrote an interesting analogy relating to the three hundred prophecies in the Old Testament concerning the coming of the Messiah. McDowell referred to Peter Stoner, a statistician who applied the laws of probability to the chance of one person fulfilling only eight of those three hundred prophecies four centuries after they were made—the likelihood of that happening is one chance in ten to the seventeenth power (ten with sixteen zeros behind it). Yet, Jesus fulfilled all three hundred!

God has given us His written Word as a personal affirmation that He will help us find answers of hope to problems that we thought unsolvable. God has given us this incredible Book through which He speaks to us about the Living Word. The Bible provides all the answers, even to our most perplexing problems.

Eternity's Mathematics 101

In his book *Systematic Theology*, theologian Wayne Grudem described a miracle as "a less common kind of God's activity in which He arouses people's awe and wonder and bears witness to Himself." I like this definition of "miracle" because it reminds me that God works on my behalf every single day. God's unique responses are great reminders that He makes all things possible—in His way.

When we hear or read a press report of a person healed of disease, we're curious about how the miracle happened, so we check it out. The same thing happened in Jesus' day—large crowds followed Him. Perhaps one of the reasons that Jesus performed signs was that He knew such extraordinary events would arouse people's interest. Miracles authenticated who Jesus was. When God works a miracle in our lives, His intervention should draw us to greater and more obedient faith. When God takes the little we have in our lives and makes it grand and wonderful, the results should always point to Jesus. Many miracles and wonders occur in this world, but unless they offer an opportunity for people to recognize Jesus Christ in them, they are counterfeit.

Another aspect of experiencing miracles is that they allow people of God to get involved with what He's doing. It has been said that 90 percent of what we learn is grasped by doing something, rather than through simply reading about it or watching it being done. As Jesus performed miracles, He began to draw His disciples into the process. Later, the disciples would perform some of the very same kind of miracles as they traveled throughout Asia to establish the Christian church.

John 6 tells the story of Jesus' feeding the five thousand. The crowds came to follow Jesus, and when He saw them, He asked Philip, "Where are we to buy bread, so that these may eat?"[2] Some Bible commentators contend that Jesus asked this of Philip because they were located close to his home turf, and perhaps he would know where there was a marketplace. But I think Jesus asked Philip in order to bring him into the process of the miracle that was about to occur.

When the disciples looked at their available resources and then surveyed the need, they saw limitations. When Jesus talked about feeding five thousand people, Philip replied that even two hundred denarii, the equivalent of two hundred days' wages, wouldn't buy enough food for the task. Andrew said, "There is a lad here who has five barley loaves and two fish, but what are these for so many people?"[3]

Traditional mathematics tells us that if we don't have much, we won't get much. But Jesus can take the very little we have and multiply it into something wonderful, something that surpasses our expectations. The disciples believed that the only resource they had was a boy's lunch. God took a scarce resource and created abundance for many. He took the impossible and made the possible.

If we choose to be satisfied with a "scarcity model" of life, we shortchange God's calling on our lives. If we believe we can accomplish only what our bank accounts say we can or only what our energy will allow us to do, we have accepted the scarcity model and the limitations it offers. But God has unlimited wealth and power. And although the tasks are daunting, taking the High Way means stepping out in faith with confidence.

FOOTNOTES: 1. John 5:6; 2. John 6:5; 3. John 6:9

GPS: God-Positioning Scriptures (to Reorient Your Life)

Encourage the exhausted, and strengthen the feeble. Say to those with anxious heart, "Take courage, fear not. Behold, your God will come with vengeance; The recompense of God will come, but He will save you." Then the eyes of the blind will be opened and the ears of the deaf will be unstopped.
—Isaiah 35:3-5

REST STOP: *Pull Over and Ponder*
Think of those you know who have been sick and in need of the connection to eternity through prayer and through healing. Have you prayed for them? Have you become closer to the individual that you prayed for?

Mile 74

Stormy Weather

When you're in the midst of a storm, you can be blind to everything else around you. You may actually believe that even God can't pull you out of this one. Don't assume that He has abandoned you simply because you can't see Him in your situation.

DURING HIS EARTHLY ministry, Jesus did so many wonderful things for the people and had provided so abundantly for their needs that the crowd wanted to proclaim Him king. Jesus knew that His ministry had only begun; the time had not yet come for public acknowledgement of His kingship. The people saw the wonderful things God did and wanted Him as liberator, the supplier of their needs. By declaring Him a temporal king, they defined their savior in worldly terms. Jesus knew that true power does not result from an elected office, but from a permanent connection with the Father. His goal was to prepare a future kingdom from among all nations over which He would reign forever.

Before He withdrew to the mountain to pray, Jesus sent His disciples on ahead to a boat to cross the Sea of Galilee to Capernaum. The Sea of Galilee measures six miles wide by fifteen miles long and lies six hundred fifty feet below sea level. The wind often comes gusting over the top of the mountains that surround the sea and rushes downward, squeezing through the ravines. By the time the wind shear reaches the water's surface, it causes waves that easily reach ten to fifteen feet high. Storms on the Sea of Galilee continue to be a common threat even today.

The disciples, some of who were fishermen, had rowed more than halfway across the sea. They knew how to handle the boat from having sailed on that body of water numerous times. They relied only on their own strength to see them through conditions that continually grew rougher. Like the disciples, when we face life's storms, we tend to rely on our own strength. And like them, some of us have been rowing in the turmoil for so long that we're exhausted. The more depleted we become, the more we anticipate catastrophe, and the more we're likely to resist intervention.

> "[God] sees us, and He doesn't ignore our struggles. It is His nature to come to us."

What we need is the kind of help that can calm the inner storms and bring peace to our soul—the kind of help that Jesus offers. When the disciples needed help, Jesus came to them; they needed help, and He showed up. He identified Himself. "It is I; do not be afraid."[1] When we're in distress, we may think that God is far away. He sees us, and He doesn't ignore our struggles. It is His nature to come to us.

So how do we live in a world where the God we expect to deliver us doesn't do it in the way we think He should? What do we do while we are waiting for Him to straighten out the universe to our liking? In many ways, life would seem easier if God were to take away our free will and control our every decision and move. But that would not draw us closer to Him. He wants us to choose to love Him out of our heart's desire, not out of coercion.

God is in control even when our personal circumstances lead us to believe that is not the situation. Pain and evil exist in this world, but Christians recognize the ultimate victory that awaits all of those who have accepted Jesus Christ as Lord and Savior. While retaining a heavenly perspective, we must also deal with today's realities. If we overlook them, we'll miss incredible opportunities to minister to others.

When I was young, I remember watching a boxing match between Muhammad Ali and George Foreman. Muhammad Ali had developed an unusual fighting strategy that he coined "the rope-a-dope." Instead of attacking Foreman, Ali retreated into a corner and protected himself from the punches, letting Foreman jab him with all his might. Throughout the fight, Ali egged Foreman on, and with punch after punch, Foreman lost more strength. Ali bided his time because he knew that the energy coming against him would be spent and eventually he would enjoy the advantage. Ali had to absorb many blows prior to achieving ultimate victory. We're all going to absorb many painful blows in life and at some point may feel that our defeat is imminent. Sometimes we don't even want to "risk" praying for fear that God will let us down. So we only pray prayers that (in the flesh) have a good chance of success without God's intervention.

Mature faith trusts fully in God in all circumstances. It "goes for it" in prayers! If God doesn't choose to answer in the way we were expecting, we are disappointed and get hurt. But at least we know we didn't fake it, just pretending we were trusting.

Here are five prayers that "go for it"—prayers that God always answers in His own way, that you can pray in the midst of life's storms:

1. *"Lord, get me out of this temptation!"* Believe it or not, when we earnestly pray this prayer, we have to climb over God's impediments to sin! Not only does He promise a way out; He also gives us disincentives.[2]

When I first entered the ministry, I was still smoking cigarettes. It was a nasty habit left over from college, and I wanted God to take it away. I prayed for help. I then stopped to buy a pack, miles away from the church, and the attendant recognized me: "Say, aren't you a minister?" I bought them anyhow, lit up in the car as I had a hundred times before and dropped the ash in my lap. Swerving, I pulled over. A young man in my youth group came up to the car and wanted a ride to the church. We may decide to overcome God's way out, but we will be both miserable and pitiful at the same time.

2. *"Lord, amaze me with a glimpse of the supernatural."* As shallow as this sounds, this isn't the same as a generation always looking for signs. This prayer is a request to see God's hand in our lives and appreciate His nearness. He loves to reveal Himself above all rational explanation, but we do not usually ask or look.

My friend and co-pastor Vernon Rainwater loves to tell the Good News to people at God's opportunity. One time, his heart was quickened to pray for opportunities only God could arrange. Soon he was invited to emcee a totally secular convention in Europe and challenged to "somehow work in the Gospel." Soon after arriving home, someone who swore he never wanted to hear the Good News asked Vernon questions about Jesus Christ.

We ask for healing in the face of illness, rescue in the face of danger, and miracles in the midst of hopelessness. Why do we not ask for glimpses of His supernatural presence every day? Isn't He "Immanuel ... God with us"?[3]

3. *"Lord, show me better ways to love and serve."* A word of caution: If you pray this prayer, you will discover that people are yelling at you for a reason. It is God's ventriloquism trying to get you to see a new perspective.

Eddie has a ministry to professionals and is very efficient. He felt convicted, though, that he might not be really compassionate. He prayed a version of this prayer and got his answer soon ... in traffic! Instead of a competitive response to a rude driver, it occurred to him to pray for the hostile driver. Then he decided to let others into the lane as a way to serve and began praying for them. He now has a ministry on the highway. If you can customize your service to people (that's what God did in Jesus), you will find new ways to serve.

4. *"Lord, use me for Your purpose in this situation."* The great adequacy of God is that He can use us when we do not know what to say or do or even think! Many times we are reluctant to enter into a potential place of ministry because we think we surely would mess it up.

Herb was an introvert. He dreaded going to the funeral home and speaking to his friend's widow. He knew anything that came out of his mouth would sound trite and stupid. He rehearsed, "You have my sympathies," but when he got in front of the widow, all he could do was break down in tears and hug her. Years later, I asked a young widow what the most helpful thing was that was said to her during her husband's funeral. She replied: "I don't remember many of the words, only the hugs. Those were God's arms for me."

We think people need a professional, rather than an available Christian. Well, unless we are talking about something like medical care, we couldn't be more wrong. Second Corinthians 3:5-6 is a reminder to pray (" ... our adequacy is from God") before we act!

5. *"Lord, glorify Your name."* There are many times when I have no idea what God wants me to pray. I can see the good and bad in each alternative. There was an old man that I had loved dearly. His wife had gone to be with the Lord. He was tired of living without her, even though he was still a great blessing to any who knew him.

He had suffered a massive stroke. I could pray for healing on this side of the curtain or perfection on the other side. What should I pray? I remembered what Jesus prayed facing death, so I figured it was still a pretty solid prayer. To this day, I simply pray, "Lord, glorify You name" when I don't know what else to pray.

Taking the High Way means leaning on God in every circumstance, in every trial, asking God to glorify His name. He always does.

FOOTNOTES: 1. John 6:20; 2. 1 Corinthians 10:13; 3. Matthew 1:23

GPS: *God-Positioning Scriptures (to Reorient Your Life)*

Encourage the exhausted, and strengthen the feeble. Say to those with anxious heart, "Take courage, fear not. Behold, your God will come with vengeance; The recompense of God will come, but He will save you." Then the eyes of the blind will be opened and the ears of the deaf will be unstopped.
—Isaiah 35:3-5

REST STOP: *Pull Over and Ponder*
Have you ever prayed a prayer similar to any of the five listed in this Mile? How did God respond? Lean on God in prayer today and expect Him to answer.

Mile 75

Fender Benders

Life can hit you hard sometimes. Sometimes it's your fault; sometimes it's not. Instead of looking for something or someone to blame, look for a higher purpose instead.

L IFE IS FULL of imperfections. And we expend a great deal of energy trying to figure out the cause of those imperfections rather than considering their purpose. It's while we're still imperfect that Christ comes to us and uses our weaknesses to exhibit His glory. Imperfections beg His involvement.

In the ninth chapter of John, we read the story about Jesus' healing a blind man and what the Lord said regarding this man's impairment. Ironically, the experience of the blind man gives us a heavenly perspective about troubles that we experience. The Jews believed that every mishap and imperfection in life were the result of someone sinning. In the blind man's case, they believed either his parents' sins or some sin committed in the womb resulted in his blindness.

We are used to thinking in terms of cause and effect, but Jesus said that sometimes life will reveal an effect before the cause becomes apparent.

I believe that the blind man represents all of us. We're all born spiritually blind. When God opens our eyes, however, we have a choice of keeping our sight fixed on the imperfect world or of letting God give us His perspective. He can and will change our lives. He will use the totality of all that we are, not just the good and successful aspects that others recognize, to bring glory to His name.

We need to adopt God's perspective, and when we experience tough times, we especially need to look at our situation from His point of view. His perspective is beyond the boundaries of the present moment, and, in fact, beyond the boundaries of time. What we are going through could be just as much about the future as about the past or the present.

> *"What we are going through could be just as much about the future as about the past or the present."*

From heaven's perspective, there is a way of loving people that protects and provides for them. Jesus showed us a way to love, lead, and live in community so that everyone benefits. He showed the religious leaders of His time, through a simple metaphor about shepherding, a style of leadership that they never could have imagined. Jesus said, "I am the good shepherd, and I know My own and My own know Me, even as the Father knows Me and I know the Father; and I lay down My life for the sheep."[1] Jesus invites us into a life with Him. He does not strong-arm or control us, but He leads and protects us and calls us into a relationship with Him. His invitation was radically different from the authoritarian, demanding style of leadership of the time. To choose to follow Christ was at that time and is today a willingness to abdicate our self-interest for the benefit of others. That is what gives us the eternal perspective that results in selfless love.

Sometimes love does not respond in the way or within the time frame we desire. And when it doesn't, it may not seem like love at all. When it does not provide immediate comfort, relief, or rescue, when we experience things that we can't comprehend, we may need to remind ourselves how much we need to trust God. The Bible tells us that God's thoughts are higher than our thoughts and

His ways are higher than our ways. So it naturally follows that sometimes we simply won't understand the process, or the result of a circumstance.

In John 11, Jesus let his friend Lazarus die. Jesus could have prevented Lazarus' death—He was only two miles away when He received news of his illness. Martha, Lazarus' sister, clearly communicated her feelings about the situation: "Lord, if You had been here, my brother would not have died."[2] Like Martha, many times we rationalize, "If only God had done this or that, my life would have been better." If we truly believe in the sovereignty of God, however, then we would never say, "If only God had … " Lazarus had been dead for four days by the time Jesus arrived. Martha reminded Jesus that there would be a stench. But He replied, "Did I not say to you that if you believe, you will see the glory of God?"[3] Imagine the impact the dramatic scene made on the witnesses standing a distance from the tomb. "The man who had died came forth, bound hand and foot with wrappings, and his face was wrapped around with a cloth. Jesus said to them, 'Unbind him, and let him go.'"[4] The raising of Lazarus was proof of the power of the Lord Jesus over death.

In light of the eternal things of God, energy needs to be directed toward productivity and significance. And we see in Scripture that the same God who re-engages the dead into life, is willing and able to disengage any parts of the living that hinder eternal productivity and significance. In John 15, Jesus referred to Himself using a metaphor. He said that he was the "true vine" and His Father was the "vinedresser."[5] Grapevines need considerable attention to reach the stage that they produce a bountiful harvest. They might show a lot of leaf growth and look productive, but to actually bear fruit, they must be pruned in order to direct energy into the vines. Left to itself, the vine's spurious growth dissipates its energy and renders it incapable of being productive. Busy people—going in a million directions at once—are comparable to the wild vine. Stressed by their pursuits in every direction, they are of negligible benefit to anyone or any purpose.

Pruning is the act of shaping and strengthening the vine for the harvest. It appears to the untrained eye to be a profoundly drastic treatment, as much of the plant is cut off and discarded, but it is that drastic treatment that allows the plant to flourish and bless others. That's true for vines and true for people. Sometimes even when we do the right things, God will continue to prune us. As a result, when we eventually come up against opposition or a roadblock, we're prepared to cope with whatever injustices and problems we face. We'll be even more fruitful than if we had been left alone in our successes. Taking the High Way means trusting God even in issues of life and death. And it means expecting that what He prunes will bear fruit.

FOOTNOTES: 1. John 10:14-15; 2. John 11:21; 3. John 11:40; 4. John 11:44; 5. John 15:1

GPS: *God-Positioning Scriptures (to Reorient Your Life)*

*Jesus said, "For judgment I have come into this world, so that the blind will see and those who see will become blind." —*John 9:39 (NIV)

REST STOP: *Pull Over and Ponder*
Where can you see that God's "pruning" in your life has had a purpose? How do those examples help you trust God as He prunes you today?

Mile 76

Start to Finish

*How can you exemplify a godly life in such a way that those who come
after you will want to follow?*

THE NIGHT BEFORE Jesus died, He created two lasting memories that
enable us to capsulate His life of loving service: He washed the disciples'
feet, and they partook of a last meal together. Because of His great love,
Jesus wanted to prepare His followers for a future without Him. His preparations encourage us to consider our own legacies as well.

Jesus lived in such a way that He left a spiritual legacy for all time. He established a model of how to be a faithful servant while living in a sinful world. Too
often, people attempt to withdraw from God ordained relationships. How many
teenagers consider running away from home because they think their lives will
be better? Some married people think the family would be better off without
them, or the flip side of this self-focused approach: "I'd be better off without

them." Running away or giving up won't produce the results God intends for our relationships.

Jesus demonstrated a number of ways for us to infuse life into relationships, but the story of Jesus' washing the disciples' feet from John 13 is one of my favorites. As the Lord of the universe modeled servanthood, surely the observing disciples realized that no act of servitude was beneath their undertaking. The disciples could not grasp the concept that he who has the most power and influence is under the greatest obligation to be the most humble servant. Such an idea turned the values of the day upside down.

People are tempted to seek authority, position, wealth, and influence as a way to leave a legacy. But Jesus, through His example, showed us a way to leave a better legacy. He spent His life in such a way that others were better off as a result of their encounter with Him. Will we leave a legacy through our example that encourages our family and friends to love Jesus and serve others?

> "Will we leave a legacy ... that encourages our family and friends to love Jesus and serve others?"

On the night of His betrayal, Jesus dined with His disciples and left symbols of the heavenly cost of human salvation. Several emblems identified with this event have become part of the Christian ceremony of remembrance called Communion. We are in the very presence of God whenever we partake of the wine, symbolic of His blood shed for us, and the bread, a symbol of His body. In His teachings, He told us that we can be partakers of the divine nature. Whenever we participate in this commemorative act, we acknowledge what He has done on our behalf to assure our salvation. Symbolically, this partaking of the divine nature reverses the partaking of the forbidden fruit in the Garden of Eden. The ceremonial meal foreshadows a future banquet around the heavenly table. No other ceremony binds heaven and earth more closely.

Jesus followed up that Last Supper communion with His disciples by telling them that He would be leaving them to go and prepare a place for them. In John 14 we find those words of hope that are often used at funerals today, but the imagery was actually appropriate for a traditional Jewish marriage of that day. During the betrothal, the groom built a dwelling place for his future bride. No one knew exactly how long it would take him to finish the house, but the groom's father decided when it was ready. At the appointed time, the bridegroom would return to claim his bride. Since many New Testament verses state that Jesus is the bridegroom and the church is His bride, the analogy is hard to miss.

John goes on to tell us that Jesus continued to comfort His disciples with the assertion "You know the way to the place where I am going."¹ But Thomas, who was skeptical of everything he didn't understand, interrupted with a question: "We don't know where you are going, so how can we know the way?" Jesus took Thomas' questioning in stride and simply reassured him that he did, indeed, know the way. "I am the way, and the truth, and the life; no one comes to the Father but through Me."² If there is one verse in the Gospel of John that sums up the plan of salvation for all of us, this has to be it.

I have heard people claim that this verse is too exclusive, since it indicates that there is only one way to God—one way to salvation. But even for those frustrated with its exclusivity there surely must be some consideration of the miracle that access to Him exists at all. Imagine, for a moment, being trapped in a burning building with only one exit. We would see that way out as an invitation to escape, and would not be asking why there aren't more ways to get out. The fact that there is any way out at all should make us ecstatic.

Before Jesus and His disciples left the room that evening, He told them that He would ask the Father to send them a helper who would be with them forever. The word "helper" can be interpreted either to mean "another, other than I" or "another Me." Through the ministry of the Holy Spirit, Jesus promised to abide in the life of each of His disciples in every generation. Christ invests Himself in us so we can know Him and feel His love. This is an intimacy with Jesus that we could never get if we were limited to only physical contact.

When His Spirit resides in us, our relationship with Him is one of awe and reverence and of the heart. Taking the High Way means loving others and demonstrating His compassion for them. The power of the Holy Spirit is not governed by our abilities; it's poured out according to the way He works through us.

FOOTNOTES: 1. John 14:4 (NIV); 2. John 14:6

GPS: *God-Positioning Scriptures (to Reorient Your Life)*

To this you were called, because Christ suffered for you, leaving you an example, that you should follow in his steps. —1 Peter 2:21 (NIV)

REST STOP: *Pull Over and Ponder*

Do your actions and words draw others toward Jesus? Will you be pleased with the legacy you're leaving with your friends and family?

Mile 77

Giving Others a Lift

When your greatest desire in life is to see people be a part of the kingdom of God, you are the most like Christ.

A T A CERTAIN point in life, we may think that we should have arrived ... spiritually speaking. That doesn't happen while we're on this side of heaven.

God somehow, though, over time in our relationship with Him, uses our conversation with Him to give us a heart that desires what He desires. We do come to point where we can pray without reservation, "Lord, I don't know exactly what to pray, so please pray through me. Whatever I pray, let Your will be done."

A while back, I received an e-mail about Mike Vance, one of our church members serving as a missionary to Namibia, Africa. Mike's team went into the bush country throughout the year to preach the Good News. On one occasion, his team ran out of money, and they debated whether or not to continue their travel throughout southern Namibia. As they spent time in prayer, they all received the distinct impression that they should continue. That day, it took forty-five minutes to get the truck started. But they felt sure that God wanted them to move on, so they continued the journey through a very barren, seldom traveled area. During the first few hours, they saw only two cars that passed them and disappeared on the road ahead. As the truck rounded a bend, they came upon one of the two cars that had passed them earlier. The car had flipped over and was on fire, trapping two elderly people inside. The team members rushed out of their truck and pulled the accident victims free. It was two hours before another car came down the road. Had Mike and his team not arrived just when they did, the two people wouldn't have survived. Looking back, we can understand why God impressed upon the team to go on that day. It had nothing to do with money or even their ministry to the African people. It had everything to do with God's plan to rescue those two people.

So often, our prayers are not answered according to our requests. But the promptings to pray have to do with God's much broader plan. Like Jesus so often did, we should speak these things aloud and watch what God does with our intercessions.

Jesus lived an undistracted, unhurried existence that focused on issues of eternal life. He wanted that to be our focus as well. Now let me go out on a limb here and make an assumption that this is as difficult for you as it is for me. But God leaves us in this world to sanctify and cleanse us as well as to spread the Gospel. So God will allow us, on occasion, to come to a point of crisis through which we can learn and grow. It's often through a crucible of pain that God strips away what we think is important to help us become the people He wants us to be. C.S. Lewis said "God whispers to us in our pleasures, speaks in our conscience, but shouts in our pains."

In order to gain an eternal perspective, let's be praying that God will reshape and consecrate us so that we may be sanctified in His truth. Sanctification is a lifelong process of growing and enduring that reshapes our sinful nature into a Christ-like character.

If we Christians don't really understand God's heart for people, we will likely believe ourselves to be more sanctified if we only spend time with those who are sanctified. But if we only congregate with like-minded believers and separate ourselves from the rest of the world, we've missed the point entirely. That's why churches filled with those who are serious about sanctification, will not be fixated on how many people they can pack into the pews on a weekend, but will be measuring their commitment to fulfill Christ's Great Commission. It is how many people a church sends out into the world to minister that reflects the sanctification of its members. Let me say that again: The impact of a church should be measured in how many it sends, not how many it seats.

> "The impact of a church should be measured in how many it sends, not how many it seats."

Jesus sent His disciples out into the world for those who would come to believe through them. Jesus prays for their sanctification, and for their unity and oneness: "even as You, Father, are in Me and I in You, that they also may be in Us, so that the world may believe that You sent Me."[1] There is a "so that" in this verse—the consequence that God promises as a result of an association. The "so that" in this verse does not end with believers becoming one, but rather has an even greater result: that the entire world might believe in Jesus.

When Jesus prayed, He always interceded for those who were not part of His family. When our greatest desire in life is to see people be a part of the kingdom of God, we are the most like Christ. John Stott, author of *Basic Christianity* once commented, "We must be global Christians with a global vision because our God is a global God." Genuine Christian unity, of the kind Christ prayed for His disciples, is a powerful witness to the world. We need to associate with people, whether we agree with them or not, because that is God's way. An old adage comes to mind: If your Gospel isn't touching others, it hasn't touched you! Taking the High Way means recognizing that being sent, not being separated, sanctifies us. We are united by whom we have in common not by what we share in common.

FOOTNOTES: 1. John 17:21

GPS: *God-Positioning Scriptures (to Reorient Your Life)*

[Jesus said] Here's what I'm saying: Ask and you'll get; Seek and you'll find; Knock and the door will open. Don't bargain with God. Be direct. Ask for what you need. This is not a cat-and-mouse, hide-and-seek game we're in. —Luke 11:9-10 (The Message)

REST STOP: *Pull Over and Ponder*

How might you be able to improve your prayer life so that you can improve your relationships with others? Take a moment today to encourage someone today whom you would not normally talk with.

Mile 78

Headed for Betrayal

In an effort to stay on track in your journey to spiritual maturity, you will be tempted to simply try harder. Beware! Self-righteousness leads to self-betrayal, which leads to shame. There's a better way ...

THE CRUCIFIXION OF Jesus Christ stands at the center of God's plan to restore mankind to the rightful place Adam and Eve originally occupied. Our eternal destiny hinges on that significant promise that Jesus should become "the Lamb of God who takes away the sin of the world."[1] John 18 helps us understand the great price Jesus paid by dying for our sins. The final drama begins with His being betrayed in the Garden of Gethsemane. The garden is strangely reminiscent of another garden and another scene of betrayal—the Garden of Eden. The cycle of betrayal, however, began even before the history of mankind. In Ezekiel 28 and Isaiah 14, we read that Satan defected from the heavenly courts for basically the same reason Adam and Eve chose to disobey—a selfish desire for a position more elevated than the one God had assigned His created beings.

As we read in John 18 about the second garden and the second Adam, Christ, we see the cycle broken. The second Adam would rather die than disobey God. Instead of taking power for Himself or taking what we might consider the easy way out, Jesus chose to stay close to God, a relationship that carried Him through the betrayal to the ultimate victory on the cross. Jesus' actions in the Garden of Gethsemane overturned the dire consequences of the failure of Adam and Eve in the Garden of Eden.

> *"Forgiveness always trumps revenge."*

An act of betrayal typically occurs on familiar territory and makes apostasy even more shocking and hurtful. John 18:2 tells us that Judas knew that Jesus often met in the Garden of Gethsemane with His disciples. Judas arrived at the garden with a cohort of Roman soldiers and chief priests. The crowd brought with them lanterns, torches and weapons. What kind of implements were these to try to conquer the Light of the World and the Prince of Peace? The mob obviously didn't know the character of Jesus.

The verses of John 18 express at least two principles. First, betrayal is an impersonal act that takes place for selfish gain. Loyalty, on the other hand, is personal. Adam and Eve listened to Satan because they believed he was offering them something that God was not. In this case, the prize was wisdom that would make them "like God."[2] They disobeyed God for the same reason people today damage and even sever relationships—they thought they could get a better deal elsewhere.

The second principle we should note in this passage is that Jesus "went forth."[3] Jesus wasn't thinking of Himself, but rather of His followers. He intentionally drew the attention of the attackers to Himself so that He could protect His disciples. Our first reaction when we're betrayed might be to enlist others as allies to fight against the betrayer. When we truly care about others, however, we attempt to shelter them from the residual effects of our pain. That's what Jesus did.

We need to realize what's at stake if we react to betrayal only out of our pain. The fallout can be enormous. One single act can destroy many years of being a witness for Christ. Our obligations as Christians are to be proactive and to forgive those who have hurt us. Until we do that, we will be distracted from our mission.

The late Lewis Smedes, a professor of theology and ethics for twenty-five years at Fuller Theological Seminary, wrote, "Forgiving does not erase the bitter past. A healed memory is not a deleted memory. Instead, forgiving what we cannot forget creates a new way to remember. We change the memory of our past into a hope for our future."

His comments on forgiveness bring clarity to a simple, but difficult to practice, concept. I heard the following true story about a profound ramification of forgiveness. After being freed from a Nazi concentration camp, one ex-prisoner asked another if he had been able to forgive the Nazis for what they did. The man answered that he had. The first prisoner confessed that he had not. In fact, every single day, he thought about the pain the Nazis inflicted and said his desire was that they should feel the same pain he had endured. His comrade replied, "Then they still have you as a prisoner."

Forgiveness always trumps revenge. Jesus overcame Judas' act of betrayal because He did for us what all of us needed Him to do—He died on a cross for the forgiveness of our sins. Because of His willing sacrifice, we never have to be prisoners of revenge or of any other sin. We can, instead, choose to be captives of Jesus Christ, free to move forward in our eternal journey with the One who will never betray us.

Dealing With Self-Betrayal

Often betrayal comes from within—we sabotage our own happiness and undercut the very thing we desire. Peter's response to the arrest of Jesus illustrates this in John 18. There are many people who think these verses are about Peter's cowardice, especially since he lied to a lowly slave girl. But a coward would not have drawn his sword to challenge the Roman soldiers in the garden. When Peter cut off the ear of the high priest's slave, he was ready to fight to the death by taking on the army of Rome!

Peter's reaction wasn't prompted by cowardice; it was motivated by pride. We see that character flaw in Peter even more clearly in Matthew 26:33 when Jesus had just predicted His own death and the scattering of the disciples. At that time, Peter responded that he wouldn't abandon Jesus, even if everyone else did.

Yet, in spite of all his boasting, Peter later denied even knowing Jesus. This is a valuable lesson for us: Pride leaves footprints that lead toward betrayal.

When Peter was asked, "You are not also one of His disciples, are you?"[4] his three denials sabotaged his relationship with Christ. His denial of Christ separated him from what he most desired. Are we so very different from Peter? We dedicate our lives to something we deem important, only to lose it all with one stupid mistake. We have within us a self-sabotaging element. Following one of our failures, we often determine never to make that mistake again. We set up boundaries and rules for ourselves. When we break them, in our shame, we establish even more limits.

There are times when we think we need to try harder. Taking the High Way means conquering self-deception not by trying harder, but by surrendering our lives to God and living in the freedom that releases us from sin. The cure for sin is grace—God's grace. Even in our failures, God makes us fail forward.

FOOTNOTES: 1. John 1:29; 2. Genesis 3:5; 3. John 18:1; 4. John 18:25

GPS: *God-Positioning Scriptures (to Reorient Your Life)*

He saved us, not because of works done by us in righteousness, but according to his own mercy, by the washing of regeneration and renewal of the Holy Spirit, whom he poured out on us richly through Jesus Christ our Savior, so that being justified by his grace we might become heirs according to the hope of eternal life. —Titus 3:5-7 (ESV)

REST STOP: *Pull Over and Ponder*
When has leaning on God's grace allowed you to fail forward? How did it feel?

Mile 79

No Accidents!

Jesus' death and resurrection were the fulfillment of prophecy written hundreds of years before. Knowing this, do you really think anything in your life happens by accident?

W E HAVE NEARLY reached the last Mile of our Inner State journey together. And I'd like to point out that there have been no accidents! That shouldn't surprise us, because nothing happens by accident. God created and faithfully superintends everything. So we can rest assured in the following key facts:

It was not by accident that Jesus died. When we look at the crucifixion, we are reminded of David's cry of despair in Psalm 22 that questions, "My God, my God, why have You forsaken me?" In the book of John, we see that Jesus cries out those same words from the cross. In addition, Psalm 22 contains details about Jesus' thirst, the piercing of His hands and feet, and the division of His garments. All these prophetic utterances were fulfilled! The circumstances of Jesus' crucifixion were no surprise to God the Father, or God the Son. *It is not by accident that you are where you are.* Our struggles, whether large or small, are not a surprise to God. Our tests of faith range from being excruciatingly painful to simply annoying, but God uses each of them for our good and His greater glory.

Scripture tells us that the soldiers removed Jesus' outer garments before His crucifixion. Typically during a crucifixion, the soldiers would divide the spoils, but they ran into a problem with Jesus' robe. They didn't want to tear His seamless tunic because it would become useless, so they decided to roll dice for it. This fulfilled an old testament prophecy, "They divide my garments among them, and for my clothing they cast lots."[1]

"It is not by accident that you are where you are."

It was not by accident that Jesus wore a robe that was woven into one piece. The high priest of that day wore that exact kind of tunic. Jesus' clothing was symbolically linked to His role as our High Priest. The seamless robe, however, symbolized even more than Jesus as a high priest. The early Christian fathers saw the garment as a metaphor for the church. The church is not something that man has put together by seaming and sewing. The church is something God has woven together, and is therefore indivisible. *It is not by accident that He has woven you together with believers who are very different from you.*

Following the death of Jesus, the Bible gives us a number of details pertaining to His body and the people who cared for it. Joseph of Arimathea and Nicodemus didn't care who found out that they wanted to care for the body of Christ. They had to express their love.

On Sunday, the third day after Jesus' death, Mary Magdalene went to visit His tomb. When Mary arrived, the heavy stone that covered the opening of the tomb—a stone that could be moved only with extraordinary strength—had been rolled aside making it possible for everyone to see for themselves that Jesus was no longer inside. When Jesus came back to life, He certainly could have left His tomb without moving that rock. But it's God's nature to remove barriers to our understanding and believing. John 20 describes the miraculous setting in detail so everyone would know that the body had not been stolen. No Jew or Greek would have unwrapped a dead body just to carry it out. The dead body would have contaminated them. And the Roman soldiers would not have stolen the body since they were supposed to guard the tomb to prevent that from happening. In fact, Jesus' disappearance meant certain death for them. And no one would have taken the time and effort to unwrap the linens from the corpse, yet the wrappings were found neatly folded, as if someone had tidied up before leaving the site. The headcloth had been rolled up in a separate place. Nothing in the passage indicates there was anything rushed or chaotic about Jesus' leaving the tomb. *It was not by accident that Jesus rose on the third day.*

When the disciples saw the empty tomb and the linens, they realized that Jesus had risen from the dead. They remembered the Scriptures said He would come to life again. From there, they would eventually change the world! Jesus' resurrection was and is the key. It causes the ignition of our faith and is the basis for the Christian church's witness to the world. C.H. Spurgeon said, "Jesus is as strong now as He ever will be, for He changes not. At this moment He is as able to convert souls as at the period of the brightest revival, or at Pentecost itself. There are no ebbs and flows with Christ's power. Omnipotence is in the hand that once was pierced, permanently abiding there. Oh, if we could but rouse it; if we could but bring the Captain of the host to the field again, to fight for His church, to work His servants! What marvels should we see, for He is able." The same Spirit that raised Christ from the dead dwells in you![3] *It is not an accident that you were called.* In our own strength, we will never change the world for His glory. Taking the High Way means coming to grips with the fact that His resurrection power is in us to transform so that He may transform the world through us.

FOOTNOTES: 1. Psalm 22:18; 2. Romans 8:11

GPS: *God-Positioning Scriptures (to Reorient Your Life)*

It stands to reason, doesn't it, that if the alive-and-present God who raised Jesus from the dead moves into your life, he'll do the same thing in you that he did in Jesus, bringing you alive to himself? When God lives and breathes in you (and he does, as surely as he did in Jesus), you are delivered from that dead life. With his Spirit living in you, your body will be as alive as Christ's!
—Romans 8:11 (The Message)

REST STOP: *Pull Over and Ponder*

What does it mean to your faith to believe that nothing in life happens by accident? Where do you need to employ a confidence in the transforming power of God?

Mile 80

Follow Me

The journey you're on ends not on Earth, but in heaven. As you go on your way, remember ... keep your eyes on the road and your hands on the wheel, and keep moving forward until you're finally home.

THE STORY OF the life of Jesus Christ does not end with His crucifixion or resurrection. Jesus remained on Earth forty days after He left the tomb. The Bible tells of the transferring of Jesus' spiritual authority to His believers. This process began when Jesus appeared suddenly to His disciples ... behind locked doors. "So when it was evening on that day, the first day of the week, and when the doors were shut where the disciples were, for fear of the Jews, Jesus came and stood in their midst and said to them, 'Peace be with you.'"[1]

Then, we observe a method God uses when He is about to do something significant. First, He selects people who know they are inadequate for the task they are called to do. John records the event where Jesus first empowered His disciples with the Holy Spirit. The Bible says, "He breathed on them and said to them, 'Receive the Holy Spirit.'"[2] The word used for "breathed" in this passage is *ruach*, the same word used in Genesis 2:7 when God first breathed His Spirit into man and Adam became a living being. The Hebrew word *ruach* means wind, breath, and spirit.

Even though the disciples had witnessed Jesus' miraculous visitation in the locked room, without Jesus, they were rudderless. While waiting to see what God would do next so they could follow His lead, they decided to do something they routinely did. They went fishing. They felt like they were accomplishing nothing, but their decision to do something constructive while looking for the Lord's specific guidance is a model for all of us to follow.

About the time that the disciples were dejected, thinking they couldn't do anything more to produce the results they wanted, Jesus showed up and instructed them to try another tactic. He told them to throw the net on the other side of the boat. They obeyed and experienced incredible success.

> "Our limitations [on this side of heaven] ... don't alter our responsibility as believers."

After eating a fresh fish breakfast with His disciples, there was another issue that our resurrected Jesus addressed. He took Peter aside and gave him a chance to repent of his sin: his recent three-time denial of knowing Him. Jesus said to Simon Peter: "Simon, son of John, do you love Me more than these?"[3] It was a question with a life-changing impact. Simon was Peter's name prior to his becoming a disciple. By referring to Peter as Simon, it was as if Jesus were saying that the two of them had to go back to the very beginning of their relationship in an effort to give Peter an opportunity to recommit himself.

Peter was grieved that Jesus repeated the phrase three times, because he was reminded how many times he had denied Christ. When we recognize our sin after being confronted with it, we are dismayed on the one hand, yet relieved on the other to have the opportunity to be free of that sin.

When Peter first began following Christ, he might have thought that he was such a strong-minded man that he could do anything, much like we might have felt when we began to follow Christ. But he could not and neither can we. Peter did confront his failure and his weakness as Jesus repeated the same command that He had given him years before—"Follow Me."[4] This time Christ told Peter what he would face in the future: "I tell you the truth, when you were young, you were able to do as you liked; you dressed yourself and went wherever you wanted to go. But when you are old, you will stretch out your hands, and others will dress you and take you where you don't want to go."[5] Jesus said this to let Peter know that one day, his death would glorify God. When Jesus told Peter about his future, Peter was taken aback. Who could blame him! Tradition says that Peter was crucified upside down for preaching the Gospel.

Peter's response to Jesus' pointed comments is so surprising. Peter looks around, sees John, the disciple Jesus loved, and asks, "What about him, Lord?" As amazing as that twist in the conversation seems, even today, many followers of Jesus are distracted from their calling as they spend time comparing themselves with others. We want to see how our status and situation compare to everyone else's. When Jesus replies to Peter about his "need to know" Jesus makes it clear that Peter needs only to be concerned with following the Lord. He told Peter, "If I want him to remain alive until I return, what is that to you? As for you, follow me."[6]

Like Peter, we also have a tendency to get distracted with things that God's handling. We may spend time and energy worrying about world events. We wonder how certain happenings will affect our lives and even become anxious because we can't influence the outcome of the situation. Jesus says, "Follow Me." In Greek, the command is intensely personal and calls for repeated and continuous action. It means, "You keep following Me—follow Me, and follow Me, and follow Me."

Nothing will ever come right in the world until we take care of the sin in our own hearts. After that, our prayers and efforts in this world on behalf of God can do remarkably more than we can ever ask or think to make the world better.

On this side of heaven, we'll never fully understand God's big picture. Our limitations, though, don't alter our responsibility as believers. We are to act on the aspects of the big picture that we do understand and faithfully follow Christ. Mark Twain captured the heart of this point when he commented, "It ain't the parts of the Bible that I can't understand that bother me, it is the parts that I do understand." As we are diligent in what we know to do, we will become a blessing to others. God will manage the complexities of the world, and there will be fewer complexities if each of us who profess to be Christian will be faithful on our spiritual journey. Taking the High Way means praying for the Holy

Spirit to perfect our Inner State and fill us with compassion for each one we meet along the way.

FOOTNOTES: 1. John 20:19; 2. John 20:22; 3. John 21:15; 4. John 21:19; 5. John 21:18 (NLT); 6. John 21:20-22 (NLT)

GPS: *God-Positioning Scriptures (to Reorient Your Life)*

Then the Angel showed me Water-of-Life River, crystal bright. It flowed from the Throne of God and the Lamb, right down the middle of the street. ... Never again will there be any night. No one will need lamplight or sunlight. The shining of God, the Master, is all the light anyone needs. And they will rule with him age after age after age ... Oh, Yes! —**Revelation 22:1-5, 21 (The Message)**

REST STOP: *Pull Over and Ponder*

Contemplate the journey you're on. Are you taking the High Way? Whom are you following? And who's joining you? Invite someone to join you on the road to spiritual maturity.

Road Atlas

Mile 78:
page 367

Taking the High Way means conquering self-deception not by trying harder, but by surrendering our life to God and living in the freedom that releases us from sin.

Mile 79:
page 371

Taking the High Way means coming to grips with the fact that His resurrection power is in us to transform so that He may transform the world through us.

Mile 80:
page 275

Taking the High way means praying for the Holy Spirit to perfect our Inner State and fill us with compassion for each one we meet along the way.